W9-ARI-801

WHENCE THE POWER?

WHENCE THE POWER?
THE ARTISTRY AND
HUMANITY OF SAUL BELLOW

M. GILBERT PORTER

University of Missouri Press
1974

ISBN 0-8262-0165-2
Copyright © 1974 by The Curators of the University of Missouri
Second printing, 1975
Library of Congress Catalog Card Number 74-79165
Printed and bound in the United States of America
University of Missouri Press, Columbia, Missouri 65201

1. Bellow, Saul — Criticism and interpretation

For my mother and father,
who made the center hold,
and for my wife, Georgeanne,
who has made the circle whole.

ACKNOWLEDGMENTS

Parts of the work on this book were supported by research grants. The University of Oregon's Cuthbert Collingwood Fellowship enabled me to draft major parts of an early version, and the Research Council at the University of Missouri—Columbia provided a grant-in-aid for the summer of 1973 that released me from teaching duties to write the chapter on *Mr. Sammler's Planet* and to make extensive revisions. The Council also provided funds to meet incidental expenses. I am very grateful to both sources for their assistance.

To my other set of parents, Frank and Marge Barlow of Portland, Oregon, I extend my thanks for unstinting encouragement and the provision of an idyllic place to write.

For permission to quote from his work, I am indebted to Saul Bellow and his publishers: to The Vanguard Press, Inc., for *Dangling Man*. Reprinted from *Dangling Man* by Saul Bellow, by permission of the publisher The Vanguard Press, Inc. Copyright ©1944 by The Vanguard Press, Inc. Renewed 1972 by Saul Bellow. For *The Victim*. Reprinted from *The Victim* by Saul Bellow, by permission of the publisher The Vanguard Press, Inc. Copyright © 1947 by Saul Bellow. To The Viking Press: From *The Adventures of Augie March* by Saul Bellow. Copyright © 1949, 1951, 1952, 1953 by Saul Bellow. Reprinted by permission of The Viking Press, Inc. From *Seize the Day* by Saul Bellow. Copyright © 1956 by Saul Bellow. Reprinted by permission of The Viking Press, Inc. From *Henderson the Rain King* by Saul Bellow. Copyright © 1958, 1959 by Saul Bellow. Reprinted by permission of The Viking Press, Inc. From *Herzog* by Saul Bellow. Copyright © 1961, 1963, 1964 by Saul Bellow. Reprinted by permission of The Viking Press, Inc. From *Mr. Sammler's Planet* by Saul Bellow. Copyright © 1969, 1970 by Saul Bellow. Reprinted by permission of The Viking Press, Inc.

Excerpts from T. S. Eliot's "The Waste Land," "The Love Song of J. Alfred Prufrock," and "Burnt Norton" are from his

Three chapters of this study have appeared elsewhere in slightly different form. For permission to reprint that material here I would like to thank John DeStefano, Editor, *New England Review* (Cheshire, Connecticut); Lee Pryor, Editor, *Forum* (University of Houston); and Earl Rovit, Editor, *Saul Bellow: A Collection of Critical Essays* (Prentice–Hall, Inc.), the Twentieth Century Views Series, Maynard Mack, General Editor.

Through an Honors College Preceptorship at the University of Missouri—Columbia, Ms. Lao Rubert aided me greatly in the preparation of the bibliography.

Mrs. Nina Casto, in the Humanities Library at the University of Oregon, smoothed my way time and again through her enormous knowledge of research materials, and her irrepressible cheerfulness was a constant source of encouragement to me.

One can never fully acknowledge his debt to all those teachers who have helped to shape his sensibilities and literary responses, and a mere listing would certainly be inadequate, but I would like to mention one who has been a major influence on my life with books: Dr. William J. Handy, author, among many other works, of *Kant and the Southern New Critics, Modern Fiction: A Formalist Approach,* and (with Max Westbrook) *Twentieth Century Criticism.* Dr. Handy has encouraged my study from its inception. He has read the entire manuscript, sharing with me his critical acumen, his suggestions for revision, and his excitement over Bellow's fiction. Much of the strength of the book derives from his influence, though he is blameless of whatever weaknesses remain. "Whence the power?" is Dr. Handy's phrase, suggesting at once awe and humility before the imaginative presentation and the desire to approach an understanding of it on its own terms.

Finally, I wish to thank all my students in contemporary literature who have shared with me over the last ten years their enthusiasm, their questions, their thoughts, and their insights. They have given me a great deal more than I have given them, and my book is richer for their many catalytic discussions.

Beyond the limits—and the limitations—of this study, my debt is greatest where the book is dedicated.

M. G. P.
Columbia, Missouri
May, 1974

CONTENTS

Introduction, 1

1. *Dangling Man:*
Condemned to Freedom, 6

2. *The Victim:*
A Cast of Millions, 29

3. *The Adventures of Augie March:*
Tension of Opposites, 61

4. *Seize the Day:*
A Drowning Man, 102

5. *Henderson the Rain King:*
Tuning a Soul, 127

6. *Herzog:*
Law of the Heart, 146

7. *Mr. Sammler's Planet*
Objectives Without Correlatives, 160

8. Bellow's Vision:
To Live and Not Die, 181

Bibliography, 199

INTRODUCTION

"The New Criticism, which despite its vociferous detractors works quite well with lyric poetry, is helpless when
confronted by the large irregular masses of prose fiction
which we call novels."[1] So says Robert Scholes in the
introduction to what is an otherwise sound anthology devoted to critical theories of the novel. The statement is
unsound. It can be made at all only because the New Critics have had relatively little to say about the application of
their theories to fiction. But they have not been silent. John
Crowe Ransom, whose "structure/texture" approach to
poetry is well known, has written about the possibilities of
a formalist approach to fiction in *The New Criticism* (1941),
in "The Content of the Novel: Notes Toward a Critique of
Fiction" (*The American Review*, 1926), and in "The Understanding of Fiction" (*Kenyon Review*, 1950). Cleanth
Brooks and Robert Penn Warren in *Understanding Fiction*
(1943) and Allen Tate and Caroline Gordon in *The House
of Fiction* (1950) have further advanced the cause of formalist criticism of fiction by showing its usefulness in the
classroom. Mark Schorer has called attention to the unity
of theme and form in fiction in "Technique as Discovery"
(*Hudson Review*, 1948) and to the importance of metaphor
in "Fiction and the Matrix of Analogy" (*Kenyon Review*,
1949). Allen Tate has devoted significant space to the critical problem of point of view in "The Post of Observation
in Fiction" (*Maryland Quarterly*, 1944) and has acknowledged the importance of scene in fiction:

> I should, myself, like to know more about the making of the
> single scene, and all the techniques that contribute to it; and
> I suspect that I am not asking the impossible, for this kind of
> knowledge is very likely the only kind that is actually within
> our range. It alone can be got at definitely and at particular

1. Robert Scholes, *Approaches to the Novel* (San Francisco, 1961), p.v.

1

moments, even after we have failed . . . to retain the image of the book.[2]

More recently, New Critical methodology as applied to fiction has been strengthened by a number of critics and theorists in the formalist tradition or, as in the case of Aristotelians and Structuralists, in traditions akin to it. In *The Rhetoric of Fiction* (1961) Wayne C. Booth has made a sophisticated study of point of view, and David Lodge has emphasized the importance of language in the novel in *Language of Fiction* (1966) and *The Novelist at the Cross-roads and Other Essays on Fiction and Criticism* (1971). Dorothy Van Ghent's *The English Novel: Form and Function* (1952) is an excellent example of formalist methods at work. Murray Krieger's *The New Apologists for Poetry* (1956) as well as his work on contextual and phenomenological theories (particularly his essays "The Existential Basis of Contextual Criticism" and "Mediation, Language, and Vision in the Reading of Literature") have important implications for intrinsic theories of fiction, as does the renewed interest in Russian formalism. Examples in this area are Robert Scholes's essay "The Contributions of Formalism and Structuralism to the Theory of Fiction" in the winter, 1973, issue of *Novel,* or Tzvetan Todorov's "Some Approaches to Russian Formalism" in the December, 1972, issue of *Twentieth Century Studies,* an issue devoted entirely to Russian formalism. Like several other contemporary critics, Harry R. Garvin attempts to unite formalism and phenomenology in his essay "The Novel as Structure: An Ontological Approach" in the fall, 1972, issue of the *Bucknell Review.* Though he does not acknowledge his predecessors, he is clearly indebted to Ransom and the New Critics.

This brief survey of critics roughly in the formalist tradition who have written on fiction by no means exhausts the field, but perhaps it is sufficient to suggest that New Criticism is neither helpless nor dying in the field of fiction. Critical polemic, though, is not really the purpose here, and this book does not presume to be a model of New Critical

2. "Techniques of Fiction," *Sewanee Review,* 52 (Winter 1944), 213.

theory or practice. The readings that follow, however, are based on the assumptions of New Criticism[3] and draw heavily from analytical work in that tradition.[4] Candor and an honest relationship with the reader make it impera-

3. Cleanth Brooks has stated the major assumptions concisely under the rubric of the ten "articles of faith" for the formalist critic:
   1. That literary criticism is a description and evaluation of its object.
   2. That the primary concern of criticism is with the problem of unity . . . and the kind of whole which the literary work forms or fails to form, and the relation of the various parts to each other in building up this whole.
   3. That the formal relations in a work of literature may include, but certainly exceed, those of logic.
   4. That in a successful work, form and content cannot be separated.
   5. That form is meaning.
   6. That literature is ultimately metaphorical and symbolic.
   7. That the general and the universal are not seized upon by abstraction, but got at through the concrete and the particular.
   8. That literature is not a surrogate for religion.
   9. That, as Allen Tate says, "specific moral problems" are the subject matter of literature, but the purpose of literature is not to point a moral.
   10. That the principles of criticism define the area relevant to literary criticism; they do not constitute a method for carrying out the criticism.

"The Formalist Critic," *Kenyon Review,* 13 (1951), 72. In this study of Bellow I consider these articles as valid now as when they were written and as applicable to fiction as to poetry.

4. In addition to those already cited and among others to be cited later, specifically the following: William J. Handy, *Kant and the Southern New Critics* (Austin, Tex., 1963). John Crowe Ransom, "The Concrete Universal: Observations on the Understanding of Poetry," in *Poems and Essays* (New York, 1955), pp. 159–85; "Criticism as Pure Speculation," in *Literary Opinion in America,* rev. ed., Morton D. Zabel, ed. (New York, 1951); "The Understanding of Fiction," *Kenyon Review,* 12 (Spring 1950); "The Content of the Novel: Notes Toward a Critique of Fiction," *The American Review,* 7 (April 1926). José Ortega y Gasset, "Notes on the Novel," in *The Dehumanization of Art* (New York, 1956). Susanne K. Langer, *Feeling and Form* (New York, 1953). A. Kingsley Weatherhead, "Structure and Texture in Henry Green's Latest Novels," *Accent,* 19 (Spring 1959). Boris Tomashevsky, "Thematics," in *Russian Formalist Criticism,* Lee T. Lemon and Marion J. Reis, eds. (Lincoln, Nebr., 1965). Allen Tate, "Techniques of Fiction," *Sewanee Review,* 52 (Winter 1944). Edwin Muir, *The Structure of the Novel* (London, 1928). R. S. Crane, "The Concept of Plot," from *Critics and Criticism,* in *Approaches to the Novel,* Robert Scholes, ed. (San Francisco, 1961). Northrop Frye, *The Anatomy of Criticism* (Princeton, 1957). Mark Schorer, "Fiction and the Matrix of Analogy," *Kenyon Review,* 11 (Autumn 1949). R. P. Blackmur, *Eleven Essays in the European Novel* (New York, 1943). René Wellek and Austin Warren. *Theory of Literature* (New York, 1956). C. C. Walcutt, *Man's Changing Mask: Modes of Characterization in Fiction* (Minneapolis, 1966).

tive that the critic make clear where he stands and, in the style of Archimedes, what fulcrum he intends to use and which cosmos he proposes to move. The critical stance here, then, is formalistic (nonmilitant); the critical tool is close analysis of intrareferential relations, the interaction of themes and forms, or what Ransom calls structure and texture; the cosmos is the rich world of Saul Bellow's long fiction, and the aim is, first, to account for its artistry and, second, to measure its humanity—to answer the question, "Whence the Power?"

Chapter one examines the identity crisis of Joseph (*Dangling Man*) as it is revealed in his journal, tracing his progressive alienation from family, friends, and society, and his final desperate attempt to accommodate himself to others with all their imperfections because he makes the frightening discovery that he lacks the resources to survive alone. Character foils are used skillfully to reveal Joseph's condition, as are mythical situations, and allusions in his dreams. Chapter two treats the issues of guilt and responsibility as they are raised in the relationship between the Jew Asa Leventhal and the gentile Kirby Allbee (*The Victim*). Critical attention is devoted especially to the dual level of presentation in the novel, the realistic and the symbolic, and the wealth of mythical allusion subtly introduced into the symbolic level. Taking its cue from Robert Penn Warren's essay "Pure and Impure Poetry," Chapter three charts the play of opposites in *The Adventures of Augie March,* in which Augie, a free and optimistic spirit, is exposed to conditions designed to limit his freedom and destroy his optimism; yet he emerges at the end a character still largely in control of his fate. He is more aware than he was, but his laughter is able to reconcile the ambivalences in his world. Following W. J. Handy's equation of the fictional scene with the poetic image and Joseph Frank's concept of "spatial form" in the novel, Chapter four examines the scenes in *Seize the Day* as nearly as possible as poetic images and relates each scene to the organic central metaphor in the novel, the image of a man drowning. Water imagery and an archetypal pattern of descent are analyzed carefully. Chapter five, written somewhat in the spirit of

Henderson the Rain King, traces the physical and spiritual regeneration which Eugene Henderson undergoes. The major emphasis in this chapter is on Bellow's skillful use of music to enhance Henderson's spectacular transformation. Chapter six follows Moses Herzog as he tries painfully but with heroic comedy to understand the actual chaos of his personal life in terms of the theoretical wisdom he possesses as a holder of a doctoral degree in history. An anatomy in Northrop Frye's terms, the book emphasizes erudition more than plot. Thus critical focus is directed mainly to the subject matter of Herzog's reflections and his unmailed letters. Herzog solves the conflict between his sensibilities and his intellect by moving through existentialism to transcendentalism. Chapter seven examines the uneasy relation between themes and fictional concretions in *Mr. Sammler's Planet,* a novel in which Bellow's moral indignation seems to overshadow his artistic control. His reflective hero emerges not so much a fully realized character with a life of his own as much as he does a thinly disguised mouthpiece for the author's didacticism. This didacticism is timely, sound, even admirable, but it is too expository, nonfictive, and therefore distracting from the novel *qua* novel. Though occasional cross reference is made to the other novels, these eight chapters stand largely as discrete readings of each novel to emphasize the special qualities of the individual work. Chapter eight makes more extensive cross references to Bellow's protagonists in the interests of aggregation and synthesis, offers a brief statement about Bellow's vision of man as reflected in the living experiences of his seven heroes, and relates his vision to a literary tradition.

Because this study is intended as much for the general reader as for the specialist, summaries of plots and central episodes have been supplied where appropriate. The specialist who knows Bellow well may wish to skip such passages (though they are neither frequent nor extensive), but the general reader should find the summaries useful both for refreshing his memory of the individual novels and for the full illustration of critical points.

1.

Dangling Man: Condemned to Freedom

The hero of *Dangling Man,* Bellow's first novel, is named Joseph. His surname is never given. He is a young man, married, a Canadian citizen who has been living in Chicago for eighteen years. He is employed by the Inter-American Travel Bureau. In the spring of 1942 he receives an induction notice from the Army, as a result of which he quits his job, submits to a physical, and is accepted for service. But before he actually becomes a soldier and joins himself to the war effort, questions about his past and present are raised by officialdom. For almost a year he is kept in a state of uncertainty as a "friendly alien," a "1A," then a "3A"; he is classified and reclassified, finally accepted, but not drafted. This official search for Joseph's identity stimulates his personal quest for identity. No longer an active member of the civilian world, and not yet committed to the military, he becomes, in Sartre's phrase, "condemned to freedom." His philosophic mind is given full rein. Since his wife's library job is adequate to support the two of them, he is thrown completely on his own resources. He begins to measure out his life in aimless days and ways. He dangles not merely between the military world and the civilian world, but between the material world of action and the ideal world of thought, between detachment and involvement, between life and death. He becomes more and more introspective and isolated. As time drags on and the disparity between the ideal world and the real world becomes more apparent to him, he grows less confident of his ability to make sense out of the universe or to discover his proper relationship to it. At last, in some desperation, Joseph decides that he will find no answers in his detached state, and he goes to his draft board to submit himself to the same fate his countrymen are enduring. The novel records this progress from Joseph, with the philosophical coat of many colors, to G.I. Joe.

As Hemingway managed in *The Sun Also Rises* to depict the empty and aimless groping for direction of the post-World War I expatriates, Bellow has in *Dangling Man* captured the mood of philosophical malaise which marked the generation of World War II. The two books are alike in that both examine from a distance the ravages of war on the human spirit, but they differ in several ways. Jake Barnes ends where he began, an impotent Fisher King whose wound cannot be healed and whose future in the symbolic wasteland is as bleak and absurd as his past. Drinking in Paris, fishing in Burguete, partying in Pamplona, he has replaced disquisition with a studied code of silence. With his impossible love, Brett Ashley, he has concluded that "Talking's all bilge."[1] The informing principles in the novel are action and sensation within the now famous Hemingway tradition of stoic private misery. Except for the rare times when Jake breaks his code of silence in late-night soliloquies, any philosophical reflection is the reader's own. It is against this close-mouthed tradition that Bellow's Joseph reacts in setting forth his personal problems—and the ethos of his era—in journal form:

> For this is an era of hardboileddom. Today the code of the athlete, of the tough boy . . . is stronger than ever. Do you have feelings? There are correct and incorrect ways of indicating them. Do you have an inner life? It is nobody's business but your own. Do you have emotions? Strangle them. . . .
>
> If you have difficulties, grapple with them silently, goes one of their commandments. To hell with that! I intend to talk about mine, and if I had as many mouths as Siva has arms and kept them going all the time, I still could not do myself justice. In my present state of demoralization, it has become necessary for me to keep a journal—that is, to talk to myself—and I do not feel guilty of self-indulgence in the least. The hardboiled are compensated for their silence; they fly planes or fight bulls or catch tarpon, whereas I rarely leave my room.[2]

1. Ernest Hemingway, *The Sun Also Rises* (New York, 1926), p. 55.
2. Saul Bellow, *Dangling Man* (New York, 1944), p. 7. Subsequent page

Joseph's journal is an anatomy of the sensitive human being seeking to discover and maintain a sense of selfhood in a complex world. Complicating his world further, warfare's threat of annihilation has accentuated the need for discovering meaningful identity. Where *The Sun Also Rises* is mainly dramatic and concrete, *Dangling Man* is discursive and abstract. Where Jake at the end has come full circle, Joseph has committed himself to a new direction. Neither book, of course, celebrates the triumph of order in the world, but there is a broader base for possible positive vision in *Dangling Man* than in *The Sun Also Rises.* Joseph's final willingness to seek meaning through community is more hopeful than Jake's resignation or Hemingway's ecclesiastical assertion that, despite vanity, "the earth abideth forever." [3]

Joseph's journal consists mainly of successively dated entries from December 15, 1942, to April 9, 1943, his last day as a civilian. These entries contain information about daily events, strategically placed flashbacks to earlier periods of Joseph's life, accounts of several dreams, and imaginary conversations with his divided self, *Tu As Raison Aussi,* the Spirit of Alternatives. This form provides Bellow maximum flexibility to explore the character of his protagonist and the implications of his conflict, and he has carefully coordinated the narrative manner with the nature of his narrator. That is, though a substantial body of the novel is composed of what appears to be mere expository abstract reasoning, the reasoning is placed in the mind of a completely realized tortured self whose propensities to abstraction are habitual, indeed compulsive. The structure of the novel, then, as John Crowe Ransom would say, is adequately embodied in its texture. It is a novel of ideas,

---

numbers are in parentheses in the text.

3. Marcus Klein has seen the movement toward community, the "strategy of accommodation," as a dominant theme in the contemporary American novel. "Joseph," he says, "must give himself to idiopathic freedom, and that way is madness, or submit to the community's ordinary, violent reality. He hurries his draft call. He surrenders." *After Alienation* (Cleveland, 1965), pp. 35–36.

but the protagonist is an intense idea man in whom philo-sophical analysis is totally natural.

Early in the book Joseph distinguishes between the New Joseph and the Old Joseph he was before he began to dangle:

> Very little about the Joseph of a year ago pleases me. I cannot help laughing at him, at some of his traits and sayings.
>
> Joseph, aged twenty-seven, an employee of the Inter-Ameri-can Travel Bureau, a tall, already slightly flabby, but, neverthe-less, handsome young man, a graduate of the University of Wisconsin—major, History—married five years, amiable, gen-erally takes himself to be well-liked. But on close examination he proves to be somewhat peculiar. . . . He is a person greatly concerned with keeping intact and free from encumbrance a sense of his own being, its importance. Yet he is not abnormal-ly cold, nor is he egotistic. He keeps a tight hold because, as he himself explains, he is keenly intent on knowing what is happening to him. He wants to miss nothing. (19)

The Old Joseph, the preinduction Joseph, was mainly a "creature of plans." His life had been devoted to formulat-ing an answer to the central question that he had posed for himself: "How should a good man live; what ought he to do?" That he qualified as a "good man" was clear to the Old Joseph. He was uncomfortably aware that historical evidence existed to support the view that "man was born the slayer of his father and of his brother, full of instinctive bloody rages, licentious and unruly from his earliest days," but the Old Joseph "could find in himself no such history of hate overcome. . . . He believed in his own mildness, believed in it piously" (27). Because he believed in his own goodness, he believed also in the goodness of others like him. Consequently, he sought what he called a " 'colony of the spirit,' or a group whose covenants forbade spite, bloodiness, and cruelty" (27). Through fellowship with such kindred spirits Joseph hoped to escape from those lesser mortals "in whom the sense of the temporariness of life had shrunk"; he sought to establish a kind of spiritual Brook Farm, to refute if he could the the Hobbesian view that life was necessarily nasty, brutish, and short. But as Robert Balzer has said, "Life is what happens to you while you're making other plans." With the tension of war came the disruption of the Old Joseph's plans and the creation of the New Joseph, whose confidence is shaken, whose values are undermined, and whose plans for the future are as uncertain as his dangling stance in the present.

Where the Old Joseph had attempted to erect a "colony of the spirit" the New Joseph now discovers "craters of the spirit" (26). Through the magnifying pressure of the times, he sees in himself and in others capacities for violence and duplicity that he had never before acknowledged. He becomes aware that his early plans had caused him to make "mistakes of the sort people make who see things as they wish to see them, or, for the sake of their plans, *must* see them" (27). The question, "How should a good man live?" still cries out for an answer, but Joseph finds himself increasingly incapable of formulating one. His own life, he is painfully aware, provides no answer, and the novel makes clear that his life is a representative one. Joseph lives in an inexpensive apartment house surrounded by an interesting variety of neighbors, and during his daily routine he encounters an extensive cross section of the human species. He has an uneven relationship with his wife, Iva, and his relatives, and he finds himself frequently at odds with a curious assortment of friends. Joseph is in the actual world, then, a "plain Joe" with the same kinds of daily problems that everyone faces. Because of his sensitivity, his training in history, and his intensely analytical mind, however, Joseph is set apart from the average man in the Platonic world of ideas. Joseph's attempt to strike a balance between the world of affairs and the world of ideas, a difficult task in the first place, is complicated by his new insight into his past mistakes, his situation, and his exposure to too many pressures at once—social, domestic, and philosophic.

In a long journal entry dated December 22, Joseph reflects on a springtime party given by his friends Harry and Minna Servatius. It is at this party that Joseph seems to get his first dramatic evidence of weaknesses in the matrix of the colony of the spirit. Though most of his old friends are present, the party is a failure. The hostess, Minna, is an overbearing yet well-intentioned woman whose husband is a philanderer. To compensate for her fear of abandonment, she drinks too much, laughs too loudly, and tries desperately to whip the others into a sense of communion and a spirit of gaiety. When the compulsive drinking and the oft-repeated jokes of these mock-revellers fail to produce the desired effect, she compels George Hayza, who once "had played at being a surrealist," to record on her phonograph one of his poems which used to be popular among them. The poem is no longer relevant. The attempt falls flat. Finally, Minna coerces Abt Morris, her former sweetheart, into hypnotizing her. Piqued and jealous, he agrees and subjects her to both physical pain and mental anguish. With its dancing, its drinking, its poetic incantation, and its symbolic sacrifice, the party is, Joseph notes, a spring rite, a shabby modern counterpart of the Eleusinian Mysteries, but the land is no longer fertile, and the worshippers no longer believe:

> And it came to me all at once that the human purpose of these occasions had always been to free the charge of feeling in the pent heart; and that, as animals instinctively sought salt or lime, we, too, flew together at this need as we had at Eleusis, with rites and dances, and at other high festivals and corroborees to witness pains and tortures, to give our scorn, hatred, and desire temporary liberty and play. Only we did these things without grace or mystery, lacking the forms for them and relying on drunkenness, assassinated the Gods in one another and shrieked in vengefulness and hurt. (31–32)

The desperation that Joseph witnesses in this gathering is disturbing enough—especially when he senses the same feeling in himself—but what really disturbs him is his new awareness of his best friend's capacity for violence, even hate. Joseph suspects this capacity when Abt casually mentions in a kidding fashion that he could stab Dr. Rood, his college dean; the suspicion is confirmed when Abt harshly, and with apparent pleasure, pinches the helpless, mesmerized Minna. The insight into Abt, whom Joseph considers his most kindred spirt, casts doubts on his own character. He asks, "If, in Abt, cruelty and the desire for revenge were reduced to pinching a woman's hand, what would my own mind give up if one examined its tiniest gaps and runnels?" (38).

The questions raised in Joseph's mind open the way for a progressive disillusionment:

> In the months that followed I began to discover one weakness after another in all I had built up around me. . . . It would be difficult for anyone else to know how this affected me, since no one could understand as well as I the nature of my plan, its rigidity, the extent to which I depended on it. Foolish or not, it had answered my need. The plan could be despised; my need could not be. (39)

"The plan" of the Old Joseph proved inappropriate to the new world, which Joseph sees now with new eyes, just as the religious ritual symbolized by the party is no longer relevant to a Nietzschean world in which all gods are dead. But Joseph knows, nonetheless, that the impulses that prompted both the plan and the party are valid ones (and are perhaps the same impulse); they simply need appropriate forms and viable directions for development. In his groping, blundering, frequently abject, often arrogant way, Joseph continues searching for the forms and the directions.

Not all of Joseph's insights are as dramatically represented as in the Servatius party, and not all of his responses are as clearly reasoned. Paradoxically, his very detachment from life sometimes narrows his vision and distorts his judgment, particularly where his sense of selfhood is concerned. Because as a dangling man he is not an active member in any productive world, his identity in the community is nebulous; and when he finds himself tacitly censured by the community because he does not seem to belong anywhere, he becomes defensive; he overreacts. This dimension of his dangling life is most evident in his casual relationships with community servants.

As the uncertainty and boredom of his life begin to take their toll of Joseph, little things assume unreasonable proportions. He declares himself very weary of having to remember a day as the day he " 'asked for a second cup of coffee,' or 'the day the waitress refused to take back the burned toast' " (55). And he finds himself overly sensitive to the attitude of those who serve the public. When Marie, the maid, comes to clean his room, she smokes a cigarette, an action which Joseph interprets as a personal affront: "I think I am the only one before whom she dares smoke; she recognizes I am of no importance" (11). He avoids patronizing any restaurant too regularly, for he does not wish to become "friendly with sandwich men, waitresses, and cashiers, and compelled to invent lies for their benefit" (11). Because he has no role in society, Joseph feels a curious guilt in the presence of those who do have a social role, however menial. Hypersensitive and defensive, Joseph experiences an implied indictment wherever he goes.

As his patience diminishes and the question of his identity presents itself with ever-mounting intensity, Joseph begins stubbornly to resist the censure which, real or imagined, he encounters. In the fall Joseph tries to cash Iva's check, which she has endorsed to him, in their local bank. He is greeted by a vice-president, Mr. Frink, who questions his identification ("How do I know you're this person?"), calls him by his first name, and refuses to cash the check because he is unemployed. Joseph reacts instantly, creating a scene:

> "Here you'll notice I have a surname, Frink," I said, holding one of the cards up. "I realize it's difficult to deal with the public efficiently and still politely. All the same, people don't like to be treated like suspicious characters and patronized at the same time." (116)

A similar scene occurs in December in the Arrow, a restaurant in which Joseph has joined Myron Adler for lunch. Waiting for Myron, Joseph sees at a neighboring table a man named Jimmy Burns, who had been Joseph's comrade when they were both idealistic young communists in the thirties. Burns will not acknowledge Joseph's greeting because Joseph is no longer part of the movement. Joseph interprets this slight as a refusal to acknowledge his existence. He becomes enraged, confronts Burns, and forces him into a begrudged response. He tries to explain his uncharacteristic action to the bewildered Myron:

> Listen. He has no business ignoring me. This is always happen-

ing to me. . . . I have a right to be spoken to. It's the most elementary thing in the world. Simply that. I insist on it. (23)

It is not, of course, "simply that" which disturbs Joseph. To be ignored by Burns, deluded though he is, is similar to being censured by maids, waitresses, and bank officials, insignificant though they are to Joseph. Although none of these people is important to Joseph personally, they represent to him, in his agitated state, withdrawal of social recognition. One may question oneself, but one does not like to be questioned by others, especially if one's own questioning is not going well. Joseph's is not going well, and his alienation from friends and society has its parallels in his domestic relations.

Joseph has never been close to his brother, Amos, who married a wealthy woman and has become a successful businessman, a big-town Babbitt. The schism between the two widens over the issues of the war and Joseph's independence. Joseph refuses to profit from the war by seeking an officer's commission, as Amos urges him to do, and he rejects the many offers of financial aid which Amos frequently tries to impose on him, thinking that to accept Amos's money is to give tacit approval to those profiteering values for which Amos stands and from which his money is derived. Amos cannot understand. He thinks Joseph a fool.

Joseph's fifteen-year-old niece, Etta, Amos's daughter, is a source of irritation to him, too. She is a vain girl, Joseph notes, and she bears a remarkable resemblance to himself. As Amos's daughter, she has espoused Amos's values and has been "brought up to identify poverty not so much with evil as with unimportance." Since Joseph is poor, he is unimportant to her. When he protests her interruption in the music room, she reminds him that "beggars cannot be choosers." Losing all control, he spanks her. In several ways Etta mirrors Joseph. They are both vain, young, and physically alike. Her bitchiness is matched by his stubbornness; her "movie talk" is answered with movie talk of his own. They both are danglers, Joseph between the ideal and the real worlds, Etta between childhood and

adulthood. Her immaturity is paralleled by his extreme re-
actions. In attacking her, he is really attacking those traits
in himself which are frustrating his attempts to achieve
clarity. She represents those remnants of his past self
which still prevent him from gaining "pure freedom," "to
stop living so exclusively and vainly for [his] own sake"
(102). Vanaker is to serve a similar function to Joseph,
showing him a glimpse of what his life will be like if he
fails to unlock "the imprisoning self." Etta is the ghost of
Joseph past; Vanaker portends the shape of the Joseph to
come. Joseph is extremely uncomfortable with both figures, but he doesn't consciously recognize their full significance.

Relations with Iva's family also sustain an added strain.
Joseph offends Mr. Almstadt by expressing wonder that
the man has been able to live so long with the witless
prattling of Mrs. Almstadt, and he rejects in disgust a glass
of orange juice offered to him by Mrs. Almstadt, thought-
lessly served (in lieu of an adequate lunch) on the kitchen
sink, where a partially disembowelled chicken lies drain-
ing. The juice has a feather in it. This is an assault on his
sensibilities; to Joseph it is further evidence of a symbolic
disregard for him as a person.

Joseph's relation with his wife begins to deteriorate. Iva
is a sensible, hard-working, devoted wife. She tries to
make a difficult situation as easy on Joseph as possible.
She does not question what he does with his time, she does
not complain that he is not working, and she nurses him
tenderly when he falls ill. She begins to show signs of
impatience only when he has driven her to it by his growing paranoia, when he makes public displays of temper or
private displays of petulance (the fight with Briggs, for
example, or the refusal to cash her checks). Her only com-
plaint to Joseph is of neglect: "And it's months and months
since you took an interest in me. Lately, for all you care,
I might just as well not be here" (63). Joseph's feeble response to this charge is that they are both victims of an
impossible situation.

The situation is impossible, but it has caused Joseph to
see Iva as another flaw in his rapidly disintegrating plan,

a plan which included salvation through a colony of the spirit. In his entry for February 17, Joseph remarks that Iva is "as far as ever from what I once desired to make her. I am afraid she has no capacity for that." The "that" he refers to is a share in his ideal world, the world of unshakable values and pure ideas, a world distinct from the material world of disorder where orange juice has chicken feathers in it and men experience genocidal world wars. He reflects on Iva's failure to fulfill his expectations for her:

> Was it possible that she should not want to be guided, formed by me? I expected some opposition. . . . No one came simply and of his own accord, effortlessly, to prize the most truly human traditions, the heavenly cities. You had to be taught to struggle toward them. . . . But it was now evident that Iva did not want to be towed. Those dreams inspired by Burckhardt's great ladies of the Renaissance and the no less profound Augustan women were in my head, not hers. Eventually I learned that Iva could not live in my infatuations. There are such things as clothes, appearances, furniture, light entertainment, mystery stories, the attractions of fashion magazines, the radio, the enjoyable evening. . . . Women—thus I reasoned—were not equipped by training to resist such things. You might force them to read Jacob Boehme for ten years without diminishing their appetite for them; you might teach them to admire Walden but never convert them to wearing old clothes. (65)

Joseph wishes to see a "difference between things and persons and even between acts and persons," that is, between existence and essence, for only in separation can Joseph come to terms with them. With Whitman, Joseph wishes to assert "Apart from the pulling and hauling stand what I am/ Stands amused, complacent, compassionating, idle, unitary" (*Song of Myself,* IV, 75–76). But in Iva and the life she leads—their life—Joseph sees a disturbing lack of distinction between the actual and the ideal.

Distanced from Iva, Joseph seeks solace in the arms of Kitty Daumler, a "warm, uncomplicated" girl who flatteringly finds him desirable. Their affair lasts two months before Joseph discovers that such activity is out of character for him. Though their relationship becomes strictly Platonic, Joseph is angered when, coming to her apartment unexpectedly to retrieve his copy of *Dubliners,* he discovers her in bed with another man. Again, Joseph feels his identity threatened, his place usurped by another. Like Hamlet, Joseph finds all occasions informing against him.

In the tradition of Henry James's Isabel Archer, Joseph wants to carry his life to a certain height, to escape the trivial and the routine. "Shall my life," he asks, "by one-thousandth of an inch fall short of its ultimate possibility?" (59). But Joseph's vision of what constitutes a meaningful life is shown to be too circumscribed. He does not, as Arnold said of Sophocles, see life steadily or whole. One great blind spot is his inability to reconcile himself to the ineluctable routine of everyday life. On December 17 he records his response to a moving passage in Goethe's *Poetry and Life,* a passage to which Joseph refers repeatedly in his journal:

> This loathing of life has both physical and moral causes. . . . All comfort in life is based upon a regular occurrence of external phenomena. The changes of the day and night, of the seasons, of flowers, and fruits, and all other recurring pleasures that come to us, that we may and should enjoy them—these are the mainsprings of our earthly life. The more open we are to these enjoyments, the happier we are; but if these changing phenomena unfold themselves and we take no interest in them, if we are insensible to such fair solicitations, then comes on the sorest evil, the heaviest disease—we regard life as a loathsome burden. It is said of an Englishman that he hanged himself that he might no longer have to dress and undress himself every day. (13)

This is disturbing reading for a man who waits listlessly every day for "the maid's knock, the appearance of the postman, programs on the radio, and the sure cyclical distress of certain thoughts" (9). Goethe cites the "recurrence of the passion of love" as the greatest source of the weariness of life, but Joseph's despair clearly comes from other sources. First, the "external phenomena" that he is exposed to are particularly squalid, and, second, his internal condition is too congested to allow him to distinguish between the meaningful and the trivial, the eternal and the ephemeral.

When Joseph does venture out into the "external phenomena," he rarely discovers flowers and fruits. What he finds instead are "odors from the stockyards and sewers" and a winter-ravaged city groaning itself into spring:

> The streets . . . looked burnt out; the chimneys pointed heavenward in openmouthed exhaustion. The turf, intersected by sidewalk, was bedraggled with the whole winter's deposit of deadwood, match cards, cigarettes, dogmire, rubble. . . . And the houses, their doors and windows open, drawing in the freshness, were like old drunkards or consumptives taking a cure. . . . I even saw in a brick passageway an untimely butterfly, out of place both in the season and the heart of the city, and somehow alien to the whole condition of the century. (114)

With its butterfly in an alley amid the debris of the city, the scene is to Joseph one of "impossible hope," the life force trying to assert itself against insurmountable odds. It is beauty fighting a losing battle against decay, and the people he encounters in such scenes are to Joseph either victims or victimizers.

The most disturbing element in his environment is Mr. Vanaker, his senile neighbor. Like Joseph, he is given only one name and, like Joseph, he is isolated and unhappy. As Joseph seeks a colony of the spirit and yet alienates himself from his friends and family, Vanaker seeks companionship and yet offends those with whom he seeks contact. Iva calls him a "werewolf," and Joseph judges him to be a "queer, annoying creature," even though he acknowledges that Vanaker's frequent coughing is "a sort of social activity" designed "to draw attention to himself"; it is a perverse form of shared activity, as is his exasperating habit of leaving the toilet door open when he urinates.

In "Terence, This Is Stupid Stuff" Housman offered two approaches to the world:

> Ale, man, ale's the stuff to drink
> For fellows whom it hurts to think.
> Look into the pewter pot
> To see the world as the world's not.

Housman suggested that there is thought, or escape from thought. Joseph adopts the first approach, Vanaker the second. His drinking is a counterpart to Joseph's thinking. Both activities are performed in their respective adjoining rooms; they are opposite sides of the same coin, both trying in vain to change an unacceptable life into an acceptable one. Neither are there flowers and fruit outside Vanaker's room, only his empty bottles in the snow. In their personal lives, moreover, Joseph and Vanaker have similar contradictions. While Vanaker takes instruction to be converted to Catholicism, he continues to receive "large quantities of mail from the Masonic Scottish Rite." When he moves, the maid discovers among the things he leaves behind an erotic magazine and a copy of *Pilgrim's Progress.* Joseph, on the other hand, is a man capable of devoting himself to a series of empathetic essays on the rational philosophers of the Enlightenment, yet he can also immerse himself in the *Weltschmerz* of Goethe and the mysticism of Jacob Boehme. He suffers the dilemma of the idealist caught between the Platonic world of ideas and the Aristotelian world of experience.

The parallels in the lives of the two men are many, from the insignificant to the profound. Joseph joins the maid in privately condemning Vanaker for his unsightly underwear, but Joseph's own underwear is so shabby that he sometimes puts his "leg through the wrong hole." Though Joseph is infuriated by Vanaker's disregard for "decency and politeness," he himself is reprimanded by Briggs for "rowdyism . . . making a row." Vanaker steals Iva's perfume; Etta accuses Joseph of stealing something from her mother's bedroom. It is in Vanaker's theft of Joseph's socks, however, that the symbolic significance of the men's relationship is made clear. When he discovers the theft and finally confronts Vanaker directly for his careless toilet habits, Joseph curses him, charges him with stealing, and accuses him of "going before the priest at St. Thomas the Apostle and standing in my socks and stinking of my wife's perfume" (119). Joseph has not consciously "put himself in Vanaker's shoes," but Vanaker has done him the favor of putting himself in Joseph's socks, the next best thing. He has provided Joseph a glimpse into his future if he continues to practice detachment and escape. Joseph senses that there, but for his youth and possibilities, goes he himself. Though Joseph doesn't articulate these matters for himself, it is clear that Vanaker is his alter ego, a Conradian secret sharer. A Death-in-Life figure, he stands daily before Joseph as an object lesson in the price of continued isolation. The violence of Joseph's final outburst against Vanaker is an acknowledgment of his subconscious awareness of the old man's significance and a measure of his resistance to such a future. It is this outburst that drives him in desperation to the draft board.

The conflict with Vanaker is the physical manifestation which triggers Joseph's change of direction, but it has been set up by substantial mental conditioning involving his childhood, chance encounters on the street, his dreams, and his continuing dialogue with his divided self.

One of Joseph's reflections carries him back to an incident in his childhood. When he was four years old and wearing his hair in curls, his Aunt Dina insisted that his hair be cut. His mother, who was vain about his youthful beauty, refused. But his aunt, the family Atropos, had "arbitrary ways." She had his hair cut in Buster Brown style and presented the severed curls to his tearful mother, who preserved the curls in an envelope in a drawer which also contained a picture of her father taken just before his death. When Joseph was fourteen, about Etta's age, he discovered both curls and picture and imagined the curls encircling the old man in the "shroudlike" clothing:[4]

> Then, studying the picture, it occurred to me that this skull of my grandfather's would in time overtake me, curls, Buster Brown, and all. Still after I came to believe (and this was no longer an impression but a dogma) that the picture was a proof of my mortality. (51)

This first encounter with the proof of his mortality leads the hypersensitive Joseph to greet all further evidence of his own death with heightened awareness. With the war

4. It should be mentioned in support of my interpretation of Vanaker that his skull, too, is fringed with curls. Joseph describes him as having a "somewhat concave face, with its high forehead overarched with gray curls in a manner that suggested a bonnet" (53). This observation comes on the heels of Joseph's recollection of his grandfather's picture.

serving as a constant backdrop to the personal drama
which is Joseph's life, Death seems to appear with increasing frequency, and always assumes a human form.

As he goes downtown on January 20 to meet Iva for
dinner on their sixth anniversary, Joseph has a mythic
experience with the ancient Antagonist. He descends from
the El at the Randolph and Wabash station, and he encounters the urban counterpart of Dante's gateway to oblivion. The Styx is a lake and the ferry is a train, but it is
clear from the imagery that the crowds and their ultimate
destination are the same:

> There were crooked streaks of red at one end of the street, and
> at the other, a band of black, soft as a stroke of charcoal; into
> it were hooked the tiny lights of the lake front. On the platform
> the rush-hour crowds were melting under the beams of oncom-
> ing trains. Each train was followed by an interval of darkness,
> when the twin colored lamps of the rear car hobbled around
> the curve. (76)

At the end of a "smoky alley . . . where the south-bound
cars emerge," a man falls down in front of Joseph. The
victim's broad coat was hitched up behind, his chest and
belly rose hugely together as he labored, snoring, for
breath" (77). A mounted policeman is immediately on the
scene:

> His features were sharp, red, wind-scarred, his jaws muscular,
> his sideburns whitish, intersected by the straps of his stiff blue
> cap. He blew his steel whistle. The signal was not necessary.
> Other uniformed men were already coming toward us. (76)

As the ambulance carrying the body slips from the narrow
passageway, Joseph watches the policeman on "the calm
horse stepping away from the car." The policeman is
Death's functionary, a modern Charon, and the fallen man
has provided Joseph with "a prevision":

> Without warning, down. A stone, a girder, a bullet flashes
> against the head, the bone gives like glass from a cheap kiln;
> or a subtler enemy escapes the bonds of years; the blackness
> comes down; we lie, a great weight on our faces, straining
> toward the last breath which comes like a gritting of gravel
> under tread. (77)

Several nights later, on January 26, Joseph has a dream which enables him to descend even further into the Underworld. He dreams he is in Constanza or Bucharest, where "those slain by the Iron Guard were slung from hooks in a slaughter house." His mission is to reclaim for a particular family a corpse from all the massacred bodies around him. He identifies himself to his guide as "an outsider," one who did "not even know the family well." The guide, a man with a "pointed face," smiles in approval of his neutrality. But the smile is offensive to Joseph: It too quickly acknowledges the estrangement he has just claimed from the family of man and from the processes of life that naturally lead to death; it leagues him with the bloodless creature at his side, and he resists the identification. "Could I be such a hypocrite?" he asks.[5] "Do you think he can be found?" (80). The dream ends before the questions are answered, but Joseph has been sufficiently exposed to the nether kingdom to be shaken.

The guide reminds him of a grizzled man who once impressed a bristly kiss on him when he was a boy walking through a muddy back lane. It was a kiss of death. Cerbere-

---

5. The scene at the El (read Hell) and this dream episode suggest in combination the last section of Eliot's "Burial of the Dead" from *The Waste Land.* The city, the crowds, the labored breathing of the fallen man, the Dantean allusions, the search for the corpse, and the mirrored self as Baudelairean "hypocrite" are close enough to cause speculation that Bellow here was constructing his mythic scenes under the influence of Eliot:

> Unreal City
> Under the brown fog of a winter dawn,
> A crowd flowed over London Bridge, so many,
> I had not thought death had undone so many.
> Sighs, short and infrequent, were exhaled,
> And each man fixed his eyes before his feet.
> Flowed up the hill and down King William Street,
> To where Saint Mary Woolnoth kept the hours
> With a dead sound on the final stroke of nine.
> There I saw one I knew, and stopped him, crying: "Stetson!
> "You who were with me in the ships at Mylae!
> "That corpse you planted last year in your garden,
> "Has it begun to sprout? Will it bloom this year?
> "Or has the sudden frost disturbed its bed?
> "Oh keep the Dog far hence, that's friend to men,
> "Or with his nails he'll dig it up again!
> "You! hypocrite lecteur!—mon semblance,—mon frére!"

T. S. Eliot, *Collected Poems and Plays* (New York, 1962), p. 39.

an dogs howled maniacally behind snaggled boards. The policeman at the El, the guide in the charnel house, the man in the alley are interchangeable in Joseph's mind. They are death figures. They are painful reminders to Joseph that he must die, and he knows them for what they are:

> We know we are sought and expect to be found. How many forms he takes, the murderer. Frank, or simple, or a man of depth and cultivation, or perhaps prosaic, without distinction. Yet he is *the* murderer, the stranger who, one day, will drop the smile of courtesy or custom to show you the weapon in his hand, the means of your death. (81)

And there are other reminders. On March 29, two days after the attack on Vanaker and Briggs, and after Joseph has committed himself to the draft board, Mrs. Kiefer dies. She too has been dangling, between life and death, for several weeks. Her funeral seems to commemorate the death of Joseph's plan, or at least the end of his isolation. And on the street he repeatedly encounters the Christian Science woman. She talks mindlessly to him of salvation, but her body speaks to him of death: "Her skin was the color of brick dust; her breath was sour" (107). Because Joseph must constantly view himself in relation to the war, he imagines his end in a wartime situation:

> How will it be? How? Falling a mile into the wrinkled sea? Or, as I have dreamed, cutting a wire? Or strafed in a river among chopped reeds and turning water, blood leaking through the cloth of the sleeves and shoulders? (82)

But once he has confronted his own death, examined it exhaustively, and acolwledged its inevitability, he can either accelerate it by suicide (the first philosophical question, as Camus said), go insane, or turn back to life. Joseph refuses "to worship the anti-life." He exclaims that "there are no values outside life. There is nothing outside life" (110). He turns, then, back to life despite its disorder and apparent meaninglessness and despite his alienation from it.

It is natural that Joseph should continue trying to "sound creation" because he has been a "creature of plans," and even though the theoretical plans have not worked out in the chaotic realm of actuality, the impulse that formulated the plans is still present. Like the untimely butterfly he saw in a brick passageway, Joseph is capable of harboring an impossible hope. To give his hope direction, he seeks to replace the old plan with an "ideal construction" which will enable him to come to terms with the actual world and its war and still retain a sense of his personal identity, a plan that will allow him to reconcile the ideal world with the real world. He is aided in this philosophic search by the voice of his divided self, to whom he gives a local habitation and a name: *Tu As Raison Aussi,* the Spirit of Alternatives.

As the occasion for both death and dramatic human conflict in the realm of actuality, the war is a central problem for Joseph. He does not wish to profit from it indirectly as Fanzel the tailor has done or as his brother, Amos, is doing. Nor does he wish to profit directly by seeking a commission that would give him immediate military advantage and have carry-over value for his later civilian life. If he goes, he tells Amos, it will be in emulation of Socrates, as a hoplite, a common foot soldier. But Joseph is not sure that he should go. It is not so much a question of his death, which he has come to accept, but his destiny. He declares that he would "rather be a victim than a beneficiary of the war," but he is also resigned to the possibility that he may victimize others:

> Yes, I shall shoot, I shall take lives; I shall be shot at, and my life may be taken. Certain blood will be given for half-certain reasons, as in all wars. Somehow I cannot regard it as a wrong against myself. (57)

If his destiny is to kill, then he will kill. The question that puzzles him—and keeps him dangling—is this: Is it indeed his destiny? Is his fate linked with all the Frinks, Burnses, Briggses, and Formans in the world? Does his life of quiet desperation have no unique qualities to distinguish it from the mass of men? Must he submit his individuality to an institution as totally limiting as a wartime army? These are questions which he takes up with the Spirit of Alternatives.

In his first talk with the Spirit of Alternatives, Joseph seeks, through reason, to come to terms with his world. He mentions that the present century falls short of ancient civilization; the Hollywood dream is a travesty of Hellenic culture. He wonders what has happened to man, to himself. The Spirit of Alternatives mentions Joseph's alienation; he suggests that Joseph relies too heavily on reason at the expense of instinct and feeling. "Then what are we given reason for?" Joseph asks. "To discover the blessedness of unreason? That's a very poor argument" (90). Joseph desires a plan that will enable him to proclaim, "This is the only possible way to meet chaos." The Spirit of Alternatives gives it a name: an "ideal construction." Yes, Joseph wants an ideal construction, but he is aware that such constructions in the past have been unable to encompass the complexity of the real world. He asks the Spirit if the "gap between the ideal construction and the real world" can be bridged. The Spirit reminds him that his province is alternatives, not answers. To Joseph the Spirit is another alter ego, an opposing self; he is also here the devil's advocate. He throws Joseph back on his own resources, which are proving inadequate. Luther fashion, the furious Joseph flings orange peel at him to banish him from the room.

At the next appearance of the Spirit of Alternatives, Joseph is calmer about the war and about his isolation in his room. He tries to explain his position to the Spirit:

> I would be denying my inmost feelings if I said I wanted to be bypassed and spared from knowing what the rest of my generation is undergoing. I don't want to be humped protectively over my life. I am neither so corrupt nor so hard-boiled that I can savor my life only when it is in danger of extinction. But, on the other hand, its value here in this room is decreasing day by day. Soon it may become distasteful to me. (110)

He admits that there is vanity in thinking that he can make his "own way toward clarity," and he wonders if he is justified in trying to preserve himself from the "flood of death that has carried off so many." He wants to preserve the integrity of his mind, "the self that we must govern," despite the war. He wishes to view the war as an incident, something comparable to the childhood diseases which he managed to survive "to become Joseph."

> The war can destroy me physically. That it can do. But so can bacteria. I must be concerned with them, naturally. I must take account of them. They can obliterate me. But as long as I am alive, I must follow my destiny in spite of them. (112)

Then the Spirit of Alternatives asks the question which Joseph has been wrestling with in vain for much of the past year. He asks if Joseph truly has a separate destiny? That is, can he define himself in any essential way apart from the others who make up his world? Has the freedom to which Joseph has been condemned allowed him to see an ideal Joseph whom he can reconcile with the actual Joseph in the real world? Joseph pales. He cannot answer the question. This conversation is recorded in the entry for March 16. Ten days later occurs the scene with Vanaker when Joseph decides to give up his freedom.

Joseph does not answer the question, but neither does he acknowledge that the answer is "no" nor that the question is unanswerable. His decision to force his induction is simply a sign that his present method of examining the issue has failed. In one of his reflections he admits his failure:

> I had not done well alone. I doubted whether anyone could. To be pushed upon oneself entirely put the very facts of simple existence in doubt. Perhaps the war could teach me, by violence, what I had been unable to learn during those months in the room. Perhaps I could sound creation through other means. Perhaps. But things were now out of my hands. The next move was the world's. I could not bring myself to regret it. (126)

His last entry (April 9) records a kind of affirmation:

> I am in other hands, relived in self-determination, freedom cancelled.
> Hurray for regular hours!
> And for the supervision of the spirit!
> Long live regimentation! (126)

This conclusion is, of course, ironic. Whatever joy there is in it is supplied by relief. He does not praise regimentation, which he knows nothing about, or regular hours, though Goethe recommends them; he celebrates instead the end of his long, painful isolation, the return to community experience, however imperfect, and the bare possibility that he may indeed find answers to his questions in a new way of life. But there is no illusion here. He has long since recognized that the world allows man's reason only limited access to the nebulous principles according to which it operates: "I know now that I shall have to settle for very, very little. That is, I shall have to accept very little, for there is no question of settling. Personal choice does not count for much these days" (83).

This is a sadder Joseph than the Joseph of a year ago. He is still, characteristically, sitting in a room, but this time it is his old room in his father's house. He has only one day left as a civilian. On the wall is a picture of a dead Persian youth in his grave, upon which his bereaved sweetheart drops a flower. This is the final isolation, the end. Joseph thinks of the picture and of his youth, and suddenly he has a mystical experience:

> The room, delusively, dwindled and became a tiny square, swiftly drawn back, myself and all the objects in it growing smaller. This was not a mere visual trick. I understood it to be a revelation of the ephemeral agreements by which we live and pace ourselves. I looked around at the restored walls. *This place which I avoided ordinarily had great personal significance for me.* But it was not here thirty years ago. Birds flew through this space. It may be gone fifty years hence. Such reality, I thought, is actually very dangerous, very treacherous. It should not be trusted. (126) [My italics.]

The room has become a room with a view; it has provided historical and metaphysical perspective, teaching Joseph the finality of death, the ephemeral—and therefore precious—nature of life, and the dangers of isolating oneself from "this place which . . . had great personal significance." Such isolation leads to questioning that, as Joseph has noted, puts "the very facts of simple existence in doubt." The baffling symbolic walls by which Joseph has been surrounded have finally given way a little. They have not revealed any universal secrets, but they have at least provided Joseph with a way back into the universe of man, where, amid the dust and heat of a Miltonic battlefield, he can still seek to answer, intellectually and morally, the old question, "How should a good man live?"

2.

The Victim: A Cast of Millions

Bellow's second novel, *The Victim,* tells the story of Asa Leventhal, a middle-aged New York Jew who, during a difficult period in his career, unknowingly causes a gentile named Kirby Allbee to lose his job. The loss of his job causes the weak-willed Allbee to lose his wife, first by separation, then by death in a highway accident. With the insurance money from his estranged wife's death, Allbee makes a perverted attempt through drunkenness to relieve himself of the guilt he feels for his wife's tragedy. His drinking and distraction soon cause his sense of guilt to give way to the suspicion that Leventhal is the real cause of his wife's death and his own degradation. He becomes intent on making Leventhal expiate his alleged guilt for the error which led to Allbee's degeneration. Confusing Leventhal with accusations, Allbee insinuates himself into Leventhal's home, where he intensifies his persecution by bringing filth into the house, by reading intimate letters from Leventhal's wife (who is temporarily visiting her mother in Charleston), and by entertaining a prostitute in Leventhal's bed. At first Leventhal denies any responsibility for Allbee's plight. Later, compassion and a complex of other feelings lead Leventhal to accept in an ambivalent way some measure of guilt for Allbee's condition, but when Allbee's excesses become too great—including a murder attempt thinly veiled as suicide—Leventhal throws him out, freeing himself finally from this macabre personal nemesis. A few years later they meet accidentally in a theater. Both men have come to terms with their personal problems, Leventhal substantially, Allbee only superficially. Allbee is the gigolo of a once-famous actress, and Leventhal, more relaxed and younger looking, is a successful editor and father-to-be. Allbee expresses a vague sort of debt by way of apology to Leventhal for his earlier behavior, and the two part in an ambiguous fashion.

The Victim is a difficult book. The problems it presents have received a good deal of critical attention, and the various ways critics have approached it testify to its complexity. Chester Eisinger sees the central problem of Asa Leventhal as that of "a man who falls short of love and understanding and humanity. . . . His plight is a function of the anti-Semitism, real and imagined, that he feels engulfs him. Loaded with these disabilities [self-interest and fear of victimization]. . . Asa is asked to consider the nature and extent of one human being's responsibility to another."[1] For Eisinger the main thematic concerns are anti-Semitism and existential responsibility. Marcus Klein also sees a theme of responsibility in the novel but believes that the ordering strategy involves a tension in "the basic conflict between the self that demands preservation and the society that demands self-sacrifice,"[2] that is, between what one owes oneself and what one owes to others. Irving Malin interprets *The Victim* as "a novel of fathers and sons."[3] Leventhal rejects his natural father, is tyrannized by business fathers (Williston, Rudiger, Harkavy, Dunhill), disturbed by a kind of paternal conscience (Allbee), and becomes himself first a surrogate father (to Mickey, Philip, and Max) and at last, with Mary's pregnancy, a real father, thus finding a natural and psychological resolution to his ambivalence toward fatherhood.

Jonathan Baumbach assigns to Allbee the role of psychological and symbolic double; he "is not the cause but the occasion of Leventhal's victimization—the objectification of his free-floating guilt. . . . Allbee is . . . the personification of his evil possibilities, . . . the grotesque exaggeration of his counterpart. He represents Leventhal's failings carried to their logical insanity."[4] Only by acknowledging that

1. Chester E. Eisinger, *Fiction of the Forties* (Chicago, 1963), p. 350.
2. Marcus Klein, *After Alienation* (Cleveland, 1965), p. 37.
3. Irving Malin, *Saul Bellow's Fiction* (Carbondale, Ill., 1969), pp. 59 ff.
4. Jonathan Baumbach, *The Landscape of Nightmare* (New York, 1965), pp. 40–42.

he has such a counterpart can Leventhal come to terms with the evil in himself (and Evil, as Baumbach makes clear) and thus become truly human. "Bellow is suggesting here that ultimately the best and worst instincts of man are not always distinguishable. Heaven, which is redemption, can only and finally be reached through Hell." [5] A similar view is expressed by Keith Opdahl: "Bellow subordinates the theme of man's fear of imaginary evil to that of man's denial of the real evil in the world and himself. Each of the characters, Bellow shows, views the other as a symbol of the evil he would deny. The moral issue between the two men becomes an issue concerning the nature of the world and man's ability to face it."[6] John Clayton claims that the theme of the book lies in Asa's "casting-off of his self-imposed burdens by learning to accept himself and others rather than to judge and blame, by learning to have an open heart."[7] Asa must move from suspicion and blaming (of himself and others) to acceptance and loving (of himself and others). In their discussions of the plot of *The Victim,* Klein, Opdahl, and Clayton all point to the many parallels in Dostoevski's *The Eternal Husband.* [8] James Hall, on the other hand, sees Kafka's *The Trial* and Joyce's *Ulysses* as the two books "that obviously stand behind" *The Victim.* "The large movement of the novel," he asserts, "depends on setting Leventhal against a grotesque of his own fears and anger; moving him to a point where he

5. Ibid., p. 45.

6. Keith Opdahl, *The Novels of Saul Bellow: An Introduction* (University Park, Pa., 1967), p. 59.

7. John J. Clayton, *Saul Bellow: In Defense of Man* (Bloomington, Ind., 1968), p. 139.

8. John Clayton and Keith Opdahl give full discussions of these parallels, but Marcus Klein's general summary will suffice here: "Velchaninov becomes the victim of a man whom many years ago he had wronged. The parallels between *The Victim* and *The Eternal Husband* are in fact numerous and detailed, and there can be no doubt that Bellow had this Dostoevski novella in mind. Velchaninov finds himself one sultry summer alone in St. Petersburg. He becomes aware suddenly that he is being haunted by a man he faintly recognizes. Pavel Pavolovich, whom he had once victimized[through cuckoldry],gradually intrudes himself into Velchaninov's intimacy and at last moves into his apartment with him. It is when Pavel tries to murder him that Velchaninov can begin to unravel the complications of guilt and expiation that bind him to Pavel, and thereby free himself." *After Alienation,* p. 37.

identifies with the fear and where only its total removal promises relief; then bringing him, as much from exhaustion as wisdom, to distinguish between the extreme and his own actuality."[9]

Clearly there is a large area of agreement among these views on thematic matters and on the basic strategy which pits Allbee against Leventhal and finally frees each from the other as a changed man. There are also, however, numerous differences in focus and emphasis which point up the several levels Bellow is working on. Everyone seems to agree, for example, that "*The Victim* . . . is traditionally plotted, well-made in the Jamesian sense,"[10] a fully realistic novel in the tradition of the American novel in the forties. Opdahl concludes, however, that "we miss the expected denouement of a realistic novel because *The Victim* is finally not realistic," [11] and he blames the obscurity of the novel on this shift—"thematic escalation"—from the social level to the religious one. Similar observations have been made by others. Alan S. Downer, for instance, believes that there is too much contrivance for a realistic novel, insisting "it is never clear what *The Victim* is about." [12]

"Thematic escalation" seems a fair enough description, but not in the sense of a shift. It is more in the nature of a parallel development, a kind of epiphenomenal progression from the realistic to the symbolic. But both levels are constantly present, like a little boy on the sidewalk and his elongated shadow in the gutter—or, to use Bellow's epigraph, the merchant on the ground and Ifrit in the sky. "The novel," Howard Harper has said, "may be read either as realism (as most casual readers see it) or as symbolism (as many critics see it) without reference to the other level; yet each level is powerfully strengthened, and in no way twisted, by the other."[13] My purpose here is to show that

9. James Hall, *The Lunatic Giant in the Drawing Room* (Bloomington, Ind., 1968), p. 143.

10. Baumbach, p. 39.

11. Opdahl, p. 52.

12. Alan S. Downer, *New York Times Book Review*, 52 (November 30, 1947), 29. Downer also mentions Bellow's closeness in *The Victim* to Kafka and Joyce.

13. Howard M. Harper, Jr., *Desperate Faith* (Chapel Hill, N.C., 1967),

the themes involving fear of failure, anti-Semitism, and existential responsibility are embodied at the realistic level in characterization, dialogue, and metaphor, and that these themes at the symbolic level expand to encompass the larger problems of Evil and Death, suggested in a shadowy and appropriately ambiguous way in setting, allusion, and situation. The subtle way in which the two levels overlap—the natural with the supernatural, the actual with the imaginary, the mythic, or the symbolic—seems an objective correlative for the way the two realms merge in human experience. The interaction of the two becomes at last the rhetorical stance of the novel.

Asa Leventhal is a ponderous physical presence in *The Victim.* He stands anxiously at the center of the narrative tumbrel that moves steadily toward a guillotine that finally never really appears. A big man at 210 pounds, Leventhal is described as "burly," "ordinarily not neat"; he has "thick brown wrists," and his trousers sag "loose at the knees."[14] He does not have the hypersensitive brilliance of a Herzog but has instead "an intelligence not greatly interested in its own powers, . . . indifferent." He is most often characterized as "impassive." He gives the impression of an unaccommodating, taciturn, moderately successful businessman.

This is the public Leventhal. Underneath this impassive exterior he is a cauldron of feelings. He can consider smashing the face of an offensive woman behind him and Mary at the movies, he does lose his temper with Rudiger, and he attacks the derelict Allbee. Yet he is also capable of troubling to take his nephew Philip to the zoo, of putting his hand gently to the cheek of the dying Mickey, or of kissing tenderly a love letter from his absent wife. He is, moreover, frightened of failure despite his relatively comfortable success: an ambivalent man. It is this ambivalence that leads him to be vulnerable to the accusations of Allbee.

---

p. 23.

14. Saul Bellow, *The Victim* (New York, 1947), p. 20. Page numbers, hereafter in parentheses in the text, are from the readily available Signet edition (New York, 1965).

Leventhal's insecurity stems from two sources: his early hard times and his Jewishness (though he is not orthodox). The son of an authoritarian, turbulent father and a mother who died insane when he was eight, Leventhal had an unhappy and unstable childhood. His first job as an adult in the senior Harkavy's auction house resulted from an uncle's influence and ended when the business closed. Months of hardship followed as he worked part time in a shoe store, full time as a fur dyer, and then as a clerk in "a hotel for transients on lower Broadway." By luck, a civil service job in the Baltimore customhouse lifted him out of these sordid surroundings and ultimately led him to Burke–Beard and Company, but he is still haunted by the seamy side of life which he barely escaped, by those who represent the price of failure, "the part that did not get away with it—the lost, the outcast, the overcome, the effaced, the ruined" (26). That he may be returned by the indifferent shuffle of things to such a condition is his constant fear.

His fear is intensified by the vulnerability he feels as a Jew in what seems to him an environment charged with anti-Semitism. In the business world he has felt the sting of anti-Semitism in the hostility of Rudiger and, more recently, in the unjustified suspicions of Beard that Leventhal is malingering: "Takes unfair advantage," Beard charges when Asa goes to Elena's aid, "like the rest of his brethren. I've never known one who wouldn't" (13). Among his relatives, too, he feels threatened. He is certain that Elena and her mother (both Catholic) will use his Jewishness as an excuse for blaming him for the death of Mickey. In his personal life he is explicitly exposed to the anti-Semitism of Allbee. Leventhal even accuses his long-time friend and ally Williston of being anti-Semitic because he sides with Allbee:

> You think that he[Allbee] burned me up and I wanted to get him in bad. Why? Because I'm a Jew; Jews are touchy, and if you hurt them they won't forgive you. That's the pound of flesh. Oh, I know you think there isn't any room in you for that; it's superstition. But you don't change anything by calling it superstition. (106–7)

Leventhal's distaste for the persecution to which he feels Jews are subject makes him hypersensitive to the possibility of a similar persecuting spirit in himself. He also fears that the squalor he escaped from as a bumbling youth may still be visited on him as a man either unworthy of success or one, like the merchant in the epigraph, who has accidentally offended the power who "runs things." Both feelings prepare the way for the admission of Allbee into his life.

Although his personal history is very sketchy, Allbee is as vividly rendered physically as Leventhal: "His cuffs were frayed, the threads raveled on the blond hairs of his wrist. His hands were dirty. His fair hair, unevenly divided on his scalp, was damp" (67). As Leventhal stands with Philip at the zoo, his sense of Allbee's presence is so strong that he can "see the weave of his coat, his raggedly overgrown neck, the bulge of his cheek, the color of blood in his ear; he can even evoke the odor of his hair and skin" (99). Leventhal is constantly repulsed by the odor of sweat and alcohol that Allbee gives off; yet Stan and Phoebe Williston insist that Allbee was once a charming, fastidious man. He is a realistic, fully rounded character, and though he may be sporadically deranged, his claim on Leventhal is finally compelling enough to force Leventhal's partial acknowledgment of its validity.

Why does Allbee single out Leventhal as his victim, as the cause of his own victimization? Opdahl, following Sartre, offers a perceptive explanation:

> Anti-Semitism is "fear of the human condition" and is "at bottom a form of Manichaeism." The bigot's hatred is an "explanatory myth," in which he prefers a world ordered by "the struggle of the principle of Good with the principle of Evil" to a world of accident. The anti-Semite's projection of evil onto the Jews is his attempt to order the world by giving tangible shape to his fears.[15]

At the realistic level, then, Allbee is a man who feels that the world is chaos and is frightened by it. He allays his fears in part by ordering the world in his distracted mind according to a deterministic theory, a principle of persecu-

15. Opdahl, p. 51.

tion. He attributes to his individual enemy a larger malevo-
lent force, in this case an international Jewish conspiracy.
His action is to him both a curious comfort and, he hopes,
a source of restitution. Leventhal does help him, of course,
but only by throwing him back on his own resources, by
dispelling his illusions.

It is not difficult to understand, either, why Leventhal
allows himself to be manipulated by such a man, though
Leventhal himself is puzzled both by Allbee's accusations
and by his own response:

> In a general way, anyone could see that there was great unfair-
> ness in one man's having all the comforts of life while another
> had nothing. But between man and man, how was this to be
> dealt with? Any derelict panhandler or bum might buttonhole
> you on the street and say, "The world wasn't made for you any
> more than it was for me, was it?" The error in this was to forget
> that neither man had made the arrangements, and so it was
> perfectly right to say, "Why pick on me? I didn't set this up any
> more than you did." Admittedly there was a wrong, a general
> wrong. Allbee, on the other hand, came along and said "You!"
> and that was what was so meaningless. For you might feel that
> something was owing to the panhandler, but to be directly
> blamed was entirely different. (77)

Like the panhandler, Allbee steps into Leventhal's path
and says, *"J'accuse."* Suddenly Leventhal's insularity is
shattered. With his wife away and his absent brother's
family in his charge during a crisis, Leventhal is already off
balance. Allbee's appearance forces Leventhal into an une-
quivocal confrontation with his own values and his relations with others.

To Leventhal, Allbee represents the spectre of failure to
which he himself was—and still is—subject. His empathy
with Allbee is vivid and deep: When Allbee explains that
he is down and out, Leventhal imagines his condition:

> There rose to Leventhal's mind the most horrible images of
> men wearily sitting on mission benches waiting for their coffee
> in a smeared and bleary winter sun; of flophouse sheets and
> filthy pillows; hideous cardboard cubicles painted to resemble
> wood, even the tungsten in the bulb like little burning worms
> that seemed to eat up rather than give light. . . . He could smell
> the carbolic disinfectant. And if it were *his* flesh on those

sheets, *his* lips drinking that coffee, *his* back and thighs in that winter sun, *his* eyes looking at the boards of the floor . . .? Allbee was right to smile at him; he had never been in such a plight. (67–68)

Although he has been exposed to such conditions, Leventhal has never really "been in such a plight"; consequently, the law of averages is against him: He may be in line for such a fate yet. He cannot deny Allbee's assertion that "the things we sometimes think are permanent, they aren't permanent. So one day we're like full bundles and the next we're wrapping paper, blowing around the streets" (73). Taking Allbee in, then, is both an act of compassion and an attempt by Leventhal to compensate for what he has acknowledged as a general wrong in the order of things. It is also an attempt to placate a mysterious fate and thus ensure his own future security, a self-interested casting of bread on troubled waters.

Leventhal's actions can be explained, furthermore, as a refutation of the charge that the anti-Semitic Allbee has made against him. Allbee believes that "the world has changed hands" (203), that the Jews, "the sons of Caliban" (131), are now running things, and that they are hostile to the interests of gentiles. (That this deterministic view is inconsistent with his theory of an indifferent universe doesn't trouble Allbee, logic not being an attribute of a drunken, deranged mind.) He resents Harkavy's singing of Christian spirituals and is angered to discover that a critique of Emerson and Thoreau has been written by a Jew named Lipschitz. Allbee's accusation is leveled against Leventhal emphatically and unequivocally:

> You try to put all the blame on me, but you know it's true that you're to blame. You and you only. For everything. You ruined me. Ruined! Because that's what I am, ruined! You're the one that's responsible. You did it to me deliberately, out of hate. Out of pure hate! (74)

Because Leventhal has been a victim of anti-Semitism and despises that kind of prejudice, he is anxious to purge any taint of a similar feeling in himself. By helping Allbee despite his anti-Semitism, Leventhal dramatically under-

mines the grounds of Allbee's charges and frees himself
further from what Baumbach calls his "free-floating guilt"
over his relative success and security. The motives and
actions of both men are fully explored, completely realistic, and wholly human.

What is human and where guilt and responsibility lie are
much discussed in *The Victim,* by Harkavy, by Schlossberg, and by Allbee; Leventhal stands in relation to these
men as Herzog stands in relation to his "reality instructors." Leventhal does learn from them, and what he learns
(sometimes merely confirming his own thoughts) affects
his evaluation of himself and his final treatment of Allbee.

Harkavy believes that Leventhal strives for insularity as
a kind of human perfection and that this isolation makes
him oversensitive to slights from others and vulnerable to
unreasonable impositions. When Leventhal voices his fear
of professional reprisal by Rudiger for the recent scene in
his office over Leventhal's application for a job, Harkavy
comforts and cautions him: "He can't persecute you. Now
be careful. You have that tendency, do you know that?"
(48) And when Leventhal continues to seek Harkavy's
counsel on Allbee's persistent harassment, Harkavy warns
him that he is trying to deal with the matter beyond the
limitations of the human:

> If you don't mind, Asa, there's one thing I have to point out that
> you haven't learned. We're not children. We're men of the
> world. It's almost a sin to be so innocent. Get next to yourself,
> boy, will you? You want the whole world to like you. There're
> bound to be some people who don't think well of you. . . . I
> happen to have found out that a young lady I always liked said
> I was conceited. . . . What about this girl? I know she has
> reasons that she doesn't understand herself. All I can say is,
> "Lady, God bless you, we all have our faults and are what we
> are. I have to take myself as I am or push off. I am all I have
> in this world. And with all my shortcomings my life is precious
> to me." My heart doesn't sink. Experience has taught me to
> expect this once in a while. But you're so upset when some-
> body doesn't like you, or says this or that about you. A little
> independence, boy; it's a weakness, positively. (83–84)

Despite the Polonius-style posturing here, Leventhal recognizes a persuasive element of truth. Later at Harkavy's

house the evening of the birthday party for Julia's daughter Leventhal, untypically, gets drunk in order to escape momentarily the weight of his problem.[16] The next morning, when Leventhal explains that he has been distraught over the death of Mickey, Harkavy urges him again, in the name of life, to free himself from Allbee:

> You admitted you wanted to get the man off your neck. Don't hide behind the child. That's not good. It's dishonest. Wake up! What's life? Metabolism? That's what it is for the bugs. Jesus Christ, no! What's life? Consciousness, that's what it is. That's what you're short on. For God's sake, give yourself a push and a shake. It's dangerous stuff, Asa, this stuff. (231)

This conversation occurs when Harkavy learns that Leventhal is considering involving himself even deeper with Allbee by sending him to Shifcart with a reference. Harkavy reminds Leventhal that initially he judged Allbee insane. Leventhal denies he said so. The scene parallels the scene in which Max (the real brother as opposed to Allbee as psychological brother) denies Leventhal's suspicion that Elena and her mother are probably insane, an example of Bellow's extensive use of parallel plotting in the novel.

Allbee's comments to Leventhal are close to those of Harkavy, but his words are prompted by a very different motive, the desire to use Leventhal to his own advantage. Usually what he says is a reflection of his immediate condition and hastily formed plan. When as a derelict he first talks seriously with Leventhal, Allbee offers himself as an example of victimized humanity in a deterministic universe, merely another creature buffeted about by powerful external forces: "I don't know how you look at it, but I take it for granted that we're not gods, we're only creatures"

---

16. Leventhal's atypical drunkenness is a link with Allbee's habitual drunkenness; it emphasizes, as Baumbach has noted, the doubleness of the men's relationship; but it also may be at the subconscious level Leventhal's refutation of another of Allbee's charges against the Jews: "You're a true Jew, Leventhal. You have the true horror of drink. We're the sons of Belial to you, we smell of whiskey worse than of sulphur. When Noah lies drunk—you remember that story?—his gentile-minded sons have a laugh at the old man, but his Jewish son is horrified. There's truth in that story. It's a true story" (73). Leventhal belies the story with a hangover.

(73). Later, however, when he is offering to "settle" with Leventhal in return for an interview with Shifcart—and thereby an opportunity for work and advancement—Allbee claims (again contradicting his early view) to be ready to exercise the option for change available to all men within a Christian framework:

> Now let me explain something to you. It's a Christian idea but I don't see why you shouldn't be able to understand it. "Repent!" That's John the Baptist coming out of the desert. Change yourself, that's what he's saying, and be another man. You must be and the reason for that is that you can be, and when your time comes here you will be. (199)

In part Leventhal considers Allbee's resolve genuine, but also he wishes to get Allbee out of his life, to "settle" with him. He agrees to contact Shifcart for him, but throws Allbee out subsequently when he discovers him in bed with a whore. Allbee considers his ouster a ploy by Leventhal to get rid of him. He accuses Leventhal of cynicism and being less than human: "You certainly are not the same as everybody else" (238). Leventhal counters with an almost identical charge: "You're not even human if you ask me." The climactic hostility generated here leads to the abortive suicide/murder scene and the final expulsion of Allbee, the dramatic evidence that Leventhal has changed himself and become "another man."

The new stance that Leventhal takes toward life has been present in embryo all along. Early in the novel Leventhal observes to himself the inescapable complexity of individual existence in a world of masses:

> Well, the world was a busy place. . . . You couldn't find a place in your feelings for everything, or give at every touch like a swinging door, the same for everyone, with people going in and out as they pleased. On the other hand, if you shut yourself up not wanting to be bothered, then you were like a bear in a winter hole, or like a mirror wrapped in a piece of flannel. And like such a mirror you were in less danger of being broken, but you didn't flash either. But you had to flash. That was the peculiar thing. Everybody wanted to be what he was to the limit. (92)

Allbee at first prevents Leventhal from being what he is "to the limit," but by coming to terms with Allbee, Leventhal, paradoxically, achieves a larger view of himself and his world, a more balanced humanity. Because man has to act ("you had to flash"), he is, as Sartre said, "condemned to freedom." Because actions are based on inadequate knowledge of their possible results, the world is absurd and therefore, as Leventhal acknowledges, there is a "general wrong." He is willing, then, to accept some existential responsibility for Allbee's plight; but he is not willing to admit any deliberate guilt in the matter, for he is, after all, an imperfect and limited creature, a human being. He acknowledges the imperfections in the universe and accepts his own limitations, and he learns to strike a balance between what he owes to himself and what he owes to others. Paradoxically again, by throwing Allbee on his own resources, Leventhal enables the derelict to make a similar adjustment in his turn, though his final choice of life over death becomes an improvement in his condition only at the financial level.

Leventhal's development receives its most explicit explanation in the comments Schlossberg makes on two different occasions. Late in the novel Schlossberg echoes Leventhal's observation that everybody wants to be what he is "to the limit." At the birthday party he makes this statement on life and death:

> But I have to be myself in full. Which is somebody who dies, isn't it? That's what I was from the beginning. I'm not three people, four people. I was born once and I will die once. You want to be two people? More than human? Maybe it's because you don't know how to be one. (223)

He concludes by decrying the evasive practices of funeral homes: "Paper grass in the grave makes all the grass paper." That is, to falsify death, a natural part of life, is to falsify life—to give a semblance of a cheap immortality and thus to be less than human: A serious denial of what is both natural and human. Earlier, on a Sunday afternoon in a cafeteria on Fourteenth Street, Leventhal runs into Harkavy, Goldstone, Shifcart, and Schlossberg. He joins them for lunch, and the conversation turns to the merits of

individual actors and actresses. After many exchanges of
diverse opinion, Schlossberg delivers a long discourse on
the relation of acting to the human:

"I'll tell you. It's bad to be less than human and it's bad to be
more than human. What's more than human? Our friend—"he
meant Leventhal, "was talking about it before. Caesar, if you
remember, in the play wanted to be like a god. Can a god have
diseases? So this is a sick man's idea of God. Does a statue have
wax in its ears? Naturally not. It doesn't sweat, either, except
maybe blood on holidays. If I can talk myself into it that I never
sweat and make everybody else act as if it was true, maybe I
can fix it up about dying, too. We only know what it is to die
because some people die and, if we make ourselves different
from them, maybe we don't have to? Less than human is the
other side of it. I'll come to it. So here is the whole thing, then.
Good acting is what is exactly human. And if you say I am a
tough critic, you mean I have a high opinion of what is human.
This is my whole idea. More than human, can you have any
use for life? Less that human, you don't either. [My italics.]'. . .
You say less than human, more than human. Tell me please,
what is human?' And really we study people so much now that
after we look at human nature—I write science articles myself—after you look at it and weigh it and turn it over and put
it under a microscope, you might say, 'What is all the shouting
about? A man is nothing, his life is nothing. Or it is even lousy
and cheap. But this your royal highness doesn't like, so he
hokes it up. With what? With greatness and beauty. Beauty
and greatness? Black and white, I know. I didn't make it up.'
But I say, 'What do you know? No, tell me, what do you know?
You shut one eye and look at a thing, and it is one way to you.
You shut the other and it is different: I am as sure about
greatness and beauty as you are about black and white. If a
human life is a great thing to me, it *is* a great thing. Do you
know better? I'm entitled as much as you. And why be meazly?
Do you have to be? Is somebody holding you by the neck?
Have dignity, you understand me? Choose dignity. Nobody
knows enough to turn it down.' Now to whom should this
mean something if not to an actor? If he isn't for dignity, then
I tell you there is a great mistake somewhere." (121–22)

Harkavy responds to this impassioned, Yiddish-flavored
address with a "Bravo!" and Shifcart, a theatrical agent,
tosses his card to Schlossberg and suggests mock-seriously
that he come in for a test. It is Leventhal, though, who
solemnly retrieves—and keeps—the card, symbolizing,

however obliquely, that he is the "good actor" who will achieve the "exactly human."

Not only does Schlossberg's speech explain the human balance that Leventhal eventually strikes, but it also ties together a number of related threads having to do with tickets, acting, and the theater, providing what is at last a unifying metaphor in the novel. Leventhal's early difficulties in securing a job made him fear that there was no place for him anywhere, and this feeling came to a climax in Rudiger's office when Leventhal gave angry vent to his frustration. Rudiger made him feel that "the lowest price he put on himself was too high" and, as Leventhal tells Williston, "He made me believe what I was afraid of" (110). What he is afraid of is a black list that will ensure his permanent displacement, and though his job with Burke–Beard and Company thrusts this fear to the back of his mind, he is slow to escape from it, and he is never totally free from it.

Situations conveying a sense of displacement and misplacement recur frequently in the novel and are often objectified by situations involving tickets. In the first scene, for example, Leventhal, riding on the Third Avenue train, almost misses his stop; he shouts angrily at the conductor, squeezes through the closing door and descends to the street "bitterly irritated" (11). On his way to Mickey's funeral, he almost misses his bus; he has to bang on the door as the bus pulls away from the curb. He squeezes himself inside the crowded doorway. "The driver raised himself in his seat and called out something, stridently" (158). Leventhal has several dreams. In one he misses his train and is prevented from catching another by a workman at a barrier who tells him, "You can't go through, I've got people working here" (150). In another dream he is confronted by a strange salesgirl whose perfume reminds him of Allbee's whore. She is trying to sell him rouge for Mary in a department store next to "an amusement park with ticket booths" (245). In the cafeteria with Harkavy, Leventhal forgets to get a ticket from the cashier (112); he frequently has trouble getting seated in crowded restaurants (186), or he gets undesirable seats (27). On his outing with Philip, Leventhal finds himself reluctantly occupying a seat he doesn't enjoy: The horror movie bores him, the theater is too hot. He kills time in the restroom, later fidgets in his seat, finally falls asleep. All of these situations suggest a general malcontent in a man who is not comfortable in his world, a man who has not really found his "place."

Early in the novel, Leventhal castigates himself for his passiveness with others:

> His difficulty, he reflected, was that when he didn't have time to consider, when pressure was put on him, he behaved like a fool. That, mainly, was what troubled him. For instance, last week at the press Dunhill, the linotyper, sold him a ticket he didn't want. He protested that he didn't care for shows and had no use for one ticket—this was before Mary left. But because Dunhill had insisted, he bought the ticket. . . . Now if only he had been able to say at the outset, "I will not buy your ticket." (30)

The ticket motif is introduced in this passage, and it is continued in the situations involving public transportation, dreams, restaurants, and movies. It is reinforced by Leventhal's reflections toward the end of the novel.

Several years have passed, and Leventhal is now a successful editor of *Antique Horizons,* a prestigious national magazine. He is a relaxed, better-adjusted man; he looks years younger, for "something recalcitrant" seems to have left him. He has found his place and no longer feels that he "got away with it." He rarely thinks of Allbee because he suspects the man is long since dead and buried in Potter's Field. Though Leventhal enjoys a degree of stability and a certain contentment, he still ponders the nature of things:

> He was thankful for his job at *Antique Horizons;* he didn't underestimate it; there weren't many better jobs in the trade field. He was lucky, of course. It was understandable that a man suffered when he did not have a place. On the other hand, it was pitiful that he should envy the man who had one. In Leventhal's mind, this was not even a true injustice, for how could you call anything so haphazard an injustice? It was a shuffle, all, all accidental and haphazard. And somewhere, besides, there was a wrong emphasis. As though a man really could be made for, say, Burke–Beard and Company, as though

that were true work instead of a delaying maze to be gone
through daily in a misery so habitual that one became absent-
minded about it. This was wrong. But the error rose out of
something very mysterious, namely, a conviction or illusion
that at the start of life, and perhaps even before, a promise had
been made. In thinking of this promise, Leventhal compared it
to a ticket, a theater ticket. And with his ticket, a man entitled
to an average seat might feel too shabby for the dress circle or
sit in it defiantly and arrogantly; another, entitled to the best
in the house might cry out in rage to the usher who led him to
the third balcony. And how many more stood disconsolately
in the rain and snow, in the long line of those who could only
expect to be turned away? But no, this was incorrect. The
reality was different. For why should tickets, mere tickets, be
promised if promises were being made—tickets to desirable
and undesirable places? There were more important things to
be promised. Possibly there was a promise, since so many felt
it. He himself was almost ready to affirm that there was. But
it was misunderstood. (248–49)

The ticket analogy is appropriate to a man whose daily life
is regulated according to the schedules of buses, ferries,
and subways, and a great deal of the minutiae of the book
have set up this reflection, but the passage is by no means
without its ambiguities. Observing that the world is not
unjust but "haphazard," Leventhal declares that a "mysterious error" leads to a misconception that promises had
been made. He then suggests that if indeed promises are
made, they do not involve "places." At last he is "almost
ready to affirm" that a promise is made, but it is misunderstood.

Leventhal's reasoning in the theater/life analogy seems
to run something like this. Since the world is not governed
by an intelligent force, inequities in ability and opportunity among men are not signs of injustice, but merely mani-
festations of universal indifference. Men get their "places,"
then, in large measure by luck, a blind shuffle. There are
no promises in the sense of contracts. No individual life is
predestined to success, fame, or fortune. Anyone (for example, Allbee) whose aspirations are built on such expectations, therefore, is highly vulnerable to frustration and
failure. If a controlling force did exist, its promises would
very likely involve human concerns more significant than

"place." Life does hold promise, nonetheless, in the sense of opportunity, potential meaningfulness, and love is its greatest possibility. Life has existential promise, then, and Leventhal's promise is fulfilled in his wife. The point is made, not discursively, but dramatically. She is eight months pregnant, and her name is Mary. As she sits with Leventhal in the final theater scene, he looks tenderly at her: "Her skin looked very pure, and his heart rose as he watched her" (150–51). The Divine Maternity. She is the human made divine through the radiance of life, love, and fulfillment; she is the basis of Leventhal's final adjustment. The Christian overtones of this image are not as incongruous as they might seem at first glance. Joseph's Mary was also Jewish, of course, and the Messiah she brought forth represented a promise fulfilled.

The ticket motif is complemented by the many references to acting. Schlossberg's speech is the center of this motif, but several events lead up to it and away from it. When Leventhal first discovers himself being observed by Allbee in the park, he immediately suspects some kind of eccentric histrionics: "Who's this customer?" Leventhal said to himself. "An actor if I ever saw one" (31). To add to the theatricality of the moment, Leventhal is preceded in the line at the water fountain by a heavily painted woman who "looked like a chorus girl who had slipped out of the theater for a breath of air." Leventhal denies knowing that Allbee would be in the park. Allbee says his denial is merely a transparent evasive act. " 'Just like a bad actor to accuse everyone of bad acting,' thought Leventhal, but he was troubled nevertheless" (33). If Leventhal establishes himself as the "good actor" by symbolically retaining Shifcart's card, by "choosing dignity," in Schlossberg's terms, and achieving finally the "exactly human," then Allbee is the bad actor who never gets to see Shifcart (though he tries to get his card from Leventhal), who succumbs to self-pity, and who chooses not dignity but well-paid degradation.

Tickets and acting merge neatly in the final theater scene, in which Leventhal uses the goodwill tickets to a Renaissance play from one of his business associates. Un-

like the ticket from Dunhill, these are not purchased as a
result of social coercion. They are given to him, apparently, by one who holds him in some esteem; though the
theater is hot and the play is not interesting to him, he
offers "no real opposition" because he knows Mary will
enjoy the play—the kind of compromise one expects from
a well-balanced man. Coming into the theater, Leventhal
sees Allbee in the company of an attractive wealthy woman whom Mary identifies as Yvonne Crane, a glamorous
film star of the recent past. Each man sees the other, but
the two do not have a chance to speak until the final inter-
mission. Leventhal brusquely turns aside Allbee's feeble
quasi-apology for his "suicide" attempt and asks a central
question:

> What do you do out there, are you an actor?
> An actor? No, I'm in radio. Advertising. It's a middle-sized job.
> So you see? I've made my peace with things as they are. (255)

But his appearance belies him, reveals him to be still a bad
actor: "There was very little play in the deepened wrinkles
around his eyes. They had a fabric quality, crumpled and
blank" (254). His last role is gigolo to a fading beauty.
Another dimemsion can be added here, then, to see in
Baumbach's conception of Leventhal and Allbee as "dou-
bles," the comic and tragic masks of drama, the two faces
of life.

Although Leventhal still wonders "who runs things" and
still has an awareness of a daily fight in the business world,
it is "fainter and less troubling." That the play is a Renaissance play suggest a reawakening, and Mary's pregnancy
gives promise of new life. There is greater assurance now,
too, of his "place." Not only does he have tickets, but he
has a loving companion as well, and an usher to light the
way to their row. The bell rings, and the last act begins. We
don't see the last act, so it is a qualified conclusion, but the
novel has carefully charted a man's coming to terms with
a complex, disturbing world, and it has effectively unified
his development around theatrical imagery.

Two other images culminate in this final scene, revealing
further how tightly Bellow has constructed his book. The

final impression Allbee makes is that of a man who has sold out to his own temptations. A victim of his own weakness, he is one of the permanently displaced. Allbee had characterized himself as such a type unknowingly when he asked Leventhal's assistance in meeting Shifcart, whom Allbee considered a "power," one of those who run things. Allbee explained his plight: "I'm like the Indian who sees a train running over the prairie where the buffalo used to roam. Well, now the buffalo have disappeared, I want to get off the pony and be a conductor on that train" (203). In their last conversation in the theater lobby, Allbee reminds Leventhal of the analogy and states that he is now on the train, not as conductor but as passenger. "Not even first class. I'm not the type that runs things" (255). Allbee has convinced himself that he is one of those whom God disposes of because he is not "out of the lords of the earth" (204). Allbee has so frequently reduced his aspirations in accordance with his weak will that his aspirations have disappeared altogether. He takes the easy way out. He is still in the theater, but on Yvonne Crane's tickets, and she paid the cab fare.

The other image that culminates in the last scene is introduced by Leventhal midway in the novel. It is the analogy of life as an egg race:

> We were all the time taking care of ourselves, laying up, storing up, watching out on this side and on that side, and the same time running, running desperately, running as if in an egg race with the egg in a spoon. And sometimes we were fed up with the egg, sick of it, and at such a time would rather sign on with the devil and what they called the powers of darkness than run with the spoon, watching the egg, fearing for the egg. Man is weak and breakable, has to have just the right amounts of everything—water, air, food; can't eat twigs and stones; has to keep his bones from breaking and his fat from melting. This and that. Hoards sugar and potatoes, hides money in his mattress, spares his feelings whenever he can, and takes pains and precautions. That, you might say, was for the sake of the egg. Dying is spoiling, then? Addling? And the last judgment, candling? Leventhal chuckled and rubbed his cheek. There was also the opposite, playing catch with the egg, threatening the egg. (93)

By the final scene in the theater, the applications of this analogy are clear. It was Leventhal himself who "played catch with the egg" (life) when he attacked Rudiger, potentially jeopardizing his whole career. He juggled his life again when he deferred responding to Mary's placating overtures after their initial schism. On the day that Leventhal met and fell in love with Mary at a picnic, he ran in an egg race, and the fertility suggested by that event comes to fruition in Mary's pregnancy at the end. Allbee, of course, in being less than human, in yielding to the baser side of his nature, has "signed on with the devil and what they called the powers of darkness."

At the symbolic level of the novel the "powers of darkness" get a good deal of play, but not at the expense of the realistic level. Bellow makes no attempt to provide a symbolic significance for every realistic scene or to supply an allegorical counterpart for every character. To do so, of course, would be to vitiate to a large degree the realistic quality of his narrative, a problem that Bunyan ignored and that Hawthorne and Melville dealt with imperfectly. What he does do is to infuse the novel with frequent mythical and literary overtones, which have the effect of expanding individual realistic crises into larger philosophical problems. Thus Mickey's death gives way to the problem of Death; and Leventhal's fear of failure, Allbee's degeneration and anti-Semitism, the undercurrents of adultery, and the theme of victimization give way to the problem of Evil. In employing this strategy, Bellow has drawn on several literary traditions, but always in a shadowy and ambiguous way. He has not written a neatly patterned allegory.

With his skillful use of verisimilitude, Bellow carefully evokes the nerve-jangling noise, crowds and refuse, and oppressive heat of a metropolis in midsummer. "New York," we are told, "is as hot as Bangkok" (11). During one of his frequent trips on the Staten Island ferry, Leventhal scans the view:

> The Jersey shore, yellow, tawny, and flat, appeared on the right. The Statue of Liberty rose and traveled backwards again;

in the trembling air, it was black, a twist of black that stood up like smoke. Stray planks and waterlogged, foundering crates washed back in the boat's swell. (53)

Leaving the movie theater on Forty-second Street with Philip, Leventhal receives a typical assault on his sensibilities:

The street was glaring when they emerged. The lights in the marquee were wan. There was a hot, overrich smell of roasting peanuts and caramel corn. A metallic clapping sound came to them from a shooting gallery. And for a time Leventhal felt empty and unstable. The sun was too strong, the swirling traffic too loud, too swift. (96)

Such vivid renderings of city life abound, fleshing out the realism of the novel, but behind this realistic depiction lies a descriptive level that is clearly demonic.

The Staten Island ferry, for example, plays a prominent role in Leventhal's life because he must ride it regularly in order to check on Mickey. Riding across on the day he has arranged for a specialist to examine the boy, Leventhal envisions the labor of the stokers in the hold of a passing tanker:

Leventhal stared after it, picturing the engine room; it was terrible, he imagined, on a day like this, the men nearly naked in the shaft alley as the huge thing rolled in a sweat of oil, the engines laboring. Each turn must be like a repeated strain on the hearts and ribs of the wipers, there near the keel, beneath the water. The towers on the shore rose up in huge blocks, scorched, smoky, gray, and bare white where the sun was direct upon them. The notion brushed Leventhal's mind that the light over them and over the water was akin to the yellow revealed in the slit of the eye of a wild animal, say a lion, something inhuman that didn't care about anything human and yet was implanted in every human too. (52–53)

It is modern Inferno, a hellish scene of living death. It suggests immediatedly O'Neill's Yank of *The Hairy Ape,* the damned and displaced man, who in turn suggests Allbee. Here the hint of evil, which man both fears and contains, prepares the way for further mythical reverberations.

Returning to Manhattan after taking Mickey to the hospital, Leventhal notices that the passengers around him on the ferry are "still, like a crowd of souls, each concentrating on its destination," and he wonders why a deadly disease singled out a child in Staten Island. "One child in thousands" (63). Arriving at his apartment, Leventhal is greeted by the superintendent's dog: "The dog barked raucously and leaped at the pane" (65). The pagan myth involving the souls of the dead, Charon's ferry across the river Styx, and the guard dog Cerberus looms suggestively behind these scenes. After Mickey's death the mythical significance of the ferry is weighted even more heavily by demonic imagery and specific reference to Hell and the millions undone by death. Leventhal returns from the funeral on the ferry:

> He did not say good-by to the family. It was after sunset when he reached the ferry. The boat went slowly over the sluggish harbor. The splash of a larger vessel reached it and Leventhal caught a glimpse of the murky orange of a hull, like the apparition of a furnace on the water. The searchlight on the bridge passed over it and it was lost in a moment, put out. But its giant wading was still audible seaward in the hot, black air.
>
> After getting off the subway he delayed going home. He stopped in the park. The crowd was extraordinarily thick tonight. . . . The benches formed a dense, double human wheel; the paths were thronged. There was an overwhelming human closeness and thickness, and Leventhal was penetrated by a sense not merely of the crowd in this part but of innumerable millions, crossing, touching, pressing. What was the story he had once read about Hell cracking open on account of the rage of the sea, and all souls, crammed together, looking out? (163–64)

The mythic notes here are unquestionably strong, but not so strong as to be obtrusive. An artistic balance is nicely maintained.

The underworld as a region of the dead is not really Leventhal's main problem. He is troubled by Mickey's death and vaguely uneasy about his own end, but death is one of those "antique horizons" with which he, as an able editor of the journal by that name, becomes competent to deal. Mrs. Harkavy seems to speak for Leventhal when she admits she sometimes feels "wicked still to be here at [her] age while children die" but concludes philosophically that she is "not taking it away from anybody" (216). Leventhal also knows, with Schlossberg, that to be fully human is to be "somebody who dies." He learns much from the old Jewish patriarch. But the underworld as a place of punishment for the guilty, a manifestation of evil, is a more serious problem for Leventhal, and evil surrounds him in many forms.

Most dramatically, evil appears to Leventhal in the person of Allbee, and here again Bellow makes extensive use of literary allusion. The demonic qualities of Allbee, however, do not come so much by way of Homer, Virgil, or Dante, as by way of Hawthorne. For behind the question of guilt that is at the center of the relationship between Leventhal and Allbee is *The Scarlet Letter*, the American myth of guilt, of sin and redemption.[17]

Several hints in the novel set up the association of *The Victim* with *The Scarlet Letter*. The partially autobiographical "Customhouse" section prefaces *The Scarlet Letter*, and Leventhal, before he comes to work for Burke–Beard and Company, in whose employ he meets Allbee, works for the Baltimore customhouse. Both books have twenty-four chapters, the last chapter of each being a kind of epilog revealing, after several years have elapsed, the dramatic denouement. In Chapter Twelve of *The Scarlet Letter* Governor Winthrop dies, clearing the way for a new adminstration. Allbee, who believes the "world has changed hands," claims in Chapter Eleven of *The Victim* that he is "from an old New England family" (128), that one of his "ancestors was Governor Winthrop. Governor Winthrop!" (131). The symbolic *A* for adultery (and later

17. "In our own time, the unnatural triangle involving Hester, Dimmesdale, and Chillingworth recurs in Saul Bellow's *The Victim* (1947), where it assumes a peculiarly American mutilated form, being, in effect, a triangle without an apex or with only a hypothetical one, which is to say, a triangle without a woman!" Leslie Fiedler, *Love and Death in the American Novel* (New York, 1960), p. 360. Fiedler is the only critic who devotes any space to the parallels between Chillingworth–Dimmesdale and Allbee–Leventhal, but his focus is on the thematic polarities of attraction and repulsion as they merge in *The Victim* in the relation of anti-Semitism to eroticism. Howard Harper does mention in *Desperate Faith* (p.23) that *The Victim* and *The Scarlet Letter* present similar "visions of life."

"Able," "Angel," and, in Dimmesdale's case, "Absolution") at the center of *The Scarlet Letter* has its counterpart in the *A* of the "Anti-Semitism" that forms the basis of the conflict in *The Victim* and in Leventhal's fear of adultery. The letter is echoed in the *A*'s of "Allbee" and "Asa," whose name in Hebrew means "physician." During his night vigil on the scaffold, Dimmesdale sees the configuration of an *A* "burning duskily through a veil of cloud." In the conversation with Leventhal during which Allbee mentions his ties with "an old New England family," he also mentions that Honor is foreign to New York: "You won't see it at night hereabout," he exclaims, "in letters of fire up in the sky" (128).

These are minor matters, of course, and in the implied parallels between Dimmesdale and Leventhal, and Chillingworth and Allbee, there are several inconsistencies. Allbee's relation to Governor Winthrop has no parallel in *The Scarlet Letter*, for example, and if he is to play the Chillingworth role, Allbee's name should be "Asa," and Leventhal, as the Dimmesdale figure, should be the one to mention the fiery letters in the sky. Also, Mary is only sketchily a Hester figure. But far from being careless allusions, these ostensible inconsistencies are part of the novel's strategy. There is no elaborate symbolic machinery to encumber the realistic vehicle, and in one sense Leventhal and Allbee are alter egos; they frequently do seem to exchange roles:

> The conception of Allbee (universal being, or Everyman) is brilliant. Entirely believable as a realistic character, he is equally real as the symbolic manifestion of Asa ("healer" or "physician" in Hebrew) Leventhal's darker nature. But it is not a simple allegorical relationship. Ironically, Leventhal as Jew is dark and Allbee as gentile is light, and there are flaws in Leventhal's goodness and Allbee's evil. The moral overtones and reverberations of the novel seem to be inexhaustible.[18]

Allbee has accused Leventhal of "pure hate," of being less than human. He even associates him in his turn with a demonic principle: "You're right at home in this, like those

18. Harper, p. 22.

what-do-you-call-'ems that live in flames—salamanders"
(128). Basically, however, the Dimmesdale–Leventhal/
Chillingworth–Allbee parallel holds. The overlapping simply adds to the psychological depth of the characterization,
and the depth increases as the novel develops.

It seems reasonably certain that the plot of *The Victim*
follows Dostoevsky's *The Eternal Husband* (see footnote
8), a novella involving a cuckold and his cuckolder.[19] Since
one association leads to another, the Velchaninov-Pavolo-
vich parallel strengthens the Dimmesdale–Chillingworth
parallel. The adultery which forms the basis of guilt in *The
Scarlet Letter* does not have an exact equivalent in *The
Victim,* but it is present in skeletal form. Leventhal breaks
off his engagement to Mary when he discovers that she is
continuing an affair with a married man (thus contributing
to adultery), and though he never has real cause to doubt
Mary's fidelity after they are married, he is still troubled
by the possibility of being a cuckold, for he knows well
human weakness and capacity for evil. He remembers
Mary's early transgression, he is vaguely aware of sup-
pressed desires in himself for Elena and Mrs. Nunez, and
he is strangely stirred to discover Allbee with a whore in
the bed that Leventhal shares with Mary (a surrogate adultery).[20] He resents Allbee's enthusiasm over Mary's photo-
graph (69), and he is repeatedly haunted by the ugly, adul-
terous scene he witnesses one morning on the street corner
below his window (88–89).

Although adultery is present as only a minor theme, one
more manifestation of a general evil, the relationship between Leventhal and Allbee, as victim and victimizer in a
world of collective guilt, develops more and more clearly
in the pattern of Chillingworth and Dimmesdale. When
Allbee enters Leventhal's life for the second time, Leventhal is in a strange condition. With Mary gone, he is uneasy; he leaves the bathroom light burning all night because he feels "threatened by something" while he sleeps

---

19. In an interview with Jay Nash and Ron Offen, Bellow acknowledged the parallels, though apparently he was not consciously imitating
Dostoevski. *Chicago Literary Times* (December 1964), p. 10.

20. Clayton, pp. 147–51.

(30). He thinks often of his mother's putative insanity and worries generally about the irrational; he thinks he sees mice frequently, darting along the walls (74), a curious delusion suggesting the mouse that jumps from Lilith's mouth during her dance with Faust in the *"Walpurgisnacht"* section of Goeth's *Faust*, again the hint of the "powers of blackness."[21]

On the night that Leventhal coincidentally walks to the park and is confronted by Allbee, the city has a distinctly hellish cast: "There was still a redness in the sky, like the flames in the back of a vast baker's oven; the day hung on, gaping fierily over the black of the Jersey shore" (28). Accosting Leventhal, Allbee startles him by declaring that he "still exists." Leventhal responds, "I haven't thought about you in years, frankly, and I don't know why you think I care whether you exist or not. What, are we related?" "By blood? No, no . . . heavens;" Allbee laughed (34). The fiery-oven description that precedes Allbee's introduction into the novel resembles Hawthorne's introduction of Ethan Brand into his fragmentary story of that name, a story that preceded and, apparently, was superseded by *The Scarlet Letter*. As Brand, a former lime-burner, approached his old kiln, the door of which "resembled nothing so much as the private entrance to the infernal regions," his successor, Bartram, "threw open the iron door of the kiln, whence immediately issued a gush of fierce light, that smote full upon the stranger's face and figure."[22] In his search for moral and intellectual experience, Brand

21. The validity of the allusion is strengthened by Allbee's later charge that Leventhal is a "salamander" who lives in flames (128). In the *"Walpurgisnacht"* of *Faust* supernatural salamanders and mice are closely linked: Faust, Mephistopheles, Will-O'-The-Wisp (singing in turn): "To-whit! To-whoo! Closer they sound, owl and pewit and jay: Have they all remained awake! Are those salamanders[3892] coursing through the thicket? Long legs, fat bellies! And the roots, like serpents, writhe out of rock and sand, stretch out strange fetters to frighten and catch us; out of burly living gnarls they reach out toward the wayfarer fibres like octopus tentacles. And the mice[3900] in myriad colors, hordes of them, run through the fen and over the heath!" From the prose translation of Bayard Quincy Morgan (New York, 1954), pp. 96–97.

22. Nathaniel Hawthorne, "Ethan Brand," in *Eight American Writers*, Norman Foerster and Robert P. Falk, gen. eds. (New York, 1963), pp. 722–23.

has "violated the integrity of the human heart," what Hawthorne considered the Unpardonable Sin. Brand is the forerunner of Chillingworth, the diabolical manipulator of Dimmesdale's heart. Since "Ethan Brand" is based on the Faust myth, this allusion ties in with the Faustian allusions to mice and salamanders in *The Victim,* both bringing into play a mythical sense of evil, and it helps to set up the Chillingworth-Allbee/Dimmesdale-Leventhal parallel. Allbee is not, as he laughingly notes, related to Leventhal by blood, but the two are related by their human existential condition: They exist in a world where injustice frequently occurs in the affairs of men, where evil often becomes frighteningly real. Leventhal is uncomfortable to find himself one of the lucky ones in such a world and is therefore willing to make some effort to aid the unlucky, among whom Allbee is the most immediate—and most insistent. Leventhal is willing to admit in part to what is a kind of collective guilt, but he refuses to acknowledge any deliberate malevolence on his own part. Allbee, however, insists that he has been deliberately victimized by Leventhal and contrives for his own advantage to victimize Leventhal, thus becoming himself the very face of evil.

It is significant, also, that Leventhal's encounter with Allbee should be in the park. When he gets home and discovers Allbee's note asking for a meeting in the park, Leventhal questions, "Why the park?" (39). The park is the city's remnant of woodsy frontier, a natural place surrounded by civilization. Hawthorne, too, contrasted the village and the forest, the latter being a place of danger and disorder, a "moral wilderness" where one might encounter the "Black Man," the agent of Satan who caused the damnation of souls. When he first feels himself under the scrutiny of Allbee in the park Leventhal exclaims, "My God, my God, what kind of a fish is this? One of those guys who want you to think they can see to the bottom of your soul" (31). The suggestion of Allbee as Black Man in the forest (an agent of the principle of evil—or, as victim, at least evidence that a principle of evil exists) and therefore as a member of the legion of the damned is carried out further by Leventhal's fear of a black list. Before coming to Burke–

Beard and Company, he has difficulty getting a job. "Leventhal suspected, in the days that followed, that the black list was real enough, for firm after firm turned him down" (49). He tells Harkavy that he thinks Allbee was prevented from getting a job after being fired at *Dill's* because he was placed on the black list: "All right, here's proof. You see? There is a black list" (82). Pursuing the matter further, Leventhal asks Williston about Allbee's status: " 'Was he on a black list?' Leventhal said, intensely curious" (107). In a sense there is a black list, and Allbee is clearly associated with it. It is composed of that element of humanity that Leventhal has characterized as "the lost, the outcast, the overcome, the effaced, the ruined," and Allbee has established himself as their spokesman in the life of Leventhal though with flawed justification. Despite Leventhal's claim not to have "thought about him in years,"Allbee intends to make Leventhal see that "evil is as real as sunshine" (132).

Unlike Hawthorne's Chillingworth, Allbee is not some diabolical scientist whose overreliance on intellect and scientific methods has destroyed his human sympathies, but the effect that Allbee has on Leventhal is certainly comparable to the effect Chillingworth has on Dimmesdale. Sitting with Allbee on the park bench, "Leventhal suddenly felt that he had been singled out to be the object of some freakish, insane process, and for an instant he was filled with dread" (36). During the first visit that Allbee imposes on Leventhal he characterizes himself in unmistakably demonic terms: "I'm used to low places" and "I'm on the bottom. . . . When I compare myself with you, why you're in the empyrean, as they used to say at school, and I'm in the pit. And I have been in your position but you have never been in mine" (67). On this occasion Leventhal angrily throws him out, rejecting his charges again as absurd.

Like Chillingworth, Allbee does succeed in insinuating himself into Leventhal's house, where he continues to plague Leventhal with his drunkenness, his filth, his insidious anti-Semitism and his claims of victimization. He begins to assume more and more, as does Chillingworth, the appearance of the principle that inspires him. Leventhal studies him closely one day as he ascends the stairs: "The low light crossed his face up to the brows and eyes and gave it an expression, most likely accidental, of naked malice. A stir of uneasiness went over Leventhal" (193). When Allbee reads the intimate postcards from Mary, however, he goes too far, and Leventhal begins to back away from any commitment to him. The erotic nature of these intimate cards ("scarlet letters" in a sense) appears to stimulate Allbee to bring the prostitute into Leventhal's marriage bed. This act of "surrogate adultery" infuriates Leventhal, and he throws Allbee and his whore out, recognizing later what they represent to him:

> Both of them, Allbee and the woman, moved or swam toward him out of a depth of life in which he himself would be lost, choked, ended. There lay horror, evil, all that he had kept himself from. In the days when he was clerking in the hotel on the East Side, he had been as near to it as he could ever bear to be. He had seen it face on then. And since, he had learned more about it out of the corner of his eye. Why not say heart, rather than eye? His heart was what caught it, with awful pain and dread, in heavy blows. (241)

This scene leads Allbee to try his desperate suicide-murder attempt, which results in his final expulsion. Like Henderson the Rain King, Leventhal must acknowledge the evidence of evil all around him; and he must wrestle with the spectre of evil in his own home, and the spectre is also the shape of his own guilt, but Leventhal wrestles successfully. Though he is tainted with a measure of evil and guilt like all men, he refuses to be dominated by it. The climax of the novel, then, is twofold. In what Leventhal himself calls a "showdown," it begins with Mickey's death and ends with the expulsion of Allbee, bringing together Leventhal's acceptance of death, his acknowledgment of his part in a kind of universal guilt, and his recognition of the boundaries of his responsibilities to others—an acceptance of what it means to be human. Having freed himself from his nemesis, he can call Mary to come home and restore normalcy.

The Hawthorne parallels obviously cannot be pushed too far; on the other hand, they are too evident to be ignored. But Bellow is not playing a literary detective game here. His parallels are completely functional and fully consistent with the demands of realism. By drawing on a body of New England myth whose theme of guilt has its roots in Puritan concepts of original sin and repressed sexuality, Bellow not only enhances the American quality of his work and ensures the validity of psychological motivations, but he increases the scope of his vision as well, investing his novel with tradition and a universal dimension of meaning.

The book is, finally, a study of the kind of world in which victimization; deliberate, accidental, and ineluctable; is a fact of life with which each man must come to terms. Allbee, whose name and condition insist on this meaning, describes the system which creates victims:

> We don't choose much. We don't choose to be born, for example, and unless we commit suicide we don't choose the time to die, either. But having a few choices in between makes you seem less of an accident to yourself. It makes you feel your life is necessary. The world's a crowded place, damned if it isn't. It's an overcrowded place. There's room enough for the dead. Even they get buried in layers, I hear. There's room enough for them because they don't want anything. But the living. . . . Do you want anything? Is there anything you want? There are a hundred million others who want the very same thing. I don't care whether it's a sandwich or a seat in the subway or what. I don't know exactly how you feel about it, but I'll say, speaking for myself, it's hard to believe that my life is necessary. (171)

Allbee and Leventhal are dramatically presented as seeking their "places" despite the fear that in a crowded, competitive world they are not necessary. Each is in one way or another the victim of the other, and both are in some degree—Allbee to a greater, Leventhal to a lesser—victims of their own temperaments. Overwhelmed by the challenge, Allbee sells out to the system, exchanging his sex for a seat in the theater, his soul for shekels in an ironic inversion of the iniquities he as a Christian has accused the Jews of committing. A stronger man, Leventhal rises to the challenge and adjusts to the system; but the affirmative notes in the theater scene are not unambivalent, for behind Leventhal's question "Who runs things?" lies his awareness of those victims of the system or their own weakness who still haunt his consciousness: the furious husband and his promiscuous wife (88), the men "sleeping off their whiskey on Third Avenue, lying in doorways or on the cellar hatches" (33), the dead Mickey, the Yiddish peddler bitterly grubbing out a meager living as a hustler (95), the dishwasher with "raw hands and white nails" in the restroom of the movie house, whose taste for horror movies reflects the condition of his life (96), the elderly Filipino busboy who measures out his life in dirty dishes and steam tables (119), the man bleeding to death in the subway, denied aid by a policeman who insists on "policy" (198). When Leventhal, whose "heart beat agonizingly," reminds Allbee that "millions of us have been killed" (133), he is referring to the Jews, but, symbolically, he speaks more broadly than he knows for humanity. *The Victim* involves a cast of millions. It is the troupe of Man.

3.

The Adventures of Augie March: Tension of Opposites

Speaking at Princeton in 1941, Robert Penn Warren defined and discussed "Pure and Impure Poetry," revealing his critical stance to be clearly aligned with John Crowe Ransom's concept of structure and texture in poetry:

> Poetry wants to be pure, but poems do not. At least, most of them do not want to be too pure. The poems want to give us poetry, which is pure, and the elements of a poem, in so far as it is a good poem, will work together toward that end, but many of the elements, taken in themselves, may actually seem to contradict that end, or be neutral toward the achieving of that end. Are we then to conclude that, because neutral or recalcitrant elements appear in poems, even poems called great, these elements are simply an index to human frailty, that in a perfect world there would be no dross in poems which would, then, be perfectly pure? No, it does not seem to be merely the fault of our world, for the poems include, deliberately, more of the so-called dross than would appear necessary. They are not even as pure as they might be in this imperfect world. They mar themselves with cacaphonies, jagged rhythms, ugly words, and ugly thoughts, colloquialisms, cliches, sterile technical terms, head work and argument, self-contradiction, cleverness, irony, realism—all things which call us back to the world of prose and imperfection.[1]

Though Warren acknowledged that many different versions of what constitutes pure poetry have been set forth, he suggested that "the pure poem tries to be pure by excluding, more or less rigidly, certain elements which might qualify or contradict its original impulse"—pure feeling trying to expunge ideas, for instance, or pure idea attempt-

---

1. Robert Penn Warren, "Pure and Impure Poetry," in *Critiques and Essays in Criticism,* ed. Robert W. Stallman (New York, 1949), p. 86.

ing to escape feelings. As one example of the attempt at pure poetry, Warren cited Romeo in the garden rhapsodically expressing his love for Juliet in terms of celestial bodies: Juliet is the sun; she is fairer than the stars in Heaven, and a bright angel. But this sublimation of passion is not allowed to stand alone as pure poetry. Juliet criticizes his metaphors, and the nurse, in the name of household expediency and good health, calls Juliet to bed from inside. Most damning of all to Romeo's attempt at etherealizing his love is Mercutio, who has just expressed a bawdy, genital view of love as he strolls outside Capulet's orchard wall. Romeo is aware of only two of these discordant elements, but the audience is exposed to all three, the combined effect of which forms variations on Romeo's theme.

Juliet's mock-logical criticism, the nurse's strident practicality, and Mercutio's bawdy cynicism serve as qualifying tensions to the central—and idealistic—view of Romeo. And this, Warren claimed, is as it should be:

> The poet is like the jiujitsu expert; he wins by utilizing the resistance of his opponent—the materials of the poem. In other words, a poem, to be good, must earn itself. It is a motion toward a point of rest, but if it is not a resisted motion, it is motion of no consequence. For example, a poem which depends upon stock materials and stock responses is simply a toboggan slide, or a fall through space. And the good poem must, in some way, involve the resistances; it must carry the context of its own creation; it must come to terms with Mercutio.[2]

The poet "comes to terms with Mercutio" not necessarily by a Coleridgean reconciliation of opposites, but at least by an acknowledgment that opposites exist and by a willingness to allow such modifying elements their fair share of artistic play.

The assumption on which this chapter rests is that the balancing tension of opposites is as central to prose fiction as to poetry, and though the two genres are different in form, technique, and vertical intensity, this principle of interacting opposites operates in essentially the same way.

2. Ibid., p. 102.

For Bellow, such a principle is at the very center of a novelist's achievement:

> It [the novel] becomes art when the views most opposite to the author's own are allowed to exist in full strength. Without this a novel of ideas is merely self-indulgence, and didacticism is simply axe-grinding. The opposites must be free to range themselves against each other, and they must be passionately expressed on both sides. It is for this reason that I say it doesn't matter much what the writer's personal position is, what he wishes to affirm. He may affirm principles we all approve of and write very bad novels.[3]

In short, a didactic novel is inferior because it is too much in the service of an idea; it does not earn its form honestly by submitting itself to the shaping tension of opposites. Even a novel whose idea is skillfully embodied in its form will fall short of excellence if its informing vision is too narrow. Mailer's *The Naked and the Dead,* for example, neatly embodies the naturalistic theme that "everybody loses"; the point is made with dramatic impact. But from the long perspective that is the only point made. It is a virtuoso performance by Mailer, and though the note is played well, it is played too long. There are no variations on the theme. It grates on the ear eventually and, at last, on the mind because a complex world does not lend itself to that kind of oversimplification. Whether the vision may finally be a valid one in the actual world is not as important to formalist criticism as whether it first proves its validity in the virtual world of fiction. *The Naked and the Dead* does not demonstrate its validity; it does not make its peace with Mercutio by putting any opposing views into play. It can be compared profitably with *Sister Carrie,* in which Dreiser does make peace with Mercutio by examining the "vagaries of fortune" at three different levels: with Drouet, with Hurstwood, and with Carrie. All the characters do not lose: Some win, some lose, some play to a draw; and the officials in the game are absolutely neutral, indifferent. Acknowledging the complexity of human experience and the uncertainty of Fate, the novel mimetically earns its vision and its form. *The Adventures of Augie*

3. Saul Bellow, "Where Do We Go From Here: The Future of Fiction," in *Saul Bellow and the Critics,* ed. Irving Malin (New York, 1967), p. 220.

March also earns its vision and its form, for its scope is vast and its organizing strategy is the tension of opposites.

Like its nineteenth-century predecessor *The Adventures of Huckleberry Finn*, *The Adventures of Augie March* is a picaresque novel. It is also a *Bildungsroman* and a quest novel. Augie tells his own story, but unlike Huck, he tells it in retrospect as a man, reliving his life for the reader from his boyhood in Chicago to his exotic adventures as a young man in Mexico to his most recent status as husband and businessman in France. He holds numerous jobs, from Santa's elf to WPA plumbing inspector to moderately wealthy importer, and he experiences life in all its myriad forms. "Bellow scatters with prodigal hand a huge sampling of humanity through the pages of his novel. With his taste for the bizarre and the outré, which he somehow manages to present as ordinary and credible—simply by assuming that it is—Bellow gives us a range of character and experience fully in the tradition of the picaresque novel, greater in its variety than the adventures of Captain Farrago and Teague O'Regan in *Modern Chivalry* or of Huck Finn and Nigger Jim. He has a sense of the mystery and strangeness of people."[4] The emphasis is always on people, for this is a fully human novel.

Almost every critic, in fact, has felt obligated to comment on what is frequently considered the excessive humanity which Bellow has packed into his pages, exploiting the flexibility of even the picaresque form. John Clayton's remark is typical:

> There is a grand, generous quality to the book; it is crammed with enough characters for a half dozen novels; it is as spendthrift of incidents as Simon is of money. The "cult of experience" which Rahv finds in American writing is well-illustrated here. And not only experiences but ideas: the book is loose-bellied; it contains passage upon passage of philosophical dialogue disconnected from plot.[5]

There is much in the novel that could be condensed, or perhaps even eliminated, but one wonders what the price

4. Chester E. Eisinger, *Fiction of the Forties* (Chicago, 1963), p. 356.
5. John J. Clayton, *Saul Bellow: In Defense of Man* (Bloomington, Ind., 1968), p. 243.

of such excision would be. Holden Caulfield in Salinger's *The Catcher in the Rye* complains to Mr. Antolini about the speech course in which members of the class are supposed to shout, "Digression!" at anyone who fails to stick to the point. He finds this practice particularly disturbing when the nervous boy, Richard Kinsella, talks about his uncle's polio brace, say, instead of his father's farm—his chosen topic. Properly pedagogical, Mr. Antolini asks if the boy should not have chosen the brace in the first place instead of the farm if that was the most interesting topic to him. Holden replies:

> Yes—I don't know. I guess he should. I mean I guess he should've picked his uncle as a subject, instead of the farm if that interested him most. But what I mean is, lots of times you don't *know* what interests you most till you start talking about something that *doesn't* interest you most. I mean you can't help it sometimes. What I think, you're supposed to leave somebody alone if he's at least being interesting and he's getting all excited about something. I like it when somebody gets excited about something. Its nice.[6]

Mr. Antolini has logic on his side, a legitimate consideration, but Holden has interest on his, an equally legitimate claim. The two concerns enjoy a happy coexistence in *Augie March*. There is an organic center growing out of Augie's quest for a "good enough fate"; there are also peripheral events and characters only obliquely related to Augie's development, but these need not be considered purely extraneous. They may be considered abundant rather than adventitious, instead of superfluous—cornucopian. What Dryden said of the *Canterbury Tales* is applicable also to *Augie March:* "Here is God's plenty."

Whether peripheral characters and events should be condensed, eliminated, or made more relevant is not an issue here. These matters have their own justification in the picaresque tradition and in the overall charm of a very big book. "It's nice," as Holden says, "when somebody gets excited about something." The purpose of this chapter is, instead, to trace the development of Augie as he encounters the diverse humanity that make up his world and to

6. J. D. Salinger, *The Catcher in the Rye* (New York, 1951), pp. 184–85.

chart the play of opposites in the novel, which will involve oppositions of characters, situations, and ideas.

Like most picaresque novels, *Augie March* is susceptible to a number of structural divisions, but the one most useful here is threefold, based on Augie's age and travels. Section one, Chapters one through seven, deals with Augie's childhood and boyhood in Chicago, ending with his graduation from high school. Section two, Chapters eight through twenty-five, deals with his adventures as a young man "on the road" from Chicago to Mexico to the African sea, with many points in between. The three central episodes in this section are Mimi's abortion, the adventure with Thea and Caligula, and the shipwreck experience with Bateshaw. The last section, Chapter twenty-six, provides a reflective summary of Augie's stance as a man who has learned that his past and future are inextricably linked, as his fate—though not his attitude—is necessarily linked to the fate of others. This section is set mainly in Paris, the City of Man.

Augie explains early in the novel, "All the influences were lined up waiting for me. I was born, and there they were to form me, which is why I tell you more of them than of myself."[7] Augie describes these influences vividly and lovingly, and most prominent among his childhood memories are his mother, Mama, and the family boarder, Grandma Lausch, the widow of a wealthy Odessa businessman and the mother of two successful sons in the Midwest who send her money but who do not wish to have her around. She and her old dog, Winnie, dominate the household:

> With the [cigarette holder] in her dark little gums between which all her guile, malice, and command issued, she had her best inspirations of strategy. She was as wrinkled as an old paper bag, an autocrat, hard-shelled and jesuitical, a pouncy old hawk of a Bolshevik, her small ribboned gray feet immobile on the shoekit and stool Simon had made in the manual training class, dingy old wool Winnie whose bad smell filled the flat on the cushion beside her. If wit and discontent don't

7. Saul Bellow, *The Adventures of Augie March* (New York, 1953), p. 43. Subsequent page numbers will be given in parentheses in the text.

necessarily go together, it wasn't from the old woman that I
learned it. (7)

In Augie's memory she is chief among "those Machiavellis
of small street and neighborhood" who filled his young
years. She coaches Augie in the lies he must tell to get free
glasses for his simple-minded mother from the public dis-
pensary. She berates Lubin, the welfare caseworker, to
obtain more public funds for the family income. She intimidates neighborhood merchants for discounts, while privately assigning nicknames of opprobrium to each one.
She gives the retarded Georgie the "ridgy gizzards" from
chickens and then trifles with his affections, and from her
position of ruler, she delivers lessons in living to her cap-
tive family subjects:

> On the sideboard, on the Turkestan runner, with their eyes,
> ears, and mouth covered, we had see-no-evil, speak-no-evil,
> hear-no-evil, a lower trinity of the house. . . . Still the monkeys
> could be potent, and awesome besides, and deep social critics
> when the old woman, like a great lama—for she is Eastern to
> me, in the end—would point to the squatting brown three,
> whose mouths and nostrils were drawn in sharp blood-red,
> and with profound wit, her unkindness finally touching great-
> ness, say, "Nobody asks you to love the whole world, only to
> be honest, *ehrlich.* Don't have a loud mouth. The more you love
> people the more they'll mix you up. A child loves, a person
> respects. Respect is better than love. And that's respect, the
> middle monkey." (9)

The old woman's defensiveness against the world has become her credo, her very life style. Her central theme is
"the trustful, loving, and simple surrounded by the cun-
ning-hearted and tough, a fighting nature of birds and
worms, and a desperate mankind without feelings" (10).
Use others, she teaches, before they use you. Since Augie
knows Grandma is dishonest and garrulous, he recognizes
her hypocrisy, but he can still respond to the fierceness
with which she holds her views, to the protective way she
guards her individuality, for Augie, too, has a strong desire
to cultivate a personal destiny.

With Heraclitus, Augie affirms that "a man's character
is his fate" (3), and throughout the novel the goal of his
quest is to discover a "good enough fate" (28), a " 'higher,'

independent fate" (424), a "worthwhile fate" (432). Behind
all of Augie's experiences, regardless of how passive or
casual they seem, lies his intense desire to know who he
is and what he should do. He goes to school on others,
hoping to learn from their fates something of his own. Thus
his admiration for Grandma Lausch.

A once-wealthy matron, Grandma Lausch now lives in
squalor with the Marches. She has been deprived of her
husband by death and abandoned by her sons. Her tyran-
ny over the family, Augie knows, is her way of meeting her
fate, of striking back against circumstances. But as she
grows older and Simon and Augie assume more responsibilities, her influence wanes. Sensing this loss, she makes
one final sultanic gesture: She arranges for Georgie to be
institutionalized. Though probably necessary, her act is
not done in kindness, and the cruelty in her gesture triggers
her fall from power. Returning from arranging Georgie's
future with Lubin, she falls on the sidewalk to the
Marches's house. This "election-day fall" is the literal
counterpart to her symbolic fall from power in the household. As she becomes more senile, she has to be placed in
a home in her turn, and she faces even this fate with fierceness and hauteur. She praises the Russian prose in the
letter from Stiva, her son, informing her of what is in effect
her disposal, and she leaves for the home with queenly
airs:

> Ah, regardless how decrepit of superstructure, she was splen-
> did. You forgot how looney she'd become, and her cantan-
> kerousness of the past year. What was a year like that when
> now her shakiness of mind dropped off in this moment of
> emergency and she put on the strictness and power of her most
> *grande-dame* days? My heart went soft for her, and I felt admi-
> ration that she didn't want from me. Yes, she made retirement
> out of banishment, and the newly created republicans, the wax
> not cooled yet on their constitution, had the last pang of loyalty
> to the deposed, when mobs, silent, see off the limosine, and the
> prince and princely family have the last word in the history of
> wrongs. (96)

Grandma refuses to bow to her fate, and the strength with
which she resists is the strength of desperation, for to give

in to her fate would be to accept despair. Though Augie acknowledges her excesses, he admires her power of resistance. He is moved by her defiance.

The foil to Grandma Lausch is Mama. Long abandoned by the man who fathered her three illegitimate sons, Mama has no resources to cope with a complex and confusing world. She is a meek, gentle, round-eyed woman whom Augie describes as one of those "conquered by a superior force of love, like those women whom Zeus got the better of in animal form and who next had to take cover from his furious wife" (10). Unlike Grandma, Mama meets her fate without resistance:

> When she had a grief she didn't play it with any arts; she took straight off from her spirit. She made no fuss or noise nor was seen weeping, but in an extreme and terrible way seemed to be watching out the kitchen window, until you came close and saw the tear-strengthened color of her green eyes and her pink face, her gap-toothed mouth; she laid her head on the wing of the chair sideways, never direct. When sick she was that way also. She climbed into bed in her gown, twisted her hair into braids to keep it from tangling, and had nothing to do with anyone until she felt able to stay on her feet. It was useless for us to come with the thermometer, for she refused to have it; she lay herself dumbly on the outcome of forces, without any work of mind, of which she was incapable. She had some original view on doom or recovery. (54)

In her mobcap and her floppy men's shoes, Mama accepts her fate passively, "like waiting for the grief to come to a stop; as if this stop would be called by a conductor" (178). Augie is influenced by this simple-minded woman's response to fate as much as he is by Grandma's opposite reaction, for in Mama's gentleness there is much loving devotion, and in her passiveness there is a kind of faith that there is alleviation for pain, and that sorrow eventually comes to an end.

Another figure who meets his fate with the style and the resistance of a Grandma Lausch is William Einhorn, Augie's full-time employer and part-time mentor. Paralyzed in his arms and legs and totally dependent on others for his mobility and personal needs, Einhorn still successfully conducts diversified business interests. Using some of the many epic comparisons that give historic vista to his narrative, Augie introduces Einhorn:[8]

> William Einhorn was the first superior man I knew. He had a brain and many enterprises, real directing power, philosophical capacity, and if I were methodical enough to take thought before an important and practical decision and also (*N.B.*) if I were really his disciple and not what I am, I'd ask myself, "What would Caesar suffer in this case? What would Machiavelli advise or Ulysses do? What would Einhorn think?" I'm not kidding when I enter Einhorn in this eminent list. It was him that I knew, and what I understand of them in him. Unless you want to say we're at the dwarf end of all times and mere children whose only share in grandeur is like a boy's share in fairy-tale kings, beings of a different kind from times better and stronger than ours. But if we're comparing men and men, not men and children or men and demigods, and if we don't have any special wish to abdicate into some different, lower form of existence out of shame for our defects before the golden faces of these and other old-time men, then I have the right to praise Einhorn and not care about smiles of derogation from those who think the race no longer has in any important degree the traits we honor in these fabulous names. (60)

Augie comes to work for Einhorn as a high-school junior

8. Marcus Klein has written perceptively about Bellow's frequent use of epic and historic reference and allusion, especially as these references reflect Yiddish rhetoric and the tradition of the little man, *das kleine menschele,* whose conversation, as Bellow described it in "Laughter in the Ghetto," is "full of the grandest historical, mythological, and religious allusions. The Creation, the Fall, the Flood, Egypt, Alexander, Titus, Napoleon, the Rothschilds, the sages, and the Law may get into the discussion of an egg, a clothesline, or a pair of pants." *Saturday Review,* 36 (May 30, 1953), 15. Writing of Bellow's fiction in general and *Augie March* in particular, Klein describes the ironic function of the epic reference: "On the one hand, the mock-heroics of the little man renders all conventional heroism absurd, as does that of both Bellow's protagonists and antagonists. But theirs is far from the mock-heroic of tradition, that of Chaucer and Rabelais and Swift. It is not practiced with such broad and easy security. It is, on the other hand, itself real heroism, a mode of strong self-assertion in a community that disallows the self. Given the prison of restrictive circumstances of the *shtetl,* and then those of Bellow's city, it is the one mode by which personal identity can be emphasized at all. Augie's mythical mouthfuls provide rough fun, they burlesque his own bravado and dilute all pretension, but at the same time they call upon Julius Caesar and John Dillinger to witness his daring. There is courage in the insolence of it. The bravado is a thin mask for the bravery. Augie's frisky speech is the power he puts forth to win from all oppressive circumstances a right to exist." *After Alienation* (Cleveland, 1965), pp. 61–62.

and remains under his influence until graduation the following year. Einhorn continues thereafter to function periodically as Augie's avuncular adviser. Though he is not a disciple of Einhorn, he is a close observer, and what he learns from Einhorn is not so much how to live as what attitude to take toward life.

Though Einhorn sometimes complains of the "thirtieth day" when his fate is unbearable, he usually speaks proudly of the genius and will that have enabled him to assert himself in the world against many obstacles:

> Augie, you know another man in my position might be out of life for good. There's a view of man anyhow that he's only a sack of craving guts; you find it in *Hamlet,* as much as you want of it. What a piece of work is a man, and the firmament frotted with gold—but the whole *gescheft* bores him. Look at me, I'm not even express and admirable in action. You could say a man like me ought to be expected to lie down and quit the picture. Instead, I am running a big business today . . . while nobody would blame me for rotting in the back room under a blanket or for crabbing and blabbing my bitter heart out with fresh and healthy people going around me, so as not to look. (75)

So that he himself can fill the role of Socrates, Einhorn dubs Augie an "Alcibiades beloved-of-man." The self-congratulation in Einhorn's tone does not escape Augie, but neither does the truth in the assessment of his achievement, even though Augie is intimately familiar with the daily vices which tarnish the image Einhorn holds of himself. Einhorn is a schemer and deceiver: He cheats on trial offers from magazines, commits adultery, traffics with whores, attempts to defraud his insurance company, bullies his dead father's old business cronies, intimidates his renters, and evades city taxes and utility bills. He publishes a mimeographed paper for shut-ins, but his material is plagiarized and trite, and his motive is largely to obtain insurance business. Not the kind of activities one expects from a "superior man." Yet he philosophically accepts his vast losses in the stock-market crash of 1929, refusing to be defeated by external circumstances, and he fiercely urges Augie away from a life of crime. He is a respectful and loving son to his father, a protective brother toward Ding-bat, and a proud, encouraging father to his own son, Arthur. He is also perceptive enough to see the true nature of Augie's character: "All of a sudden I catch on to something about you. You've got *opposition* in you. You don't slide through everything. You just make it look so" (117).

In his turn Augie is equally perceptive—and objective—about Einhorn. He considers Einhorn "awfully damn remarkable" and asks,

> And what if, together with this, he had his inner and personal growths of vice, passion, even prurience, unbecoming obscenity? Was it unbecoming because he was a cripple? And then if you satisfy that difficult question by saying it's not up to us to declare what a man should renounce because he is crippled or otherwise cursed, there's still the fact that Einhorn could be ugly and malicious. You can know a man by his devils and the way he gives hurts. (99)

Augie declares Einhorn to be "selfish, jealous, autocratic, carp-mouth, and hypocritical" (99), yet in the last analysis Augie has "high regard for him" because of the "fight he had made on his sickness" (100). What Augie admires in Einhorn is his refusal to be bowed down by the weight of the burden life has handed him. Like Grandma, who rationalized her condition and disguised her disappointment in ferocity, and even perhaps like Georgie, who turned his retardation in a useful direction, Einhorn represents to Augie grounds for hope that the human spirit can shape some destiny of its own despite the fearsome limiting factors with which it has to work.

Any formative influence that Einhorn has on Augie ends with Augie's graduation from high school. In celebration, Einhorn treats Augie to a trip to the red-light district, but, as usual, the trip is as much for his pleasure as for Augie's. Einhorn rides Augie's back as Anchises rode Aeneas out of sacked and burning Troy, but the scene is mock-heroic here. The burning is Einhorn's lust, and the initiating experience for Augie is less than epic: "And so it *didn't* have the luster it should have had, and there *wasn't* any epithalamium of gentle lovers" (124). Einhorn's function as teacher culminates at the end of Section one in his presence as guide at the sexual ritual which tradition associates with the coming to manhood, but he has his own reasons for being there as well. Sex for Einhorn is one compensation for his paralysis, and promiscuous sex is simply an added enrichment. Always the Machiavellian, he has made his means his end, to live and not die. He does not wish, like Sardanapalus, "to be buried right plunk in front of" his pleasures. He does not wish to, and therefore he does not. While seeing the polarities in the man's character, his folly and his wisdom, his crime and vices and his aspiring nobility, Augie can still respond to the indomitability of his spirit.

Taking with him, then, something of Mama's gentleness, altruism, and passiveness, Grandma's ferocious protectiveness of self, and Einhorn's ambivalences, Augie moves into the experiences of his young manhood. He goes "on the road," where he continues to encounter opposites and polarities, beginning with his introduction into high society and his subsequent fall into the ranks of the unemployed and the unwanted.

In order to qualify for civil-service jobs—and because there is nothing else to do—Simon and Augie attend Chicago's Crane College. Augie finds himself one more ingredient in America's melting pot, and he describes his classmates in a Whitmanesque catalogue:

> They filled the factory-length corridors and giant classrooms with every human character and germ, to undergo consolidation and become, the idea was, American. In the mixture there was beauty—a good proportion—and pimple-insolence, and parricide faces, gum-chew innocence, labor fodder and secretarial forces, Danish stability, Dago inspiration, Catarrh-hampered mathematical genius; there were waxed-eared shovelers' children, sex-promising businessmen's daughters—an immense sampling of a tremendous host, the multitudes of holy writ, begotten by West-moving, factor-shoved parents. Or me, the by-blow of a traveling man. (125)

Augie does not remain long at Crane, but he acquires enough polish from it to move him from a bargain basement where he sells women's shoes to "the millionaire suburbs—Highland Park, Kenilworth, and Winnetka—

selling things, a specialized salesman in luxury lines and
dealing with aristocrats" (129). His employers are Mr. and
Mrs. Renling, who have become wealthy catering to the
luxury tastes of the carriage trade.

Augie finds himself susceptible to the feel of luxury. He
likes the "tweeds and flannels, plaids, foulards, sports
shoes, woven shoes Mexican style, and shirts and handkerchiefs" which he must wear to be dressed appropriately
for the society clientele he serves. He enjoys the luxurious
Packard that Renling drives, and the Benton Harbor resort
that the chic Mrs. Renling visits. He discovers, however,
that these things have a price. Since Mr. Renling provides
for him, Mrs. Renling feels obligated to teach him, and her
lessons echo the words of Grandma Lausch.

She warns him that others will use him, trap him: "Augie, don't you see this little tramp wants you to get her in
trouble so that you'll have to marry her? That's all you
need now, to have a baby with her at the start of your
career" (134). As Grandma preached respect above love,
Mrs. Renling preaches security above marriage:

> When I told Mrs. Renling that Simon was going to get married
> and that Cissie was the daughter of a busted dry goods man,
> she began to work it out and do the sociology of it for me. She
> showed me the small flat and the diapers hanging in the kitch-
> en, the installment troubles about furniture and clothes, and
> my brother an old man at thirty from anxiety and cut-off spirit,
> the captive of the girl and babies. "While you at thirty, Augie,
> will just start thinking about getting married. You'll have mon-
> ey and culture and your pick of women. Even a girl like Thea
> Fenchel. An educated man with a business is a lord." (152)

In settings of hotel luxury, "greenery and wickerwork,
braid cord on the portieres, menus in French, white hall
runners and deep fat of money, limosines in the washed
gravel, lavish culture of flowers bigger than life, and triple-
decker turf on which the grass lived rich," she fills him in
on the lives of the wealthy, those who drink, fornicate,
murder. "You needed," Augie said, "a strong constitution
to stick to your splendor of morning in the face of these
damnation chats" (137). To a practiced recruit like Augie,

such instruction in reality is bearable, but he goes his separate way when his association with the Renlings begins to threaten his freedom.

Because there is something "adoptional" about Augie and because he appeals to them, the Renlings wish to make him their son. He is "supposed to become Augie Renling, live with them, and inherit all their dough" (151). When Augie protests that he already has folks, Mrs. Renling defines what family should mean: "Now, Augie, don't be a fool. A real family is somebody, and offers you something. Renling and I will be your parents because we will give you, and all the rest is bunk" (153). Augie, however, withstands the temptation which would make accessible to him debutantes like Esther and Thea Fenchel, and he rejects the consequences of refusal which Mrs. Renling paints for him from her woman's "profounder knowledge of life." He resists partly out of loyalty to the family which he already has and partly as a rebuke to the kind of human manipulation for which Mrs. Renling stands: "I was not going to be built into Mrs. Renling's world, to consolidate what she affirmed she was" (151). Mainly, though, Augie resists, as he says, because "it wasn't a fate good enough." A future with the Renlings would be equivalent to a predesigned, mail-order fate, and Augie still wishes to go freestyle, to "make the record" in his own way.

Leaving the Renlings, Augie falls on bad times, first with Ruber and his unsalable rubberized paint, and then with Joe Gorman and his abortive attempt to run immigrants across the Canadian border in a stolen car. Gorman is arrested and beaten, and Augie, luckily, escapes to find his way as a fugitive from Lackawanna back to Chicago the best way he can. His chaotic trip takes him through railroad yards, jails, flophouses, and hobo jungles. His companions have names that reflect the conditions of their lives, Wolfy and Stony, and his mode of travel is the demonic train:

> When we rolled forward the wheels creaked and bit out sparks like grindstones, and the couplings played free and hooked tight in a mechanical game into which your observation and brain were forced. Having to recognize whose kingdom you

were in, with tons of coal at the back and riding in the tiny blind gallery with the dashing dark rain at the sides. (167)

As he tries to sleep in a boxcar, Augie has to repulse a homosexual advance. Picked up as vagrants suspected as auto-part thieves, he and his two companions hear a police officer, without a trace of irony in his voice, give a jail sentence to three deaf mutes caught up in a noisy lovers' triangle: "Anyway, a night in the clink will show them they aren't alone by themselves in the world and can't be car-ryin' on as if they was" (172). Augie and his companions are also compelled to spend the night in jail, and the lesson in the experience comes home to Augie with dramatic impact:

> We had to empty our pockets; they were after knives and matches and such objects of harm. But for me that wasn't what it was for, but to have the bigger existence taking charge of your small things, and making you learn forfeits as a sign that you aren't any more your own man, in the street, with the contents of your pockets your own business: *that* was the pur-pose of it. (174)

Like the deaf mutes, Augie learns that people "aren't alone by themselves in the world"; an independent fate, there-fore, is particularly hard to retain. Surrounded by "ape-wit and defiances," suspicion, flushing toilets, filth, and an enormous heavy light "like the stone rolled in front of the tomb," Augie feels the truth in his earlier hunch that there can be "cities without civilization."

The strategy of opposites here is the shift from the high-society wealth represented by the Renlings to the social deprivation represented by Gorman, Wolfy, Stony, and the inmates of the jail, society's misfits. The movement is from the firmly established to the disestablished. Augie can move in both groups, but he belongs to neither. If life among the country-club set can deprive him of his person-al fate by appropriation and acquisition, the life of a drifter can deprive him of his fate by dispossession. Each way carries its own set of determinants. The lesson Augie learns is that "there is a darkness. It is for everyone" (175). He makes a note of his insight as a troubling fact that he must come to terms with, but he affirms that he does not "get any shock from this of personal injustice" (174). If it applies to everyone, it may be unjust, but it is not personal injustice. Augie hitchhikes into Chicago, where his adventures continue.

In Chicago, Augie discovers several changes. Grandma has died, Mama has been moved to a room in the home of the Kreindls, Five Properties is engaged to marry Cissy Flexner, and Simon has been jailed for destroying Flexner's furniture in rage over the betrayal by Cissy, his former fiancée. Augie arranges with Lubin to place his mother in a nursing home for fifteen dollars a month, and then he takes a job as an attendant in a dog club catering to a wealthy clientele. The job is demeaning, he smells of dog, he dislikes the French dog-currier's frequent use of the hypodermic needle on bothersome dogs, and he feels guilty that the fee for membership is five dollars more a month than the amount he pays to keep his mother in the nursing home. He is elated, then, to run into his old friend Manny Padilla, the skinny Chicano from Crane College who could "crack any equation on the board." Though Padilla has a scholarship at the university, he steals textbooks to supplement his income. He invites Augie to join him in this enterprise because, he explains, there is no commitment involved:

> He says, "I'll explain how I feel about it. You see, I don't have larceny in my heart; I'm not a real crook. I'm not interested in it, so nobody can make a fate of it for me. That's not my fate. I might get into a little trouble, but I never would let them make it *my* trouble, get it?" (190)

Assuring Augie that his fate is safe, Padilla easily persuades him to give up his job in the dog club and become a book thief. Not only does this new "profession" bring Augie back into contact with the university, it also stimulates him to read: "I lay in my room and read, feeding on print and pages like a famished man. Sometimes I couldn't give a book up to a customer who had ordered it, and for a long time this was all that I could care about" (193). But as it turns out, Augie's knowledge during this period in his life comes more from the events around him than from the books he reads.

The theme of this section (Chapters ten through twelve), one of the most meaningful in Augie's "road" experiences, is stated by Kayo Obermark, a bright but slovenly student in the house where Augie lives:

> Well—you understand. Everyone has bitterness in his chosen thing. That's what Christ was for, that even God had to have bitterness in his chosen thing if he was really going to be man's God, a god who was human. (260)

"Bitterness in the chosen thing" expands by the end of the novel to become the theme of the whole book and the formula for encompassing the strategy of opposites that serves as the book's organic center.

In this section Augie moves between two dominant figures, his brother Simon and his friend Mimi Villars, both of whom discover bitterness in their chosen things. Simon is the arch-materialist. He can measure success only by the size of his bank account. Mimi, on the other hand, is an arch-antimaterialist, a free spirit, and a celebrator of emancipated love. Though their values and life styles are completely opposite, their fierce dedication to their ideals—perhaps even monomania—is the same. In the way each meets the bitterness in his fate, Augie learns something valuable.

Apparently because he was abandoned by his father and grew up in poverty, Simon has a hard-headed view of marriage and an intense desire to seek the security of wealth. After some successful ventures as a youth and several setbacks as a young man, he decides to achieve his goal through marriage to a wealthy woman, Charlotte Magnus. He does not intend to be one of those who are "pondering how to marry for love and getting the blood gypped out of them" (199); Simon is marrying for money, and he sees the marriage in contractual terms:

> I'm not marrying a rich girl in order to live on her dough and have a good time. They'll get full value out of me, those people. They'll see that I won't lie down and take it easy. I can't. I have to make money. I'm not one of those guys that give up what

they want as soon as they realize they want it. I want money, and I mean *want*; and I can handle it. Those are my assets. (199)

His wife later confirms this need. "Your brother," she tells Augie in Paris, "needs money, a whole lot of money. If he didn't have it to spend, as much as he needed, he'd die" (466). Since the dependence on money is as real for Charlotte as for Simon, he gets the kind of wife he deserves, and he gets the money that he desperately seeks, but the price he pays is very high. To Augie, it is too high.

The business pressures that Simon must withstand in order to remain wealthy make him extravagant, short-tempered, savage, and suicidal. Like Gatsby presenting his love and his rich man's credentials to Daisy in his profusion of luxury shirts, Simon is a compulsive buyer of slacks, shoes, underclothes, and suits. He presents these things to himself as evidence of his success and—in vain—of his concomitant happiness. He snaps at Augie and Happy Kellerman, bullies his fellow club members, and brutally attacks Guzynski, one of his customers. He makes frequent escapes to the barber shop, but still, as Augie knows, he often breaks down:

> I knew that in the barbershop and on the shopping trips he was aiming to refresh himself; he slept badly and was looking flabby and ill, and one morning when he came to fetch me he locked himself in the toilet and cried. (224)

From the pressure of living with a woman he does not love, Simon is driven crudely to "bims" on the public beach and finally to Renee, an expensive, plotting mistress who exploits his desire and blackmails him through threatened suicide and an unjustified paternity suit. Charlotte extricates him from the mess and then, vindictively, punishes him with the truth:

> "Every minute she was with him she was collecting evidence," said Charlotte. "They never stopped at a place but what she didn't take a pack of matches and write the date inside. She even had his cigar butts for evidence. And all the time it was supposed to be for love. What did she love you for?" said Charlotte with a terrible sudden outburst. "Your fat belly? Your bald spot? It was the money. It was never anything except money." (532)

Though Augie recognizes some poetic justice in Simon's being the victim of one who simply wanted money as badly as he did, Augie feels great sympathy for his brother:

> He was ashamed, stoney with shame. His secrets were being told. His secrets! What did they amount to? You'd think they were as towering as the Himalayas. But all they were about was his mismanaged effort to live. To live and not die. And this was what he had to be ashamed of. . . . Just then I thought that the worst of it for him was not to have the child. (533)

Simon's claim to Charlotte is that he has wasted his life. Augie knows, painfully, that the claim is true. The bitterness in Simon's chosen thing is that he chose the wrong thing. Though Augie can decry the choice, he cannot reject the chooser, for Simon, too, was simply seeking a good enough fate.

In sharp contrast to Simon is Mimi Villars, a waitress in a student hash-house and a resident of the apartment house where Augie lives. Whereas Simon seeks through marriage to rise to the wealth that he thinks, mistakenly, will bring him happiness, Mimi is disdainful of both marriage and wealth. To her, marriage is a form of prostitution, a swindle involving "terrible payment for what should be a loving exchange of bodies and the foundation of all true things of life" (209), and wealth is another form of slavery. She considers Augie "too indulgent . . . about the beds that would be first stale and then poisonous because their manageresses' thoughts were on the conquering power of chenille and dimity and the suffocation of light by curtains, and the bourgeois ambering of adventuring man in parlor upholstery" (209). She has a "push-faced tough beauty," and she flaunts conventions in both language and behavior because flaunting convention is part of her credo—it is also part of the source of the bitterness which she incurs. She is dedicated to love, the emotion that is anathema to Simon; she is a servant to "her belief that all [rests] on the gentleness in privacy of man and woman—they [do] in willing desire what in the rock and water universe, the green universe, the bestial universe, [is] done from ignorant necessity" (270). She lives for that loving exchange between persons which Simon calls "getting the blood gypped out of them." Ironically, each character is a case study in the other's thesis: By her zealous, singleminded devotion to love, Mimi does get, literally and symbolically, "gypped out of her blood." Mimi endures both physical and emotional pain to abort her baby, in the name of sacrifice to the free and unencumbered love that she brings to Frazer. And Simon falls victim to the swindle that Mimi sees in the loveless marriage: For the wealth and swaggering, superficial power that his marriage of advantage brings him, Simon pays with a wasted life. Each is defensively aware of the other. Simon thinks Mimi "looks like an easy broad," and he suspects her of having designs on Augie. Though Mimi satirizes Simon's frantic pace, his clothes, and his car, she sees "something extravagant and outlaw about him" that she approves. The baby that Simon misses in Renee's faking is paralleled dramatically by the baby that Mimi aborts. Though their motives are different, their losses are the same. Love cannot fructify in misaligned lives.

Between their two positions stands Augie. Though Simon's face, as Augie sees, is "the face of a man in the wrong," Simon thinks he is right and wants Augie to follow his lead, partly to affirm the rightness of his action:

> Simon's idea was that I should marry Lucy Magnus, who had more money even than Charlotte. This was how he outlined the future to me. I could finish my pre-legal course and go to John Marshall law school at night while I worked for him. He'd pay my tuition and give me eighteen dollars a week. Eventually I could become his partner. Or if his business didn't suit me, we could go into real estate with our joint capital. Or perhaps into manufacturing.(238)

Because he has nothing else to do and because he loves his brother, Augie goes along with Simon for a while, but he does not commit himself to his brother's scheme because it is one in which he does not fundamentally believe.

Augie's temporary and half-serious courting of Lucy Magnus draws him into the critical fire of Mimi, who takes "digs at marriage" and accuses Augie of looking "like the groom himself." However, the tension of the uneasy triangle among Simon, Mimi, and Augie is broken during the events of the Christmas week, centering around Mimi's abortion. Mimi first tries to abort the child with an injection. That failing, she appeals to the Public Health Service, claiming a fallopian pregnancy. The doctors operate, find her normal, sew her up and congratulate her, with unwitting irony, on the coming "blessed event." Mimi then requests the protesting Augie to take her back to the abortionist, whose butchery relieves her of the fetus but causes great pain, bleeding, infection, and almost death. With Padilla's aid, however, Augie succeeds in getting her admitted to a hospital, where her life is saved. But Augie has been seen at the abortionist's with Mimi by Lucy's cousin Kelly Weintraub, who reports to Lucy and the Magnus family. As designing a woman as Charlotte, Lucy turns Augie out because she does not really love him and she does not wish to lose her inheritance, the price her father puts on her continued association with Augie. Consequently, Simon angrily dismisses Augie from his job in the coal yard and warns him to stay away, for he resents the blundering with which Augie has upset the carefully laid plan, and he fears that any further blundering by Augie might endanger his own relationship with Charlotte and the Magnus family.

Opposites and ironies abound in this section. There is, first, the motif of accidents. Augie dents the fender of Simon's car and shrugs it off as unimportant: It is not seriously damaged, and Simon is insured. Lucy, on the other hand, is very upset over the damage she causes to her new car by running into a fence, because her father has threatened to take the car away from her if she is careless with it during the first six months. The consequences of Mimi's physiological "accident" stand in sharp contrast to the trivial consequences of Lucy's traffic accident. Against the temporary loss of a car to a spoiled rich girl is set the physical emotional pain of abortion to a tough-minded, independent working girl. Her courage points up Lucy's childishness. There is, however, a further contrast. In Mimi's gesture there is courage and conviction, but there is also something excessive, wrongheaded. She equates her conception with mere accident and therefore sees it as an

encumbrance to the freely given, no-consequences love in
the name of which she acts. Augie feels, nevertheless, that
even illegitimate conception—like his own—is a kind of
affirmation of living, a token of "the desire that there
should be more life: from gratitude" (254). With Mimi's
view and against Augie's position is the opinion of Jimmy
Klein. He too has been the victim of an "accident":

> Don't you know how it is by now? It's all that you want from
> life comes to you as one single thing—fucking; so you and some
> nice kid get together, and after a while you have more misery
> than before, only now it's more permanent. You're married
> and have a kid. (267)

Though their views are essentially the same, Jimmy and
Mimi meet their fates in much different styles. Mimi's is a
prideful, parading martyrdom to love. She sees that her
"fate is shared" (211). Jimmy's style is a resigned plodding
in the trail of biological impluse. Though poor himself, he
loans Augie the fifty dollars he needs for the abortion in
order "to defeat a mechanism as much as . . . to help a
one-time friend" (269). "Compare a few bucks," he says,
"to a life of grief" (268).

The greatest irony of this section, however, is in the
situation itself. It is Christmas week, and Mimi, with her
barren, bleeding womb, is placed in one of the maternity
wards because, as Dr. Castleman explains, there was "no
other place to put her" (281). Unlike the innkeeper in the
Christian miracle, Castleman has a place for the womb-
sore mother, but like the Christian miracle, it is the wrong
place—and the messianic birth has been abortive. Christmas decorations form the setting: "It was a tall, big cham-
ber, and in the middle on a table was a little Christmas fir
with lit bulbs and under it a box with cotton wool and
nativity dolls" (281). The Christian parallels are nothing
more than ironic suggestion, but the suggestions are clear
enough.[9] Sounds of "suckling and crying, and the night-

9. Chapter fourteen, which begins four pages later, contains in its
opening paragraph a comment set up by these sketchy Christian allusions: "If you think, and some do, that continual intimacy, familiarity, and
love can result in falsehood, this being thrown on the world may be a very
desirable even if sad thing. What Christ meant when he called his mother

time business of mothering" mingle with the sounds of New Year's Eve: "tooting, sirens, horns, all that jubilation." Despite the season, Mimi chooses to be a non-Mary. "Her comment to me," Augie recalls, "was melancholy, about whether she had outwitted her fate or met it" (281). Other women seem caught in the same dilemma. When Augie accidentally enters the labor room, he sees women in the throes of birth:

> I passed through to another division where the labor rooms were, separated cubicles, and in them saw women struggling, outlandish pain and huge-bellied distortion, one powerful face that bore down into its creases and issued a voice great and songlike in which she cursed her husband obscenely for his pleasure that had got her into this; and others, calling on saints and mothers, incontinent, dragging at the bars of their beds, weeping, or with faces of terror or narcotized eyes. . . . And just then, in the elevator shaft nearby, there were screams. I stopped and waited for the rising light I saw coming steadily through the glass panels. The door opened; a woman sat before me in a wheel chair, and in her lap, just born in a cab or paddy wagon or in the lobby of the hospital, covered with blood and screaming so you could see sinews, square of chest and shoulders from the strain, this bald kid, red and covering her with red. She too, with lost nerve, was sobbing, each hand squeezing up on itself, eyes wildly frightened; and she and the baby appeared like enemies forced to have each other, like figures of a war. They were pushed out, passing me close by so that the mother's arm grazed me. (282)

Though it is the season during which men honor the Divine Maternity and turn their faces with renewed life toward the new year, there is no peace on earth in this place, or good will toward men. For Augie it is a severe test of his conviction that marriage is blessed and that birth is an affirmation of life. By aborting her baby, Mimi frustrates her inescapable maternal instinct and denies life, albeit in the interest of love. By bearing their babies, the women in the ward subject themselves to indignity, fear, pain, and the kind of grinding toil that Augie hears of from Jimmy Klein. Each finds bitterness in the chosen thing; all alternatives are imperfect. When Anna Coblin tries the next

---

'Woman.' That after all she was like any woman" (285).

morning to rekindle Augie's interest in his childhood play-
mate Friedl as a prospective mate and mother of his children he greets her attempt with silence, turning his eyes "at
last to the weather."

"I was no child now," Augie declares at the beginning of
Chapter thirteen "neither in age nor in protectedness, and
I was thrown for fair on the free spinning of the world"
(285). The schism with Simon and the free spinning of the
world take Augie back to his reading and then to a job as
a labor organizer. Though he has sympathy for the plight
of the working man, he is somewhat overwhelmed by the
complexities of labor organization and the many obstacles
to reform. He is not really a crusader for the fates of others;
he is too much concerned with his own. Though he performs his duties in responsible fashion and enjoys his brief
affair with Sophie Geratis, whom he meets in the line of
duty, he is relieved to escape labor conflicts—and their
concomitant beatings—in the arms of Thea Fenchel, who
returns to his life as his interest in labor reform reaches its
lowest point. As the AFL and CIO battle in alleys, streets,
and basements, Augie licks his wounds in Thea's bed:

> It wasn't even in my power to be elsewhere, once we had
> started. No, I just didn't have the calling to be a union man or
> in politics, or any notion of my particle of will coming before
> the ranks of a mass that was about to march forward from
> misery. How would this will of mine have got there to lead the
> way? (310)

Augie finds himself in love with Thea, and his love and his
fate take him to hunt iguanas with eagles in Mexico, where
he discovers writ large the "fighting nature of birds and
worms" that Grandma Lausch spoke of.

The scene shifts radically from the steamy clamor of
Chicago streets to the atavistic, torrid stillness of the Mexican badlands. From the city, Augie and Thea become one
with nature. Augie describes Thea as having "perfect life";
and she aims at perfection in everything she does, from
lovemaking to eagle-training. She even stuffs toilet tissue
in her bra to produce a perfect shape, a practice that Augie
considers superfluous. She never goes anywhere "without

an animal," and, like an animal herself, she has burrowing instincts: "She rented a big place and then settled in space-economizing style, gathering and piling things around her" (315). As her name implies, Thea is a kind of goddess, a goddess of both nature and love, and from her Augie learns something about the complexities of both forces.

The eagle, Caligula, whose fierce nature Thea seeks to exploit, is found to have a streak of cowardice in him: He flees from the iguanas he is supposed to capture. Thea abandons him in disgust and turns to snakes in her quest for something without human failing—for something with a large measure of the kind of immortality with which she seeks to identify herself. Augie's increasing boredom with her various eccentric activities places him also in her disfavor. Caligula's failure to meet Thea's expectations of fierceness in nature is like Augie's failure to share her intense desire to rise above the merely human. Thea is disdainful of Augie's "humanizing" the eagle and lizards, and when he spends a starlit night with Stella, he becomes irremediably unworthy in Thea's eyes as a love object, as a man good enough to receive the affection of one who sees herself as a superior being. After their split she tells him: "You're not special. You're like everybody else. You get tired easily. I don't want to see you anymore" (396). Thea, however, is a victim of opposing motives. She wishes to be a superior being, to avoid "sticking to the ordinary way and doing something false" (395), but she also wants to establish human contact. Thea sought to follow the principle of Diotima set forth by Socrates in Plato's *Symposium* of moving from one beloved object to others, beginning with Augie: "I thought," she explains to Augie, "if I could get through to one other person I could get through to more" (396). She fails—as she has failed with others earlier—and she moves on in her futile, contradictory pursuit. Augie is nothing more than another specimen in her oft-gathered menagerie, like her latest catch in the fishbowl, a puffy, warty creature:

> "You've started a new collection," I said.
> "I caught this one yesterday. He's about the most interesting

so far. But I'm not staying here. I'm going to Yucatan. I'm supposed to see where some rare flamingoes have migrated from Florida." (410)

Moved by two opposing desires, she can satisfy neither. She moves in a circle.

Augie's affair with Thea leads him to reflect on his own actions and to discover the ambiguity of his own motives. Thea accuses him of being vain and unreliable and of turning from rather than toward a commitment to love. Augie ponders the possible validity in her charge:

> I thought about it and was astonished at how much truth there actually was in this. Why, it was so! And I had always believed that where love was concerned I was on my mother's side, against the Grandma Lausches, the Mrs. Renlings, and the Lucy Magnuses.
> If I didn't have money or profession or duties, wasn't it so that I could be free, and a sincere follower of love?
> Me, love's servant? I wasn't at all! And suddenly my heart felt ugly, I was sick of myself. I thought that my aim of being simple was just a fraud, that I wasn't a bit good hearted or affectionate, and I began to wish that Mexico from beyond the walls would come in and kill me and that I would be thrown in the bone dust and twisted, spiky crosses of the cemetary, for the insects and lizards.
> . . . Kindly explain! An independent fate, and love too—what confusion! (400–1)

As Thea aspires to the divine while reaching for human contact, Augie discovers he has been seeking love while clinging to his freedom. Allowing himself to be compromised by Stella was his subconscious way of ending his uneasy commitment to Thea. He retains his freedom and pays lip service to love, but he sees in his actions the shabbiness of the self-deception. Remembering Kayo Obermark's comments about bitterness in the chosen thing, Augie feels he has been untrue to his purest feelings and he feels "terrible contempt" (402). Thea turns to reptiles and Talavera, and in his self-disgust and despair, Augie turns to booze, cards, and the barflies Iggy and Moulton.

If the kick in the head from the old warhorse, Bizcocho, teaches Augie something about the capriciousness of nature and the precariousness of man in it, his own infidelity and Thea's departure teach him something about the instability of human relationships:

> I had wanted to marry her, but there isn't any possession. No, no, wives don't own husbands, nor husbands wives, nor parents children. They go away, or they die. So the only possessing is of the moment. If you're able. And while any wish lives, it lives in the face of its negative. This is why we make the obstinate signs of possession. Like deeds, certificates, rings, pledges, and other permanent things. (407)

That any wish lives in the face of its negative states both the organizing strategy of the book and a vision of the world. Seeking both love and an independent fate, Augie sacrifices one to the other, admitting to Iggy that he "had done wrong" (400). Simon desires both money and happiness but destroys his chances for happiness in his zeal for acquisition. In seeking a divine perfection, Thea does violence to her human capacities; and Mimi pays too high an emotional price to serve an intellectual concept that she imperfectly understands. The life experiences related to Augie by the Russian Cossack at the end of the episode in Mexico lead Augie to a bleak conclusion:

> Well, I pretended not to understand because it suited me to make him out as ridiculous, but I knew very well what he was trying to get across. Not that life should end is so terrible in itself, but that it should end with so many disappointments in the essential. This is a fact. (412)

The bitterness in the chosen thing takes on metaphysical proportions here as the imperfection in life.

Leaving Mexico, Augie visits Georgie and Mama in their separate institutions and then checks up on the Chicago personalities of his past, perhaps in a subconscious attempt to reorient himself by returning to the place and people of his origin. He finds things essentially unchanged. Simon still rages amid his riches, Einhorn still holds court in his curious household, Mimi clings firmly to her independence, but sees still that her fate is shared by someone sensitive enough to appreciate her character, and Clem

Tambow continues to offer Augie psycho-philosophical analyses of his undirected life:

> Oh, what a case! You'd be a regular conservatory for a scientific mind. You'd be the greatest collection of unknowns ever to lie on a couch. What I guess about you is that you have a nobility syndrome. You can't adjust to the reality situation. I can see it all over you. You want there should be Man, with capital M. with great stature. . . . O godlike man! Tell me, pal, am I getting warm or not? (434–35)

Augie assents, and Clem illustrates his point further with a story about the deprived children in his old fourth-grade class. The teacher would call each to the front of the room, hand the student a piece of chalk, and ask each to describe the flower he smelled. Some would imagine sweetpea, violet, rose, or nasturtium; others, more realistic or cynical, would bait the teacher and ridicule the game: "Skunk cabbage, teach" or "wild schmooflowers," or "dreck" (435). For Clem the story represents his twofold classification of people, those who escape into fantasy and those who face reality squarely; but Augie, undaunted, sees both attitudes as valid. He refuses to condemn the children who smell flowers in chalk, who impose imaginative beauty on unresponsive reality, for they, like him, are simply refusing "to lead a disappointed life" (432). Battered though he is, Augie continues his adventures in pursuit of this ideal.

The final section (Chapters twenty-one through twenty-five) of Augie's "road" experiences is more philosophically reflective than the earlier episodes, for Augie's romantic involvement in Mexico has made him a sadly wiser man. As in the section revolving around Mimi's abortion, it is Kayo Obermark who again provides thematic focus for this last section in his comments on *moha,* a variation on his earlier statement about bitterness in the chosen thing. Appropriately, Augie is involved in this section with three quirky philosophers, Robey the millionaire, Mintouchian the lawyer, and Bateshaw the ship's carpenter and scientist. Each is a theoretician, and each experiences opposition in his life and bitterness in his chosen thing.

Doing practice teaching in a Chicago elementary school in order to get a teaching certificate, Augie encounters his old slovenly but philosophical neighbor Kayo Obermark, now a teacher. One day, in an analytical mood, Augie complains to Kayo of the difficulty the individual encounters in creating any kind of personal destiny amid the man-made things and forces which bend him to their mindless wills. "Things done by man overshadow us" (450). The dominance of things, the rigidity of schedules, and the pressures of keeping up, Augie fears, leave no time or emotional space for individual happiness or a personal life style. Kayo responds without hesitation:

> What you are talking about is *moha*—a Navajo word, and also Sanskrit, meaning opposition of the finite. It is the Bronx cheer of the conditioning forces. Love is the only answer to *moha*, being infinite. I mean all forms of love, eros, agape, libido, philia, and ecstasy. They are always the same, but sometimes one quality dominates and sometimes another. (450)

The opposition of love to the finite, *moha,* sets the pattern of development for this section. It is clear in various forms in the lives of Robey, Mintouchian, and Bateshaw, and also in Augie's uneasy marriage to Stella.

For Robey, *moha* is the real barrier to human happiness. The multiplicity of things, he feels, may inundate man and eliminate lasting values:

> M-machinery'll make an ocean of commodities. Dictators can't stop it. Man will accept death. Live without God. That's a b-brave project. End of an illusion. But with what values instead? (441)

The possibility of happiness despite the opposition of things is the subject of the book he wishes Augie to help him write. The book is to be both a historical analysis and program, showing man divesting himself of oppressive Christianity and rising to heights of godlike glory, moving from one polarity to another:

> He was saying that Christianity originally was aimed at the lowly and slaves, and that was why crucifixion and nailing and all such punitive grandeur of martyrdom were necessary. But at the pole opposite, the happy pole, there ought to be an equal thickness. Joy without sin, love without darkness, gay prosperity. Not to be always spoiling things. O Great age of generous love and time of a new man! Not the poor, dark, disfigured creature cramped by his falsehood, a liar from the cradle,

flogged by poverty, smelling bad from cowardice, deeper than
a latrine in jealousy, dead as a cabbage to feeling, a maggot to
beauty, a shrimp to duty, spinning the same thread of cocoon
preoccupation from his mouth. Without tears to weep or
enough expendable breath to laugh; cruel, frigging, parasitic,
sneaking, grousing, anxious, and sluggardly. Drilled like a
Prussian by the coarse hollering of sergeant fears. Robey
poured it on me; he let it come down. (442)

Preaching polarities, Robey is himself a study in opposites.
He will call his book *The Needle's Eye,* alluding to the
biblical teaching that it is easier for a camel to pass through
the eye of a needle than for a rich man to enter the kingdom
of heaven; yet Robey is a millionaire. He desires to establish happiness for man, a kingdom of heaven on earth, and
he sees wealth as an obstacle to that happiness; yet he
refuses to divest himself of his money. He loves knowledge
and, theoretically, considers material things unimportant,
but in practice he clings to his riches, eats mouldy ham and
canned vegetables to save on his food bill, and begrudges
Augie his $30–a–week salary. Though he aspires, like Thea,
to the godlike, the only godly thing Augie sees him do is
pump Flit into the hideaway of his kitchen roaches, destroying life *en masse* with a kind of omnipotent divine
fury. The pressure of living with his ambivalences causes
Robey to stutter, makes him moody and frequently incoherent, and drives him from one fragmentary project to
another. Finally understanding that all Robey really wants
is, like Einhorn before him, a listener, Augie moves on,
leaving *The Needle's Eye* as he found it.

Between his employment with Robey and his introduction to Mintouchian, Augie experiences an epiphany resulting from his struggle to discover who he is and what he
should do. Lying on his couch resting from his teaching
duties and his renewed affair with Sophie Geratis, he explains his new insight to Clem Tambow:

> "I have a feeling," I said, "about the axial lines of life, with
> respect to which you must be straight or else your existence is
> merely clownery, hiding tragedy. I must have had a feeling
> since I was a kid about these axial lines which made me want
> to have my existence on them, and so I have said "no" like a
> stubborn fellow to all my persuaders, just on the obstinacy of

my memory of these lines, never entirely clear. But lately I have felt these thrilling lines again. When striving stops, there they are as a gift. I was lying on the couch here before and they suddenly went quivering right straight through me. Truth, love, peace, bounty, usefulness, harmony! And all noise and grates, distortion, chatter, distraction, effort, superfluity, passed off like something unreal. And I believe that any man at any time can come back to these axial lines, even if an unfortunate bastard, if he will be quiet and wait it out. The ambition of something special and outstanding I have always had is only a boast that distorts this knowledge from its origin, which is the oldest knowledge, older than the Euphrates, older than the Ganges. At any time life can come together again and man be regenerated, and doesn't have to be a god or public servant like Osiris, who gets torn apart annually for the sake of the common prosperity, but the man himself, finite and taped as he is, can still come where the axial lines are. He will be brought into focus. He will live with true joy. Even his pains will be joy if they are true, even his helplessness will not take away his power, even wandering will not take him away from himself, even the big social jokes and hoaxes need not make him ridiculous, even disappointment after disappointment need not take away his love. Death will not be terrible to him if life is not. The embrace of other true people will take away his dread of fast change and short life. And this is not the imaginary stuff, Clem, because I bring my entire life to the test." (455)

Manny Padilla had once told Augie about mathematics: "Either this stuff comes easy or it doesn't come at all." "Of course!" Augie thought, "Easily or not at all. People were mad to be knocking themselves out over difficulties because they thought difficulty was a sign of the right thing" (192). The seed planted then in Augie's mind blossoms here in the vision he describes to Clem Tambow.

And with the vision goes a program. Augie wants to get married, buy a farm in the Midwest, and operate a kind of foster-home school for orphaned children. His mother would serve as the resident Hestia, and his brother George would teach shoe repairing. Having spent so much time in the homes of others, Augie wants others to live with him for a change, and this is the way also, he thinks, to align himself with the axial lines of life which he has been missing in his fruitless striving for a worthwhile fate. Clem accuses him of masking the will to power in a cloak of altruism (always an opposite view available), but Augie denies any bad motives. He simply wishes through love— eros, agape, libido, philia, and ecstasy—to avoid the stultifying struggle with the finite; but his insight has to be nurtured longer and his project deferred, for war breaks out to interrupt his plan.

After a painful operation for inguinal hernia, a token of his fall with Bizcocho in Mexico, Augie joins the Merchant Marine and is accepted by the Sheepshead Purser's and Pharmacist's Mate's School in New York. There he renews his romance with and becomes engaged to Stella Chesney, and through Stella he meets Mintouchian, who takes Augie further into his examination of the laws of life. It is appropriate that Augie should discuss the laws of life with Mintouchian, for the former organist in a silent-movie house is now a lawyer.

Mintouchian's view of love serves as a counterbalance to the view held by Kayo Obermark. For Kayo, love carried the power of infinity, enabling one to triumph over the limitations of the finite. Mintouchian acknowledges the nobility of the emotion, but he assigns to it a more ephemeral status. Seeing that Augie is deeply in love with Stella, Mintouchian relates for Augie's benefit several sordid stories from his law practice designed to indicate the unreliability of human feelings, the infidelities and deceptions that mark most marriages. Then he obliquely draws a conclusion about love as a law of life:

> You may be as interested as I was . . . in what a clever fellow once said to me about the connection of love and adultery. On any certain day, when you're happy, you know it can't last, but the weather will change, the health will be sickness, the year will end, and also life will end. In another place another day there'll be a different lover. The face you're kissing will change to some other face, and so will your face be replaced. It can't be helped, this guy said. Of course he was a lousy bastard himself and a counterfeit no-good mooch, and he was in and out of Bellevue, and women supported him all his life; he deserted his kid and nobody could depend on him. But love *is* adultery, he said, and expresses change. You make your peace with change. Another city, another woman, a different bed, but you're the same and so you must be flexible. You kiss the

woman and you show how you love your fate, and you worship and adore the changes of life. You obey this law. Whether
or not this bum was right, may God hate his soul! don't think
you don't have to obey the laws of life. (483)

Because he feels his attempt to align himself with the axial
lines of life is an attempt to act in harmony with universal
laws, Augie denies hotly the implication that he is avoiding
the laws of life. Despite his own experience with infidelities he rejects, moreover, Mintouchian's view of love as
adultery. To use Clem Tambow's analogy, Augie still resists identifying himself with the cynical children who cannot imagine the possiblity of flowers in a piece of chalk.
Though Mintouchian's towel fits around him in the Turk-
ish Bath "like the robe of a sage," Augie shows himself to
be on the side of Kayo in denying Mintouchian's "wisdom"
that love is mere process and that human beings are simply
objects manipulated by that process.

On the law of life pertaining to individual character,
however, Augie and Mintouchian are in close agreement.
Mintouchian confesses that through an accident he once
learned the meaning of personal identity, that to live is to
accept what he is "because to live is to be Mintouchian, my
dear man." He echoes Augie's early assertion from Heraclitus about a man's character being his fate:

Why do you have to think that the thing that kills you is the
thing that you stand for? Because you are the author of your
death. What is the weapon? The nails and hammer of your
character. What is the cross? Your own bones on which you
gradually weaken. And the husband or the wife gets the other
to do the deed. "Kind spouse, you will make me my fate," they
might as well say, and tell them and show them how. The fish
wills water, and the bird wills air, and you and me our dominant idea. (484)

Mintouchian goes on to explain that his dominant idea is
that man lives by secrets, by leading many lives, sometimes
even losing sight of the true self in practicing so many
deceptions. This baring of souls leads Augie to make a
confession:

"You will understand, Mr. Mintouchian, if I tell you that I have
always tried to become what I am. But it's a frightening thing.

Because what if what I am by nature isn't good enough?" I was
close to tears as I said it to him. "I suppose I better, anyway,
give in and be it. I will never force the hand of fate to create
a better Augie March, nor change the time to an age of gold."
(485)

Agreeing that Augie must take his chance on what he is,
Mintouchian concludes, "It is better to die what you are
than to live a stranger forever" (485). Though Mintouchian's original impulse seemed to be to deter Augie
from marriage, the effect of his last counsel is to prepare
Augie for his commitment to Stella, a commitment which
Augie had heretofore resisted in all his love affairs.

Augie detects in his venerable sage evidence of "gall,"
and soon he discovers the causes of Mintouchian's bitterness. Though he appears worldy wise and well adjusted,
Mintouchian practices deception on his wife with his mistress, Stella's friend Agnes Kuttner. This "secret" from his
wife, Augie discovers, is not a secret at all, and Mintouchian has just discovered in his turn that Agnes is practicing
deception on him. Holding as he does that infidelity is the
law of love and that deceit is a way of life, he can only
acknowledge his situation as a concrete demonstration of
his intellectual vision. Finding support for his thesis in his
own life, however, does not help him bear the turbulent
feelings toward which he has become so cynical when they
occur in others. The ironic intellectual verification does
not help him overcome the emotional pain. This is the
bitterness in his chosen thing. He may be great, as Augie
suggests, but he is also, as his wife declares, "all too human."

Released by Mintouchian, then, to try to "be what he is,"
Augie decides to marry Stella despite the war. Juxtaposing
the polarities in his situation, Augie exclaims, "What use
was war without also love?" (470). After his graduation
from Sheepshead, Augie marries Stella and becomes a bit
smug about his pursuit of happiness and a worthwhile
fate. Comparing himself to Simon, he muses:

Why, I thought I had it all over him, seeing I was married to
a woman I loved and therefore I was advancing on the only
true course of life. I told myself my brother was the kind of

man who could only leave the world as he found it and hand
on the fate he inherited to any children he might now have—I
didn't for sure know whether he had any. Yes, this was how
such people were subject to all the laws in the book, like the
mountain peaks leaning toward their respective magnetic
poles, or like crabs in the weeds or crystals in the caves.
Whereas I, with the help of love, had gotten in on a much better
thing and was giving this account of myself that reality comes
from and was not just at the mercy. And here was the bride
with me, her face was burning with happy excitement; she
wanted what I wanted. In her time she had made mistakes but
all mistakes were now wiped out.(488)

After a brief two-day honeymoon, Augie ships out as Purser and Pharmacist's Mate on the *Sam MacManus,* assuring his anxious bride that he is under the protection of
love: "I love you too much to go and get sunk, on my first
trip out" (491). Augie is soon to learn, however, that love
cannot deny fate.

At sea, Augie finds himself privy to the personal secrets
of troubled members of the crew. He becomes in fact what
Einhorn had gratuitously dubbed him as an adolescent, an
Alcibiades beloved-of-man. His status as confidant and
counselor does not last long, however, for on the fifteenth
day of the cruise the ship is sunk by an enemy torpedo
somewhere off the Canary Islands. All hands are lost except Augie and the ship's carpenter, Bateshaw, who find
themselves sharing the only remaining lifeboat.

Another theoretician and Recruiter-of-Others-to-Grand-
Causes, Bateshaw was early moved to an exceptional life-
course by the ordinariness of his childhood:

> Everybody wants to be the most desirable kind of man.
> And how does it start? Well, go back to when I was a kid
> in the municipal swimming pool. A thousand naked little bas-
> tards screaming, punching, pushing, kicking. The lifeguards
> whistle and holler and punish you, the cops on duty squash
> you in the ribs with their thumbs and call you snot-nose. Shiv-
> ery little rat. Lips blue, blood thin, scared, your little balls tight,
> your little thing shriveled. Skinny you. The shoving multitude
> bears down, and you're nothing, a meaningless name, and not
> just obscure in eternity but right now. The fate of the meanest
> your fate. Death! But no, there must be some distinction. The
> soul cries out against this namelessness. And then it exagger-

ates. It tells you,"You were meant to astonish the world. You, Hymie Bateshaw, *Stupor mundi!* My boy, brace up. You have been called, and you will be chosen. So start looking the part. The generations of man will venerate you as long as calendars exist!"This is neurotic, I know—excuse the jargon—but to be not neurotic is to adjust to what they call the reality situation. But the reality situation is what I have described. A billion souls boiling with anger at a doom of insignificance. Reality is also these private hopes the imagination invents. Hopes, the indispensable evils of Pandora's Box. Assurance of a fate worth suffering for. (503)

Another seeker after a worthwhile fate, Bateshaw has followed his quest for distinction into the realms of scientific theory, but his abstractions as a theoretician exceed those of all his predecessors in Augie's experience, for Bateshaw has become proficient in the principle of life itself.

Through an elaborate series of experiments with the cause of boredom, Bateshaw, ironically, discovered the secret of life and succeeded in creating a simple form of life, protoplasm. Because his protoplasm lacked regenerative and reproductive powers, however, six universities dismissed him for claiming to have created life. Now, he tells Augie, he has successfully improved his protoplasm, though his latest batch went down with the ship. He must continue his experiments, he argues, for the whole future of mankind is at stake:

These experiments with cells, March, will give the clue to the origin of boredom in the higher organisms. To what used to be called the sin of acedia. The old fellows were right, for it is a sin. Blindness to life, secession, unreceptivity, a dull wall of anxious, overprotected flesh, ignorant of the subtlety of God or Nature and unfeeling toward its beauty. March, when liberated from this boredom, every man will be a poet and every woman a saint. Love will fill the world. Injustice will go, and slavery, bloodshed, cruelty. (509)

Asking Augie to play Joshua to his Moses to lead the entire human race into his utopian Israel, Bateshaw tries to recruit Augie to a "great course of life." Augie protests that he already has a course of life and declares himself "dead against doing things to the entire human race." A quarrel follows, and they fight. Bateshaw subdues Augie with an oar and ties him up. Augie frees himself in the night and discovers Bateshaw is gravely ill with fever. Fortunately a passing freighter picks them up, far from the Canaries where Bateshaw claimed he was heading, and takes them to a hospital in Naples, where they both eventually regain their health and go their separate ways.

Augie sees in Bateshaw another combatant against *moha* and the "doom of insignificance." Bateshaw has sought through his reason to overcome the limitations of "the shoving multitude," and though he has formulated grandiose visions in the name of Man, he has become another Machiavellian and has destroyed his own humanity. Love to him is merely a predictable set of psychological and biological responses between creatures thrown together by happenstance. Consequently, he can sexually exploit the pulmonary phthisis of his cousin Lee and hasten her death by discarding her when it suits his purposes. He can use Augie's aid to get into the lifeboat, but he makes no reciprocal effort to aid Augie. He has no respect for the memory of his neurotic father or for his aunt who slept away fifteen years of her life because she was ashamed of her ugliness. Though he claims to have the power to chart a new course for mankind, he himself founders, lost, sick, and helpless, in an unknown sea, where Augie grudgingly—but humanely—nurses him until their rescue. The ship's doctor saves the ship's carpenter after all, and with this episode Augie's shaping experiences "on the road" come to an end.

In the final section of the novel (Chapter twenty-six) Augie, now fully matured and seasoned, is appropriately enough in Paris, the City of Man. He is a successful businessman in association with Mintouchian, and he is a veteran husband. He also has a fuller grasp of who and what he is. He knows now that Stella has never been completely honest with him and that she loves him less than he loves her; yet he accepts his situation as part of his fate and somehow an ineluctable element in the nature of things. He also realizes that his scheme for an orphan's foster-home school was visionary and improbable, but he clings with tireless resiliency to his idea of a worthwhile fate:

Guys may very likely think, Why hell! What's this talk about fates? and will feel it all comes to me from another day, and a mistaken day, when there were fewer people in the world and there was more room between them so that they grew not like wild grass but like trees in a park, well set apart and developing year by year in the rosy light. Now instead of such comparison you think, Let's see it instead not even as the grass but as a band of particles, a universal shawl of them, and these particles may have functions but certainly lack fates. And there's even an attitude of mind which finds it almost disgusting to be a person and not a function. Nevertheless I stand by my idea of a fate. For which a function is a substitution of a deeper despair. (516)

Pursuing a star, Augie captures only a starlet, but persists in believing he will reach his port in safety.

Coming full circle from his initial assertion that a man's character is his fate, Augie is now willing to affirm as well that "this fate, or what he settles for, is also his character" (514). That is, whatever conditions a man becomes willing to limit himself to necessarily reflect, in a real sense, the nature of his character. A man who has difficulty holding a job, for example, decides that he is a bum and thus he becomes a bum. The condition he accepts becomes the determinant and the reflection of his character. Augie continues to seek the axial lines of life, but he no longer struggles intensely toward them. He is willing now "to be still so that the axial lines can be found" (514). The "unborn children" (529) that he pores over—Mimi's, Simon's, his own, the *bambini* of *Les Orphelines*—are the symbols of the new life he persists in his new maturity to pursue, the symbols as nebulous as their referents. His pursuit is quieter now: "When striving stops, the truth comes as a gift—bounty, harmony, love, and so forth" (514).

An ambivalent man seeking love and an independent fate, Augie sacrifices his freedom for love, only to discover that the love he commits himself to is not the completely genuine feeling he had imagined and does not produce the axial-line life he desires. He experiences the bitterness in his chosen thing. Others whose lives have touched his along the way—Einhorn, Simon, Mimi, Jimmy Klein, Thea, Robey, Mintouchian, Bateshaw—have also followed their own ambivalent motives to discover bitterness in their chosen things; and all of them have been acting in the name of their personal destinies. Their aim has been to overcome *moha,* "the Bronx cheer of the conditioning forces," the opposition of the finite. They have failed in this essential aim, and so far Augie, too, has failed. But Augie is not yet ready to settle for failure. He nourishes yet a durable optimism. After walking across a frozen field in Normandy with the French maid, Jacqueline, Augie thinks of how they have sung to prevent their lungs from freezing in the winter cold (an objective correlative, Augie senses, for the condition of man in the world) and of how Jacqueline, though beset by many mishaps in her life, still holds to her dream of someday going to Mexico (no dreamland to Augie):

> I was still chilled from the hike across the fields, but thinking of Jacqueline and Mexico, I got to grinning again. That's the *animal ridens* in me, the laughing creature, forever rising up. What's so laughable, that a Jacqueline, for instance, as hard used as that by rough forces, will still refuse to lead a disappointed life? Or is the laugh at nature—including eternity—that it thinks it can win over us and the power of hope? Nah, nah, I think. It never will. But that probably is the joke, on one or the other, and laughing is an enigma that includes both. Look at me, going everywhere! Why I am a sort of Columbus of those near-at-hand and believe you can come to them in this immediate *terra incognita* that spreads out in every gaze. I may well be a flop at this line of endeavor. Columbus too thought he was a flop, probably, when they sent him back in chains. Which didn't prove there was no America. (536)

Augie's response to *moha* and bitterness is laughter, a symbol of his indomitable spirit of optimism and a gesture that both acknowledges the joke that life plays on man and indicates his refusal to be defeated by it. The laughter includes both polarities between which Augie moves, what life is and what he would like it to be. With clear-eyed awareness now of the complexity of his situation, Augie goodnaturedly continues his quest for a meaningful life. That he has not found it yet, he insists, is not real evidence that it does not exist. Augie has been exposed through the novel's strategy of opposites to ample experiences—his own and that of others—to transform him into an abject pessimist, but he stands firm at the end. His character and his fate are clear: He will refuse to lead a disappointed life.

4.

Seize the Day: A Drowning Man

Critical opinion of *Seize the Day* reveals almost unanimous agreement that it is the most well made of all Bellow's novels. Plot, character, mood, and language are skillfully interwoven to produce the kind of "figure in the carpet" that Henry James prized so highly. Even more than *The Victim, Seize the Day* achieves a sustained intensity and a unity of effect that approaches the condition of poetry. Indeed, Keith Opdahl has seen the pattern of water imagery in the novel as its most dominant feature. His comments are both a description of imagery and a summary of plot:

> "Seize the Day" . . . depicts the death throes of a drowning man. Tommy Wilhelm faces complete submergence in failure. He begins his day plunging downward in a hotel elevator to a city sunk metaphorically beneath the sea. The New York streets carry a "tide of Broadway traffic" which is the "current" of the city (77, 100). The baroque hotel he sees from the lobby window looks "like the image of itself reflected in deep water, white and cumulous above, with cavernous distortions underneath" (5). Although Wilhelm struggles to keep "the waters of the earth" from rolling over him, he looks "like a man about to drown" (77, 104). He has foolishly quit his job and has no money to meet the demands of his wife, who seeks to punish him for leaving her. His relations with his elderly father, whom he has denied by changing his name, reach the breaking point; the physician denies his plea for help by calling him a slob. He finally loses the little money he has left on the commodities market, where he had speculated at the urging of a phony psychologist, Dr. Tamkin.
>
> The waters roll over him when he stumbles, defeated, into a funeral home. There, "where it was dark and cool," his troubles end. The quiet chapel has the wavering, dreamlike quality of an ocean grotto. Organ music "stirred and breathed from the

pipes" and "men in formal clothes and black homburgs strode softly back and forth on the cork floor, up and down the center aisle" (116). Wilhelm feels a "splash of heartsickness" as he stands before the corpse of a stranger (117). When he begins to cry, at first softly and then hysterically, his drowning is complete. "The heavy sea-like music came up to his ears," Bellow writes. "It poured into him where he had hidden himself in the center of a crowd by the great and happy oblivion of tears. He heard it and sank deeper than sorrow, through torn sobs and cries toward the consummation of his heart's ultimate need" (118).[1]

"Wilhelm's drowning," Opdahl explains further, "is first of all the climax of his day of failure. The water in which he drowns is both the world and his masochistic self which have murdered him."[2] His death, however, is not purely negative, for in the death of the old self, there is the birth of a new self who will be, the novel implies, more capable of dealing with his own temperament and the world around him.

Clinton Trowbridge has also provided a sensitive reading of the water imagery in *Seize the Day*. Among many perceptive comments, he makes the following observation:

> The image of the drowning Wilhelm is the controlling one, but because of the book's ironic structure it is an image that functions in two ways. On a first reading, and on each rereading on the surface of our experience, it intensifies sympathy for Wilhelm's condition. Even when Wilhelm is being depicted least sympathetically, when he is most in the wrong, most a slob, we are continually made aware that we are witnessing the strugglings of a drowning man and we want to see him rescued. Thus our sympathy is continual in a way that it is not, for instance, with Dostoevski's underground man.[3]

Both Opdahl and Trowbridge have provided provocative insights into the dominance of water imagery in the novel, but Trowbridge seems mainly interested in the affective functions of language and tone, and Opdahl seems content to provide an adumbrated description of the images, point-

1. Keith Opdahl, *The Novels of Saul Bellow: An Introduction* (University Park, Pa., 1967), pp. 96–97.

2. Ibid., p. 115.

3. Clinton W. Trowbridge, "Water Imagery in *Seize the Day*," *Critique*, 9 (Spring 1968), 62–73.

ing to them but not examining in detail their cohesive function in the novel as a whole. Neither writer concerns himself with the skillful use Bellow makes of the scene as image in *Seize the Day*.

The purpose of the analysis offered here, then, is to show how the embodiment of theme in water imagery finds its larger objectification in individual scenes, for the individual scenes in this novel clearly function like poetic images, producing an integrated totality of impression that is very similar to the effect of a lyric poem. A novel is not a lyric poem, of course, and the methods of analysis that serve for poetry cannot without modification be applied to fiction, but with some allowance for the difference in genres, the formalist methods of analyzing poetic images can prove illuminating when applied to fiction. Such an analysis is especially productive in revealing Bellow's narrative strategy in *Seize the Day*.

That the scene in fiction frequently functions like the image in poetry has been established explicitly by W. J. Handy:

> The scene in fiction may be viewed as being analogous to the image in poetry. From an ontological point of view both the scene and the image possess the same fundamental characteristics:
>
> 1. Both present rather than predicate about.
>
> 2. Both comprise a single configuration of multiple meaning.
>
> 3. Both intend to formulate the particularity, the texture of experience.
>
> 4. Both are directed primarily to sense, not to abstract intellection.
>
> 5. Both exceed the concept in containing more meaning than a concept can, by its inherent nature, formulate.
>
> The fictional scene, no less than the poetic image, represents the literary artist's attempt at, in Eliot's words, "transmuting ideas into sensations." [4]

How the fictional scene functions to "formulate the particularity, the texture of experience" in the life of Tommy Wilhelm and how these scenes approximate the poetic

---

4. William J. Handy, *Kant and the Southern New Critics* (Austin, Tex., 1963), pp. 83–84.

image provide the focus of this chapter.

Ezra Pound has defined the image in poetry as "that which presents an intellectual and emotional complex in an instant of time,"[5] and I. A. Richards has shown that a metaphorical image can be analyzed according to its tenor, the idea in or the subject matter of the implied comparison, and its vehicle, the particularity in which generality is embodied. The conception of the fictional scene developed in this chapter draws on both of these observations, for it is clear that at the center of *Seize the Day* is an extended metaphor which serves as the integrating principle of the narrative. The metaphor, as Opdahl and Trowbridge have shown, depicts human failure through the image of a drowning man. Tommy Wilhelm has made a mess of his life and now, gasping for breath and grabbing, panic-stricken, at straws (Tamkin), he sinks wearily beneath the pressures of his own making. The tenor of the total image that is the book is human failure. The vehicle in which this subject matter is embodied is the image of drowning, and each scene in the novel functions as a facet of the total image, the texture of the narrative presentation. The scenes render the particularity of the diverse pressures under which Wilhelm is submerged, and function thereby to extend the central metaphor.

Pound describes the poetic image as being presented in "an instant of time," that is, in a frozen moment. The effect is a kind of timelessness. In fiction, however, characters move through time; their experience occurs in successive moments. "Works of fiction," W. J. Handy has said in a recent essay, "express man's capacity to experience his experience, not in moments merely (as reflected in the lyric poem or the painting or the sculpture), but in time."[6] The action of the novel necessarily involves the passage of time. Handy's emphasis on the scene as the basic presentational unit in fiction, however, suggests that within scene,

5. Ezra Pound, "A Few Don'ts by an Imagiste," *Poetry*, 1 (March 1913), 200.

6. William J. Handy, "Criticism of Joyce's Works: A Formalist Approach," in *James Joyce: His Place in World Literature*, Proceedings of the Comparative Literature Symposium, 2 (Lubbock, Tex., 1969), 62.

time functions in a manner not dissimilar to Pound's concept of an "instant of time." What fiction achieves in the
successful treatment of time and space within scene is
what Joseph Frank has called "spatial form," the arrangement of action and setting in accentual levels of presentational unity. He illustrates his theory with an examination
of the scene in *Madame Bovary* in which Rodolphe woos
Emma with sentimental rhetoric, while below them on the
street a country fair is in progress, the mobs being ad-
dressed by both local politicians and a livestock auction-
eer. Frank's analysis is worth quoting at length:

> As Flaubert sets the scene, there is action going on simulta-
> neously at three levels, and the physical position of each level
> is a fair index to its spiritual significance. On the lowest plane,
> there is the surging, jostling mob in the street, mingling with the
> livestock brought to the exhibition; raised slightly above the
> street by a platform are the speech-making officials, bombasti-
> cally reeling off platitudes to the attentive multitudes; and on
> the highest level of all, from a window overlooking the specta-
> cle, Rodolphe and Emma are watching the proceedings and
> carrying on their amorous conversation, in phrases as stilted as
> those regaling the crowds. . . . "Everything should sound si-
> multaneously," Flaubert later wrote, in commenting on the
> scene; "one should hear the bellowing of the cattle, the whis-
> perings of the lovers and the rhetoric of the officials all at the
> same time."
>
> But since language proceeds in time, it is impossible to ap-
> proach this simultaneity of perception except by breaking up
> temporal sequence. And this is exactly what Flaubert does: He
> dissolves sequence by cutting back and forth between the vari-
> ous levels of action in a slowly-rising crescendo until—at the
> climax of the scene—Rodolphe's Chateaubriandesque phrases
> are read at almost the same moment as the names of prize
> winners for raising best pigs. . . .
>
> This scene illustrates, on a small scale, what we mean by the
> spatialization of form in a novel. *For the duration of the scene,
> at least, the time-flow of the narrative is halted: attention is
> fixed on the interplay of relationships within the limited time-
> area.* The relationships are juxtaposed independently of the
> progress of the narrative; and the full significance of the scene
> is given only by the reflexive relations among the units of
> meaning. In Flaubert's scene, however, the unit of meaning is
> not, as in modern poetry, a word-group or a fragment of an
> anecdote, but the totality of each level of action taken as an

integer; the unit is so large that the scene can be read with an illusion of complete understanding, yet with a total unawareness of the "dialectic of platitude" (Thibaudet) interweaving all levels, and finally linking them together with devastating irony. In other words, the struggle towards spatial form in Pound and Eliot resulted in the disappearance of coherent sequence after a few lines; *but the novel, with its larger unit of meaning, can preserve coherent sequence within the unit of meaning and break up only the time-flow of narrative.*[7] [My italics.]

"Cutting back and forth between the various levels of action" in time-present enabled Flaubert, as Frank has demonstrated, to present movement within scene with a kind of simultaneity that approximates Pound's concept of an "intellectual and emotional complex in an instant of time."

Bellow performs a similar feat in *Seize the Day*. Tommy Wilhelm moves through time, from his pre-breakfast appearance outside his hotel room to his attendance at the funeral of a stranger in mid-afternoon; but the narration renders this successive movement in a series of eight stills, or scenes. Instead of cutting back and forth between levels of action in time-present, as Flaubert does, Bellow's omniscient narration most often cuts back and forth between time-present and time-past in the mind of Tommy Wilhelm. Setting and time-present form the frame which contains Wilhelm's reflections on time-past and its effect on his current situation. Since the integrating principle of time and place—and also of action—is the mind of Wilhelm, his mood is the primary device for establishing the limits of individual scene. Juxtaposing time-past and time-present within the context of setting and through the mind of the protagonist has the effect, if not of actually arresting time, of rendering it in slow motion, so that "spatial form" is achieved and the focus falls on the intrareferential relation among the parts that make up scene (language, action, character, mood, etc.) and, finally, that contribute cumulatively to the total image that is the book. Slow motion is appropriate to *Seize the Day* because it suggests the movements of a man under water.

7. Joseph Frank, "Spatial Form in Modern Literature," *Sewanee Review,* 53 (1945), 230–32.

Though it is usually easy for the critic to determine where one scene leaves off and the next begins, it is not always easy for him to explain his rationale for such division. Probably the difficulty lies in the eclectic nature of the scene in fiction. Like drama, the scene commonly involves action based on conflict. Other characters are therefore involved, and the action occurs in time and in a given place. The arrival or departure of a character or a shift in time or place is likely to entail a shift in scene—but not necessarily; for, like poetry, fiction can present attitudes or emotions in almost pure states, through dreams, say, or through omniscient narration, stream-of-consciousness, or a number of other techniques. Therefore, the mood of the protagonist or the central intelligence must be considered of major importance in determining the limits of scene. If a mood is sustained through several shifts in setting and characters, the scene must usually be judged continuous. The pace of a scene must also be considered, and narrative bridges (summaries, descriptive passages, etc.) must be accounted for. In practice these matters seem less complicated because the individual scene, like the whole work, creates a dominant impression and has an internal consistency of its own if it has been skillfully built. To discover this internal consistency, the critic must allow the scene to dictate from within the key to its analysis. The rationale behind the division of scenes in *Seize the Day* [8] will, it is hoped, become clear in the discussions of each of its eight scenes.

Scene I (3–26) begins with an archetypal descent. Wilhelm emerges from his hotel room on the twenty-third floor and goes down to the lobby. Water imagery begins immediately. "The elevator sank and sank" and the carpet in the lobby "billowed toward Wilhelm's feet" (3): "French drapes like sails kept out the sun," and outside like an anchor chain is a "great chain that supported the marquee of the movie house directly underneath the lobby" (4). The Ansonia Hotel across the street looks "like marble or like sea water, black as slate in the fog." Its image is reflected

8. Saul Bellow, *Seize the Day* (New York, 1956). Page numbers will appear in parentheses in the text.

in the sun as though "in deep water" (5). Wilhelm walks to the newsstand, which provides the setting for the first scene. In the glass cigar counter Wilhelm sees his reflection, but not clearly, because of "the darkness and deformations of the glass" (6), a watery reflection. Three times in this scene he refers to himself as a "hippopotamus," an ungainly water creature. Wilhelm lights a cigar, buys a coke and a newspaper, and exchanges small talk with Rubin, the newsstand operator. He lingers at the newsstand to avoid entering the dining room to join his father, Dr. Adler, for breakfast because he fears that the day holds something ominous for him:

> Today he was afraid. He was aware that his routine was about to break up and he sensed that a huge trouble long presaged but till now formless was due. Before evening he'd know. (4)

As Wilhelm fidgets at the newsstand, Rubin's casual remarks in time-present spark Wilhelm's reflections on time-past. Rubin remarks perfunctorily that Wilhelm is looking "pretty sharp today." Wilhelm reflects ruefully that once such an observation would have been accurate, but that now he has gone to seed. Other casual remarks by Rubin lead Wilhelm into three extended reflections, and each reveals some aspect of his past that has contributed to his present discomfort.

There is, first, his stock market investment with Dr. Tamkin, the glib, semiliterate pseudopsychologist. "With all this money around," Tamkin had told him enthusiastically, "you don't want to be a fool while everyone else is making" (9). On the strength of this recommendation and in desperation, Wilhelm had entrusted the remainder of his savings to Tamkin. Though he sees himself as a porcine hippopotamus, Wilhelm perversely allowed his money to be invested in lard. Now he justifiably fears for his investment. But Tamkin is more to Wilhelm than a financial long-shot. Despite his obvious flaws, he is a surrogate father: "At least Tamkin sympathizes with me and tries to give me a hand, whereas Dad doesn't want to be disturbed" (11).

The reflection on Tamkin leads by association into a

reflection on Dr. Adler. Wilhelm's father is a retired physician, respected, wealthy, and gracefully aged. He wishes only to spend his autumn years in peace and security, which he feels he has earned. He is vain and healthy, the socially beloved object of flirtatious young women and fawning matrons. Having quit his job, left his wife, misplaced his money, and generally lost his way, Wilhelm remembers how he had confessed his troubles to his father in an implied supplication for aid and how his father had remained indifferent:

> "Father—it so happens that I'm in a bad way now. I hate to say it. You realize that I'd rather have good news to bring you. But it's true. And since it's true, Dad—what else am I supposed to say? It's true."
>
> Another father might have appreciated how difficult this confession was—so much bad luck, weariness, weakness, and failure. Wilhelm had tried to copy the old man's tone and made himself gentlemanly, low-voiced, tasteful. He didn't allow his voice to tremble; he made no stupid gesture. But the doctor had no answer. He only nodded . . . so little was he moved from his expression of healthy, handsome, good-humored old age. He behaved toward his son as he had formerly done toward his patients, and it was a great grief to Wilhelm; it was almost too much to bear. Couldn't he see—couldn't he feel? Had he lost his family sense? (11)

The father is clearly a self-centered, uncompassionate old man, but Wilhelm is far from a blameless son. He has been, he knows, a great disappointment to his father: He was a college dropout, a bungling father, a misfit in the business world, and he has become an unhygienic slob. Unlovable though he knows he is, he yearns still to be loved. Two lines of poetry occur to him in connection with his reflections on his father: "Love that well which thou must leave ere long," from Shakespeare's Sonnet seventy-three, is the attitude that Wilhelm feels his father should take toward his declining son; and this line leads him to another even more elegiac in nature, Milton's "Sunk though he be beneath the wat'ry floor"—a line from "Lycidas" which carries out the water imagery and reflects Wilhelm's moribund personality. Then Wilhelm recalls another element in his personal history that might account in part for his father's attitude: When Wilhelm dropped out of college to go to Hollywood, he had changed his name from Wilhelm Adler to Tommy Wilhelm:

> He had cast off his father's name, and with it his father's opinion of him. It was, he knew it was, his bid for liberty, Adler being in his mind the title of the species, Tommy the freedom of the person. (25)

Acknowledging this earlier rejection of the father leads Wilhelm to retrace the circumstances surrounding that event, and into his consciousness lumbers the figure of Maurice Venice, agent for Kaskaskia Films.

Water imagery continues in this reflection. Venice, whose name suggests water, has his office in the midst of the sides and roofs of buildings—"sheer walls, gray spaces, dry lagoons of tar and pebbles" (17–18). Wilhelm remembers him as a relative of Martial Venice the producer and thus "the obscure failure of an aggressive and powerful clan" (20). In describing for Wilhelm the condition of those nameless faces that make up movie audiences, Venice really describes his own condition: "Listen, everywhere there are people trying hard, miserable, in trouble, downcast, tired, trying and trying. They need a break, right? A breakthrough, a help, luck or sympathy" (22). Venice knows what he is talking about, for he too is a drowning man; he speaks with difficulty in a "choked, fat-obstructed voice"; he is an objectification of failure whose warning Wilhelm fails to heed. To Venice, Wilhelm is the type who gets "stood up." He casts Wilhelm appraisingly as a loser, and the screen test Wilhelm makes shows Venice to be a prophet. Wilhelm goes on to California without Venice's backing, but his efforts to become an actor are futile. Wilhelm takes no pleasure in learning later that Venice has been arrested for pandering, and his true love, the bathing beauty Nita Christenberry, has been sentenced to three years for prostitution. There is a wry turn in the narrative here through allusion. The nebulous relative of "aggressive and powerful" Martial (Mars) whose last name is Venice (Venus) becomes a mock-Cupid at last in his touting of love, failing to retain the happiness he thought he had found in his water nymph. Wilhelm is too absorbed with the man's suffering to trouble himself with mythological overtones.

Having reviewed in his mind some of his major mistakes of the past, Wilhelm sums them up in a kind of self-flagellation:

> He wanted to start out with the blessings of his family, but they were never given. He quarreled with his parents and his sister. And then, when he was best aware of the risks and knew a hundred reasons against going and had made himself sick with fear, he left home. This was typical of Wilhelm. After much thought and hesitation and debate he invariably took the course he had rejected innumerable times. Ten such decisions made up the history of his life. He had decided that it would be a bad mistake to go to Hollywood, and then he went. He had made up his mind not to marry his wife, but ran off and got married. He had resolved not to invest money with Tamkin, and then had given him a check. (23)

The pressures generated by this mental recital cause Wilhelm extreme depression and anxiety. The scene ends with his silent prayer for succor:

> "Oh God," Wilhelm prayed. "Let me out of my trouble. Let me out of my thoughts, and let me do something better with myself. For all the time I have wasted I am sorry. Let me out of this clutch and into a different life. For I am all balled up. Have mercy." (26)

This is the drowning man's appeal for assistance from a divine source. Several times in this scene reference is made to Wilhelm's "panting laugh," a sound suggestive of both panic and frantic exertion to stay afloat. The anguished prayer which Wilhelm silently sends out at the end of the scene grows out of the cumulative effect of his reflections within time-present, his past mistakes, bad luck, and weakness in character culminating in his current condition. All of these are unified in a "single configuration of meaning" in the presentational form of the scene. The movement from his room to the newsstand, then, is really a single movement unified by the implied metaphor and the introspective, foreboding mood of the central character. This strategy sets the pattern for the scenes that follow.

Scene II (26–30) is very brief. Wilhelm picks up his mail

from the desk clerk, realizing as he does so—as much from the desk clerk's accusing attitude as from the day of the month—that his morning mail contains a bill for his rent, a bill that he cannot pay because all his money is tied up in his venture with Tamkin. Stimulated by the bill for his rent and his own shortness of funds, Wilhelm begins mentally to accuse his father of selfishness in knowing that his son is in trouble and refusing to offer him assistance. As if to corroborate his charge, Wilhelm then recalls the scene in which his father revealed to him that he had forgotten the date of his wife's—and Wilhelm's mother's—death. For a moment, the selfishness of the father is established and Wilhelm appears in a sympathetic light.

Almost immediately, however, the narrative strategy changes, and the focus of narration shifts. The omniscient narrator reveals Wilhelm as he appears in the eyes of his father: an overweight, jittery, whining, unkempt bungler. And then, from a still more detached view, Wilhelm's actions are described as he stands musing on his father's continued indifference:

> Unaware of anything odd in his doing it, for he did it all the time, Wilhelm pinched out the coal of his cigarette and dropped the butt in his pocket, where there were many more. (28)

Suddenly the sympathetic light in which he has just appeared dims, for he shows himself no longer entitled to claim, as he has earlier, that "from his mother he had gotten sensitive feelings." Wilhelm's misery is too real to be negated by the revelation of such character traits, but the empathy which the reader regularly develops for Wilhelm is vitiated by this strategy. Such distancing through point of view—and it occurs repeatedly in the book—adds realistic dimension to Wilhelm's characterization and prevents his suffering from becoming maudlin.[9]

Returning to the mail in his hand, Wilhelm finds a letter from his wife, protesting the recent postdated check he sent her and demanding that he pay the enclosed premi-

9. For this perception into the achievement of aesthetic distance in *Seize the Day* through a carefully vacillating point of view I am indebted to Professor Ron Billingsley, English Department, University of Colorado.

ums on the boys' educational insurance policies. One of his most painful problems comes clearly into focus—money:

> They were his kids, and he took care of them and always would. He had planned to set up a trust fund. But that was on his former expectations. Now he had to rethink the future, because of the money problem. Meanwhile, here were the bills to be paid. When he saw the two sums punched out so neatly on the cards he cursed the company and its IBM equipment. His heart and head were congested with anger. (30)

This scene accomplishes at least two major things in documenting the pressures which are pushing Wilhelm under: It elaborates on the estrangement between Wilhelm and his father and between Wilhelm and his wife, and it insists on the immediacy of his financial problem. His mood throughout the scene is one of anger resulting from a sense of persecution. In accordance with the controlling metaphor of drowning, Wilhelm's head and heart at the end of the scene are congested, and in this condition he enters the dining room, putting an end to his long delay in meeting his father for breakfast.

Scene III (30–41) takes place entirely in the dining room. The mood at breakfast is casual and, at times, almost lighthearted, at least on the surface. Water imagery pervades the scene, occasionally in mildly comic fashion. Wilhelm sees his father sitting in a sunny bay where water glasses cast light patterns on the tablecloth and the white enamel on the window frames is "streaming with wrinkles" (30–31). Seated by Dr. Adler in this aquatic circumambience is, appropriately, Mr. Perls. Wilhelm immediately dislikes the fishy Mr. Perls: "Who is this damn frazzle-faced herring with his dyed hair and his fish teeth and this drippy mustache?" (31). The faintly humorous suggestion here seems to be that one who sits down before Perls runs the risk of being classified as a swine. This is especially true of one who has invested his savings in lard and who frequently refers to himself as a hippopotamus. The initial humor in this suggestion is lost, however, in the truth of its application to Wilhelm and in his awareness of its truth.[10] Narrative summary in this scene has revealed,

10. Cf. Keith Opdahl's comments on humor in *The Novels of Saul Bellow*, pp. 114, 176. Opdahl sees the humor in *Seize the Day* as an

for example, that Wilhelm is a careless, insensitive driver, that his car is filthy, that he does not wash his hands before meals, that he uses an electric razor to avoid touching water (the hydrophobia of a drowning man), and that he lives in his room with "worse filth than a savage" (36–37). Furthermore, when the conversation turns to money, Wilhelm finds to his disgust that he is lying about his financial condition to please his father and to impress Mr. Perls, even though in his mind Wilhelm has just condemned both of them for their transparent greed. He feels dirtied by his pandering to their values, and his response is the usual one: He experiences congestion.

When the conversation turns to the dubious credentials of Dr. Tamkin, Wilhelm joins halfheartedly in the laughter while experiencing despair in his heart because the object of their ridicule is the man in whom Wilhelm has foolishly invested all his immediate financial hopes. His laugh is again his characteristic "panting laugh," an expression of panic and exhaustion. The combined weight of his misery provokes Wilhelm to see himself as a heavily laden leviathan: "The spirit, the peculiar burden of his existence lay upon him like an accretion, a load, a hump" (39). The scene ends as Wilhelm thinks anxiously of the imminent opening of the stock market and of what the day's trading may portend for him.

Unlike the previous two scenes in which reflections were dominant, this scene conveys its meaning mainly through dialogue. The dominant impression left by the scene is the intensity of Wilhelm's self-disgust. When Mr. Perls excuses himself from the table, the mood changes and the subsequent scene begins.

---

attribute of the caricature of Tommy Wilhelm and a reflection of Bellow's ambivalent attitude toward the transitory truth of human experience; it provides Bellow with aesthetic distance from the convictions which inhere in Wilhelm's experience. It seems to me, however, that what little humor there is in the book is always undercut by the genuine and intense suffering of Wilhelm. His responses necessarily condition the reader's responses. For example, when Mr. Perls and Dr. Adler laugh at the schemes of Tamkin, Wilhelm laughs with them, but his heart is not in it: "Wilhelm could not restrain himself and joined in with his own panting laugh. But he was in despair" (41). Clearly, laughter does not function in *Seize the Day* as a comic mask of personal defense, a posture of survival, as it does in *Augie March, Henderson the Rain King,* and *Herzog.*

Scene IV (42–55) continues to rely heavily on dialogue in what amounts to a kind of verbal-emotional fencing match between Wilhelm and his father. Wilhelm is attempting to engage his father, to thrust through his defenses and turn up some form of deep feeling or genuine concern for the suffering of his son. Dr. Adler attempts to evade the emotionalism that Wilhelm is imposing on him, but finally strikes back at his son with feeling; the emotion he displays is anger, however, not sympathy, and it is provoked by selfishness, not paternal love. When Perls leaves their table, Wilhelm begins to gorge himself on the remaining food, causing Adler to reflect again on his son's obesity and slovenly ways. While Adler observes his son, Wilhelm is again feeling congested, partially from the vast amount of food he has just eaten but mainly from the pressure of suppressing his desire to discuss his problems with his father. The subject matter of each man's reflections reveals the distance between them: Wilhelm is concerned about his own emotional condition and his father's indifference to it; Adler is concerned about Wilhelm's physical condition and his son's indifference to it.

When they speak to each other these differences become more explicit. Adler recommends the "baths" to his son, then exclaims that the "Gloriana has one of the finest pools in New York," but Wilhelm is repulsed by the "odor of the wall-locked and chlorinated water" (43). Adler presses his point. "There's nothing better," he says, "than hydrotherapy when you come right down to it. Simple water has a calming effect and would do you more good than all the barbiturates and alcohol in the world" (44). With unwitting irony here, Adler plays Hard-hearted Hannah to Wilhelm's drowning man. One does not prescribe hydrotherapy to a drowning man, unless, of course, one is totally indifferent to the conditions of others. It is clear from their exchange that selfish indifference is indeed Adler's condition. On the level of dramatic irony, however, Adler prescribes with more wisdom than he knows, for Wilhelm's final symbolic death by water—Adler's hydrotherapy—is necessary to restore him to psychic health.

That Wilhelm is a drowning man becomes clearer and clearer. Having overcome his feeble attempts to suppress the expression of his feelings to his father, Wilhelm explains what Margaret is doing to him, accompanying his description with an appropriate choking gesture:

> Well, Dad, she hates me. I feel that she's strangling me. I can't catch my breath. She just fixed herself on me to kill me. She can do it at long distance. One of these days I'll be struck down by suffocation or apoplexy because of her. I just can't catch my breath. (48)

But Adler is unmoved; he accuses Wilhelm of victimizing himself by allowing his wife to dominate him and by expecting from the marriage a perfection which marriage is not capable of providing. The old man even accuses Wilhelm of contributing to his marital difficulties through extramarital affairs with both men and women. Wilhelm feels the pressure of this unjust accusation in conjunction with the pressure he feels from his wife's persecution. He struggles for breath, gets "choked up and congested" and thinks: "Trouble rusts out the system" (52). "Wilhelm had a great knot of wrong tied tight within his chest, and tears approached his eyes but he didn't let them out" (53). As he sinks beneath the wrongs piled upon him, Wilhelm cries out for assistance:

> He felt as though he were unable to recover something. Like a ball in the surf, washed beyond reach, his self-control was going out. "I expect *help!*" The words escaped him in a loud, wild, frantic cry and startled the old man, and two or three breakfasters within hearing glanced their way. (53)

This cry for help (the hapless swimmer's plea for assistance) directed toward his earthly father parallels the silent prayer for aid which Wilhelm directed toward his heavenly father at the end of Scene I, but the intensity is greater here. In response, his father offers him again advice he cannot use: "I want nobody on my back. Get off! And I give you the same advice, Wilky. Carry nobody on your back" (55). A drowning man, of course, is not likely to carry anyone on his back—though Wilhelm realizes later that Tamkin has been riding on his back, another pressure pushing him down (105). Adler's indifference to his son's need confirms the validity of the sense of persecution that emerges as Wilhelm's dominant feeling in this scene. The estrangement of son from father as a result of the father's self-centeredness is established dramatically here as a condition of long standing, a major contributing factor to Wilhelm's present problems.

Swearing silently at himself for breaking down in front of his father, Wilhelm moves into the lobby, where Scene V (55–77) begins. Wilhelm's chest aches and he smells "the salt odor of tears in his nose" (56). He thinks again of the line from "Lycidas"—to "sink beneath the watery floor"—and suddenly he encounters Tamkin, for whom references in earlier scenes have made dramatic preparation. With the appearance of Tamkin, Wilhelm feels himself "flowing into another channel" (57). They exchange greetings and Wilhelm attempts, skeptically, to discover through cogitation if Tamkin is all he purports to be. Wilhelm remembers his own penchant for self-destructive choices and recalls how he thought five days ago, when closing the deal with Tamkin, that "when he tasted the peculiar flavor of fatality in Dr. Tamkin, he could no longer keep back the money" (58). Tamkin had told him to invest some money in order to learn the stock market because "to know how it feels to be a seaweed you have to get in the water" (61). Now, Wilhelm senses fearfully, he is in the water deeper than he had anticipated.

Much of this scene, which moves immediately from the lobby back to the dining room where Tamkin eats his breakfast, is taken up with Wilhelm's vacillating attitude toward Tamkin. Wilhelm's suspicions are aroused when Tamkin uses bad grammar, when he brags of his fantastic international financial deals, or when he reveals the details of his many "cases": the epileptic blonde, the eccentric nudist-dentist, the transvestite general. However, when Tamkin shows concern for human suffering, Wilhelm is drawn back to him. He believes that Tamkin reveals true insight into human aspiration when he declares: "Only the present is real—the here-and-now. Seize the day" (66). Wilhelm responds from the heart when Tamkin describes the lonely person "howling from the window like a wolf when night comes" (67). And Wilhelm thinks he finds a key to understanding his own problem in Tamkin's analysis of the two major souls in the man:

"In here, the human bosom—mine, yours, everybody's—there isn't just one soul. There's a lot of souls. But there are two main ones, the real soul and a pretender soul. Now! Every man realizes that he has to love something or somebody. He feels that he must go outward. 'If thou canst not love, what art thou?' Are you with me?"

"Yes, Doc, I think so," said Wilhelm listening—a little skeptically but nonetheless hard.

" 'What art thou?' Nothing. . . . In the heart of hearts—Nothing! So of course you can't stand that and want to be Something, and you try. But instead of being this Something, the man puts it over on everybody instead. You can't be that strict to yourself. You love a *little.* Like you have a dog" (Scissors!) "or give some money to a charity drive. Now that isn't love, is it? What is it? Egotism, pure and simple. It's a way to love the pretender soul. Vanity. Only vanity, is what it is. And social control. The interest of the pretender soul is the same as the interest of the social life, the society mechanism. This is the main tragedy of human life. Oh, it is terrible! Terrible! You are not free. Your own betrayer is inside of you and sells you out. You have to obey him like a slave. He makes you work like a horse. And for what? For who?"

"Yes, for what?" The doctor's words caught Wilhelm's heart. "I couldn't agree more," he said. "When do we get free?"

"The purpose is to keep the whole thing going. The true soul is the one that pays the price. It suffers and gets sick, and it realizes that the pretender can't be loved. Because the pretender is a lie. The true soul loves the truth. And when the true soul feels like this, it wants to kill the pretender. The love has turned into hate. Then you become dangerous. A killer. You have to kill the deceiver." (70–71)

Wilhelm sees in Tamkin's theory an explanation of his past action: In going to Hollywood, changing his name, marrying against his better judgment, and hastily investing in the stock market, Wilhelm realizes he was serving his "pretender soul," the agent of social control, and now he is enduring the bondage of his own creation. That this false self must be destroyed he is not yet ready to admit, nor is he comfortable with the knowledge that Tamkin has been "treating" him on the sly. "I don't like being treated without my knowledge," Wilhelm declares; "I'm of two minds" (73)—that is, of two minds as well as two souls.

Tamkin too, it seems, is of two minds and souls, and he demonstrates his condition dramatically when he hands

Wilhelm the stock market receipts along with one of his poems, evidence of his pretender soul on the one hand and, apparently, his true soul on the other. The poem is an anachronistic, ungrammatical, hypermetric piece of, in Wilhelm's words, "mishmash" and "claptrap." The bad quality of the poem throws Wilhelm in a panic again as he assesses the credentials of the man who represents his economic survival. "Kiss those seven hundred bucks good-by," he says, "and call it one more mistake in a long line of mistakes" (75). Wilhelm feels "choked and strangled" (76). In explicating his poem, Tamkin assures Wilhelm that in conflict between "*con*struct and *de*struct" money is "*de*struct" but nature is "creative": "It rolls the waters of the earth" (77). The scene ends with Wilhelm's portentous vision of these waters as *de*structive: "The waters of the earth are going to roll over me" (77).

With the introduction of Tamkin into the narrative, the pace of the novel increases. Movement from place to place is accelerated, and greater emphasis is placed on action and dialogue as more characters are admitted into each scene. In accordance with the metaphor developing in the novel, Wilhelm is being swept along faster by the currents that are carrying him to the sucking center of his personal maelstrom.

Scene VI (77–90) begins with Wilhelm and Tamkin "crossing the tide of Broadway traffic" (77) to enter the brokerage office. Here everything is strange to Wilhelm, and he is flooded with impressions of an impersonal, rapacious, money-mad world. Man's staples—wheat, rye, lard, eggs—are reduced in this place to flashing lights and whirring tumblers on a giant electric board. On his right and left sit secretive old men whose withered lives are devoted entirely to the pursuit of money, and all around him Wilhelm feels confusion:

> That sick Mr. Perls at breakfast had said that there was no easy way to tell the sane from the mad, and he was right about that in any big city and especially in New York—the end of the world, with its complexity and machinery, bricks and tubes, wires and stones, holes and heights. And was everybody crazy here? What sort of people did you see? Every other man spoke a language entirely his own, which he had figured out by private thinking; he had his own ideas and peculiar ways. (83)

Wilhelm is clearly at sea here, bewildered and frightened, and his fear sparks two reflections. In the first he escapes in his mind to a farm he once owned in Roxbury—where the chickens and eggs were real—and for a moment he imagines the peace and quiet of a country day. In the second, he recalls an experience he had in an underground corridor beneath Times Square:

> In the dark tunnel, in the haste, heat, and darkness which disfigure and make freaks and fragments of nose and eyes and teeth, all of a sudden, unsought, a general love for all these imperfect and lurid-looking people burst out in Wilhelm's breast. He loved them. One and all, he passionately loved them. They were his brothers and his sisters. He was imperfect and disfigured himself, but what difference did that make if he was united with them by this blaze of love? And as he walked he began to say, "Oh, my brothers—my brothers and my sisters," blessing them all as well as himself. (84–85)

Though the feeling he then had soon passed, Wilhelm concludes as he remembers his experience that "there is a larger body, and from this you cannot be separated" (84). These two reflections provide Wilhelm with momentary respite from his immediate discomfort—and his transcendental vision prepares the way for the ambivalent final scene—but the insistence of the flashing lights and clicking wheels of the exchange board call him abruptly back to the feverish activity of the stock market.

Though the brokerage is strange to Wilhelm, it is familiar ground to Tamkin, who moves knowingly from place to place and from group to group in the room. His appearance and movements suggest to Wilhelm a bird of prey, perhaps a sea hawk: "A rare, peculiar bird he was, with those pointed shoulders, that bare head, his loose nails, almost claws, and those brown, soft, deadly, heavy eyes" (82). Appealing to Tamkin to sell their rye in order to cover their losses in lard, Wilhelm finds himself chided by Tamkin for his faintheartedness. Tamkin recommends that Wilhelm try "*here-and-now* mental exercises" to compose himself:

> Nature only knows one thing, and that's the present. Present, present, eternal present, like a big, huge, giant wave—colossal, bright and beautiful, full of life and death, climbing into the sky, standing in the seas. You must go along with the actual, the Here-and-Now, the glory— (89)

As Tamkin drones on to the end of the scene, advocating through his water imagery focusing on the present, recognizing opportunity, seizing the day, Wilhelm recalls a chest condition he once had and how Margaret read to him the melancholy lines from Keats's *Endymion:*

> Come then, Sorrow!
>
> . . . .
>
> I thought to leave thee,
> And deceive thee,
> But now of all the world I love thee best.

Margaret's voice from the past forms a counterpoint to Tamkin's voice in the present; both are appropriate to Wilhelm's condition. The combined effect of the two voices—Tamkin's water imagery and Margaret's elegiac tone—produce in Wilhelm a mood of resignation. His plight is too desperate, his resolve too weak, and the forces opposing him too strong for him to resist much longer. The waters are bearing him down. On this note of resignation to fate the scene ends.

Scene VII (90–105) finds Wilhelm and Tamkin at lunch in a cafeteria with a gilded front. The scene is developed by statement and amplification. Taking his cue from Wilhelm's comments about how his estranged wife mistreats him, Tamkin provides the central statement in the scene:

> But Tamkin said, "Why do you let her make you suffer so? It defeats the original object in leaving her. Don't play her game. Now, Wilhelm, I'm trying to do you some good. I want to tell you, don't marry suffering. Some people do. They get married to it, and sleep and eat together, just as husband and wife. If they go with joy they think it's adultery." (98)

"One hundred falsehoods," Wilhelm thinks, "but at last one truth. Howling like a wolf from the city window" (98). Wilhelm knows, furthermore, that he is himself one of the compulsive sufferers that Tamkin has described:

> True, true! thought Wilhelm, profoundly moved by these revelations. How does he know these things? How can he be such a jerk, and even perhaps an operator, a swindler, and understand so well what gives? I believe what he says. It simplifies much—everything. People are dropping like flies. I am trying

to stay alive and work too hard at it. That's what's turning my brains. This working hard defeats its own end. At what point should I start over? Let me go back a ways and try once more. (99)

Tamkin makes the statement that stands at the center of this scene, and Wilhelm establishes its application through his reflections. The remainder of the scene provides dramatic corroboration of the fact that Wilhelm is "married to suffering," though it is his suffering that defines his humanity at last and enables him to break out of the imprisoning self.

As Tamkin and Wilhelm return to the brokerage, an old violinist singles out Wilhelm from the crowd, pointing his bow and exclaiming, "You!" in testimony to Wilhelm's status as a victim, a mark. On the sidewalk outside the brokerage, old Mr. Rappaport grabs Wilhelm's arm and insists that he be guided to the cigar store across the street. Begrudgingly, yet still passively, Wilhelm allows himself to be used. Rappaport delays Wilhelm, intensifies his anxiety over the status of his investment in lard, bores him with a story about Teddy Roosevelt, and causes him to be separated from Tamkin at a crucial moment. When Wilhelm finally escapes the old man and enters the brokerage, he discovers that both the lard and rye have dropped drastically. He is wiped out, and Tamkin has disappeared. The scene has demonstrated his bad judgment and passiveness and the resultant suffering. With "unshed tears" rising in his eyes, Wilhelm looks at the conclusion of the scene "like a man about to drown" (104).

In Scene VIII (105–18), the final scene, Wilhelm does drown, but not without futilely thrashing about before he surrenders to his fate. The pace in this scene is very fast, and the water imagery is overwhelming. Wilhelm dashes to Tamkin's room at the hotel, but he is greeted there only by a maid, an empty room, and the "mop water smell" of the "brackish tidal river" (106). Wilhelm then begins his final symbolic descent. Seeking his father, he goes down to the health club, past the swimming pool, into the misty massage room. He asks his father for assistance, describing his condition in desperate terms: "I just can't breathe. My chest is all up—I feel choked. I just simply can't catch my breath" (109). But again his father is deaf to his cries for help. Wilhelm dashes to a phone booth and calls Margaret, asking her to give him some financial relief. The booth is oppressively close; he breaks into a sweat and warns Margaret that he is "suffocating" (113). He yells at her—or to her—and she hangs up on him with the assertion, "I won't stand to be howled at" (114)—and in her metaphor reverberates the cry in the night that Tamkin earlier attributed to the archetypal lonely person. Wilhelm now is painfully that person.

Rushing out into the street in a panic, Wilhelm encounters "the inexhaustible current of millions of every race and kind pouring out" (115). Thinking he sees Tamkin nearby, Wilhelm gets caught in the crush of a crowd and finds himself in the "dark and cool" of a Jewish funeral home where "the stained glass was like mother-of-pearl" (116). In the press of people Wilhelm is maneuvered alongside the casket and is suddenly totally engaged by the face of the strange corpse. He feels a "splash of heartsickness" (117), and the tears he has held back so long quietly begin to fall:

> Standing a little apart, Wilhelm began to cry. He cried at first softly and from sentiment, but soon from deeper feeling. He sobbed loudly and his face grew distorted and hot, and the tears stung his skin. A man—another human creature, was what first went through his thoughts, but other and different things were torn from him. What'll I do? I'm stripped and kicked out. . . . "Oh, Father, Paul? My children. And Olive? My dear! Why, why, why—you must protect me against that devil who wants my life. If you want it, then kill me. Take, take it, take it from me."
>
> Soon he was past words, past reason, coherence. He could not stop. The source of all tears had suddenly sprung open within him, black, deep, and hot, and they were pouring and convulsed his body, bending his stubborn head, bowing his shoulders, twisting his face, crippling the very hands with which he held the handkerchief. His efforts to collect himself were useless. The great knot of ill and grief in his throat swelled upward and he gave in utterly and held his face and wept. He cried with all his heart. . . .
>
> The flowers and lights fused ecstatically in Wilhelm's blind,

wet eyes; the heavy sea-like music came up to his ears. It poured into him where he had hidden himself in the center of a crowd by the great and happy oblivion of tears. He heard it and sank deeper than sorrow, through torn sobs and cries toward the consummation of his heart's ultimate need. (118)

This is Wilhelm's death by drowning, and every scene in the book has pointed toward this culminating moment. The salt water of his tears is the medium of his suffocation. Wilhelm cries for the failure that he has been, for the death-in-life that he has experienced. He cries for the pretender soul, now put to rest, whose misplaced values caused him to be married to suffering in all aspects of his existence. He cries for the time he has wasted and the mistakes he has made. His tears are tears of sorrow shed in personal grief.

He cries also, however, for mankind, for those millions—like himself—who have howled in anguish and loneliness like wolves from city windows at night. He cries for all men who must suffer and die; he cries for what Virgil called the *lacrimae rerum,* the tears of things.

Because he is able to transcend his personal grief, Wilhelm's tears are also tears of joy. In destroying the pretender soul, Wilhelm prepares the way for the coming of the true soul, who will not lead him to torture himself over an unworthy father, will not persuade him to go to Hollywood or marry unwisely or seek a quick fortune with a charlatan. In the termination of his marriage to suffering, Wilhelm's fragmentary glimpse in the underground corridor of a transcendental "larger body" comes to fruition in the tears of relief he sheds over his ability to find refuge "in the center of a crowd by the great and happy oblivion of tears." Where there has been alienation, there is now the possibility of communion. Wilhelm's drowning, then, is also a baptism, a rebirth. It is clearly a sea change, demonstrating that, as Saint John of the Cross stated, the way down is also the way up.

The unity of effect achieved in *Seize the Day* results from the skillful blending of all the elements of fiction in tightly constructed scenic units functioning very much like poetic images built around a controlling metaphor. Each scene extends the central image of Wilhelm's drowning by embodying a particular aspect of his life which has contributed to the pressure which finally overwhelms him in literal failure and symbolic death and rebirth. Unity is enhanced further by cross references between scenes. Wilhelm's appeal to his heavenly father in Scene I is paralleled by his two subsequent appeals (in Scenes IV and VIII) to his earthly father. Adler's advice to Wilhelm to "carry nobody on [his] back" in Scene IV is given ironic significance in Scene VIII when Wilhelm declares that Tamkin was "on[his] back." Tamkin's comparison of loneliness to a "howling wolf" (Scene V) is picked up in Wilhelm's reflection (Scene VII) on truth "howling like a wolf from the city window" (98) and again in Margaret's assertion (Scene VIII) that she will not be howled at. The dramatic irony in Adler's prescription of hydrotherapy for Wilhelm (Scene IV), Wilhelm's gesture of self-strangulation (Scene IV), Tamkin's theory of the necessary death of the pretender soul (Scene V), and Wilhelm's vision of transcendental love in the underground corridor all coalesce in Wilhelm's symbolic drowning in Scene VIII. It is hydrotherapy, self-induced, which destroys the false self and opens Wilhelm's heart to true values and to communion with nature and man, ending his long alienation. "Spatial form" in a larger sense is achieved, then, both within and between scenes.

"The appeal the novel has," W. J. Handy has remarked, "must come in part from knowing that fiction is a symbolic formulation designed to give a more adequate account of the way human experience actually unfolds, not when it is merely known about or 'understood,' but when it is experienced in the course of human living."[11] The combined effect of the scenes in *Seize the Day* presents the "full unabstracted bodiness" of Wilhelm's experience and—by extension—the human experience of everyone who has struggled, stumbled, fallen, and somehow picked himself up again.

---

11. *Kant and the Southern New Critics*, p. 89.

5.

Henderson the Rain King:
Tuning a Soul

As the dust jacket on one paperback edition announces, *Henderson the Rain King* is "a feast." The novel is, of course, a feast, both movable and continuous, at which many have fed long and well; and everyone who has come to it has come away talking of his own preference from the sumptuous bill of fare. Following a hint from Leslie Fiedler (in *Waiting for the End*), Keith Opdahl has shown that the novel is in part a good-natured satire on Ernest Hemingway and the Code Hero.[1] Marcus Klein has described the parallels between *Henderson* and the camel-lion-child metamorphoses of the spirit in Nietzsche's *Thus Spake Zarathustra.*[2] The mythical patterns in the novel have been duly noted by Elsie Leach and Howard M. Harper,[3] and

1. Keith Opdahl, *The Novels of Saul Bellow: An Introduction* (University Park, Pa., 1967), pp. 124–26.

2. Marcus Klein, *After Alienation* (Cleveland, 1962), pp. 67–69.

3. Elsie Leach, "From Ritual to Romance Again: *Henderson the Rain King,*" *Western Humanities Review,* 14 (Spring 1960), 223–24. Professor Leach notes Bellow's indebtedness to the "wasteland" tradition and related fertility myths as set forth in Sir James Frazer's *The Golden Bough* and Jessie L. Weston's *From Ritual to Romance*, especially as these myths manifested themselves in the rituals of the Shilluk African tribe. Howard M. Harper elaborates on these matters and quotes Weston's summary of Frazer's discussion of the "god–king concept" among the Shilluk:

"The Shilluk . . . are a pastoral people, their wealth consisting in flocks and herds, grain and millet. The King . . . is regarded with extreme reverence, as being a reincarnation of Nyakang, the semi-divine hero who settled the tribe in their present territory. Nyakang is the rain-giver, on whom their lives and prosperity depend; there are several shrines in which sacred spears, now kept for sacrificial purposes, are preserved. . . .

"The King, though regarded with reverence, must not be allowed to become old or feeble, lest, with the diminishing vigour of the ruler, the cattle should sicken, and fail to bear increase, the crops should rot in the field and men die in ever growing numbers. One of the signs of failing energy is the King's inability to fulfill the desires of his wives, of whom

almost everyone has commented on the biblical parallels involving King David, Nebuchadnezzar, Moses, Joseph in Egypt, and Daniel in the lion's den. Following Aristotle, Kenneth Burke, and Freud, Robert Detweiler has offered a perceptive analysis of rebirth patterns in the novel,[4] and John Clayton has unevenly discussed the book as a "parody search": "In a sense Eugene Henderson is a caricature of all Bellow's characters who seek salvation. Through him Bellow can laugh at this own questing spirit."[5] The novel has variety and scope enough to encompass all of these approaches, allowing to each its proper degree of validity, without forfeiting through variety any of its unity or coherence—or without losing any of its underlying seriousness.[6]

What unifies these disparate elements is the suffering, questing, riotous, comic spirit of Henderson himself, whose Thoreauvian desire is to come to grips with what is real and meaningful in the world so that when he comes to die, he will not discover that he has not lived.[7] Henderson

---

he has a large number. When this occurs the wives report the fact to the chiefs, who condemn the King to death forthwith, communicating the sentence to him by spreading a white cloth over his face and knees during his mid-day slumber. Formerly the King was starved to death in a hut, in company with a young maiden but (in consequence, it is said, of the great vitality and protracted suffering of one King) this is no longer done; the precise manner of death is difficult to ascertain; Dr. Seligman, who was Sir J. G. Frazer's authority, thinks that he is now strangled in a hut, especially erected for that purpose." (55–66) *Desperate Faith* (Chapel Hill, N.C., 1967), pp. 44–45.

4. Robert Detweiler, "Patterns of Rebirth in *Henderson the Rain King*," *Modern Fiction Studies*, 12 (Winter 1966–1967), 405–14.

5. John J. Clayton, *Saul Bellow: In Defense of Man* (Bloomington, Ind., 1968), p. 167.

6. Page numbers, hereafter given in parentheses in the text, are from the Viking edition: *Henderson the Rain King* (New York, 1965).

7. The overtones of Thoreau's *Walden* in Bellow's *Henderson the Rain King* are many; like Thoreau at Walden, Henderson goes to Africa "to live deliberately, to front only the essential facts of life." Also like Thoreau, he adheres to a policy of "simplicity, simplicity, simplicity": Henderson leaves Charlie Albert and his wife and embarks on his journey with minimum equipment and only one guide because he is "anxious to simplify more and more" (44). Thoreau's comment on the accumulation of things—"How many a poor immortal soul have I met well nigh crushed and smothered under its load"—finds its parallel in Henderson's exclamation in the cluttered attic of the dead Miss Lenox: "Henderson, put forth effort. You, too, will die of this pestilence. Death will annihilate you

succeeds in satisfying his desire. His final celebration of life is his answer to the voice that cried "I want, I want, I want," which sent him to a symbolic Africa of the soul in the first place. Bellow's novel celebrates Henderson's triumph, and music makes a major contribution to the success of the occasion, no banquet being complete without the strains that "soothe a savage breast." Henderson's transformation from wrathful pig-man to lionlike kingly spirit is accompanied by an orchestration of sound effects, musical images, and allusions that blend dramatically with theme, plot, characterization, setting, and pace to enhance the novel's total effect. The purpose of this chapter is to follow Bellow's score as it provides musical support for Henderson's development.

Henderson begins his first-person narrative with a rapid-fire account of his life before he undertook the trip to Africa: his childhood as a descendant of wealthy and prestigious Americans, his Master's degree from an Ivy League university, his experience as a crab-infested soldier in It-

---

and nothing will remain, and there will be nothing left but junk" (40). On hunting, Thoreau said, "No humane being, past the thoughtless age of boyhood, will wantonly murder any creature, which holds its life by the same tenure that he does. . . . If he has the seeds of a better life in him, he distinguishes his proper objects, as a poet or naturalist it may be, and leaves the gun and fish-pole behind." And Henderson says, "Myself, I used to have a certain interest in hunting, but as I grew older it seemed a strange way to relate to nature. What I mean is, a man goes into the external world, and all he can do with it is to shoot it? It doesn't make sense" (94). There is a close resemblance, too, between Thoreau's concept of a man as a sculptor of his own body and Dahfu's "core-rind theory." "Every man," Thoreau said, "is the builder of a temple, called his body, to the god he worships, after a style purely his own, nor can he get off by hammering marble instead. We are all sculptors and painters, and our material is our own flesh and blood and bones. Any nobleness begins at once to refine a man's features, any meanness or sensuality to imbrute them." Henderson explains Dahfu's theory, which is derived from the psychological writings of William James and Wilhelm Reich: "What he [Dahfu] was engrossed by was a belief in the transformation of human material, that you could work either way, either from the mind influencing the flesh, back again to the mind, back once more to the flesh" (236). And it is Thoreau who provides an additional confirmation that Henderson's journey to the interior of Africa is really a symbolic search into his own soul: "What does Africa, what does the West, stand for? Is not our own interior white on the chart? black though it may prove, like the coast, when discovered."

aly, his marriage to Frances, then to Lily, his perverse career as a pig-farmer and a chronic malcontent. In an extensive catalogue, he sums up the pressures that drove him to
Africa: "A disorderly rush begins—my parents, my wives,
my girls, my children, my farm, my animals, my habits, my
money, my music lessons, my drunkenness, my prejudices,
my brutality, my teeth, my face, my soul!" (3). At the center
of this list Henderson mentions his music lessons, which
he takes on his father's violin in order to contact the spirit
of his father and to introduce some harmonious order into
the chaos that his life has become, to counterbalance what
he experiences as "madness" all around him. "Of course,
in an age of madness," Henderson declares, "to expect to
be untouched by madness is a form of madness. But the
pursuit of sanity can be a form of madness, too" (25). Henderson mentions his violin repeatedly in this section, for he
is practicing regularly, doing his Sevcik exercises under
the tutelage of the old Hungarian Haponyi, trying to restore his soul: "I was playing Sevcik and pieces of opera
and oratorio, keeping time with the voice within" (31).

In his basement, standing on Lily's old mustard-colored
carpet, wearing his red velvet robe and his Wellingtons,
Henderson tries with his pig-farmer's hands to produce
"the voice of angels"; what he gets instead is a "noise . . .
like the smashing of egg crates" (30). But he struggles val-
iantly:

> Down in the basement of the house I worked very hard as I do
> at everything. I had felt I was pursuing my father's spirit, whis-
> pering, "Oh, Father, Pa. Do you recognize the sounds? This is
> me, Gene, on your violin, trying to reach you." For it so hap-
> pens that I have never been able to convince myself the dead
> are utterly dead. I admire rational people and envy their clear
> heads, but what's the use of kidding? I played in the basement
> to my father and my mother, and when I learned a few pieces
> I would whisper,"Ma, this is 'Humoresque' for you." Or, "Pa,
> listen—'Meditation' from Thais." I played with dedication,
> with feeling, with longing, love—played to the point of emo-
> tional collapse. Also down there in my studio I sang and I
> played, "Rispondi! Anima bella" (Mozart). "He was despised
> and rejected, a man of sorrows and acquainted with grief"
> (Handel). Clutching the neck of the little instrument as if there

were strangulation in my heart, I got cramps in my neck and shoulders. (30)

Henderson tries to attune his inner voice crying "I want, I want" to some appropriate external reality or spiritual force, and the violin is his instrument of mediation:

> I bent down in my robe and frowned, as well I might, at the screaming and grating of those terrible slides. Oh, thou God and judge of life and death! The ends of my fingers were wounded, indented especially by the steel E string, and my collarbone ached and a flaming patch, like the hives, came out on my jowl. But the voice within me continued, *I want, I want!* (32)

The many conflicts in Henderson's life described in this section are accentuated by the discordant "music" of Henderson's violin. The tortured sounds he produces serve as a musical objective correlative for the condition of his soul.

The snatches of song Henderson breaks into from time to time also have thematic value. He appeals to heaven for a sign: "Rispondi! Anima bella," and, with Handel, he empathizes with a misunderstood Messiah: "He was despised and rejected, a man of sorrows and acquainted with grief." The Messianic theme as it relates to regeneration is introduced here musically and is developed as a leitmotiv throughout the novel. Though Henderson is portrayed as both ardent disciple and mock-Messiah, the regeneration that he stands for is intended seriously and is brought to a triumphant, sublimely hyperbolic conclusion.

The theme so introduced is picked up almost immediately by Henderson's further allusion to another aria from Handel's *Messiah*, "For Who Shall Abide the Day of His Coming?" Confronted at last, though reluctantly, with Ricey's Negro foundling, Henderson recognizes another displaced human being, like himself, bewildered and crying out into a confusing world. Henderson reflects,

> Nobody truly occupies a station in life any more. There are mostly people who feel that they occupy the place that belongs to another by rights. There are displaced persons everywhere.
> "For who shall abide the day of his (the rightful one's) coming?"

"And who shall stand when He (the rightful one) appeareth?" (34)

Henderson dubs the baby a "child of sorrow" (36) but
decides that Ricey is too young to assume the duties of
motherhood. The child is turned over to proper authorities
and Ricey, dismissed from her school, goes to live with her
aunt in Providence, Rhode Island. The guilt Henderson
experiences over rejecting the child and hurting his daughter causes him to get drunk and declare in the Danbury
train station, "There is a curse on this land!" (38).

When Henderson's wrath and frustration spill over into
a shouting demonstration that kills old Miss Lenox, her
literal death paralleling the spiritual death which Henderson has been experiencing, he leaves the cursed land to try
saving his soul elsewhere. With Charlie Albert and his
bride, Henderson journeys to Africa on a photographic
expedition. He does not get along with Charlie's wife, however, and taking pictures of Africa, merely focusing on
external reality, is not what Henderson needs. With Romilayu as his guide, playing Virgil to Henderson's Dante, he
leaves Charlie and his wife and descends into the ageless
interior of Africa, where he encounters the Arnewi tribe.

Henderson discovers that he has left one cursed land
only to find himself in another. The Hinchagara plateau,
where the Arnewi live, is experiencing severe drought.
They are dwellers in a wasteland and their sacred cattle
are dying from thirst because the village cistern is polluted
by frogs, taboo creatures according to Arnewi tradition.
The first sounds that Henderson hears, then, are the excited screams of children and the dirgelike crying and moan-
ing of the villagers. Responding to what he interprets first
as sadness and then as distress, Henderson burns a bush,
God-fashion, and performs a rough-and-ready manual of
arms with his rifle before he discovers the real nature of
the Arnewi's plight and thus the foolish—though hilari-
ous—inappropriateness of his actions. "Alone I can be
pretty good," Henderson declares, "but let me go among
people and there's the devil to pay" (49).

Inappropriate action typifies his stay with the Arnewi.

In the middle of a drought, his gift to Queen Willatale, the wisest woman of Bittahness, is a raincoat. When Mtalba, the most beautiful woman of Bittahness, offers herself to him, a great honor, he rejects her. And when he attempts to counter religious taboo with Western technology, he blows up the cistern with the frogs and leaves the Arnewi in worse shape than he found them.[8]

Music provides accompaniment for all of Henderson's adventures and misadventures with the Arnewi tribe. The dominant sound in the village is the weeping and mourning of the villagers and the lowing of the dying cattle, but other sounds grow out of other activities. In his interview with Willatale, Henderson learns that he exhibits "Grun-tu-molani. Man want to live" (85). He kisses the Queen's belly and feels he has "made contact with a certain power—unmistakable—which emanated from the woman's middle" (74); it is the fertile power of an earth mother, a symbol of regeneration. His exotic experience is accompanied by exotic sounds: The women flap their hands rhythmically from the wrist while the men are "whistling on their fingers harmoniously" (73). Henderson becomes greatly excited, thinking he is going to find satisfaction for the voice demanding "I want, I want." He thinks he is approaching *"the hour that burst the spirit's sleep"* (77), and he passionately sings again his favorite arias from Handel's *Messiah* : "He was despised and rejected, a man of sorrows and acquainted with grief," and "For who shall abide the day of His coming, and who shall stand when he appeareth?" (84). Casting himself, then, in the role of aspiring bush-leaguer to the major-league Messiah he has just celebrated in song, Henderson stalks off, saviorlike, to rid the cistern of frogs and thus lift the plague, shouting as he goes, "Grun-tu-molani. God does not shoot dice with our souls, and therefore grun-tu-molani"(85).

However, as he makes his bomb and plots his strategy he is visited by Mtalba, who offers herself to him through gestures, gifts, and erotic dances. The rhythmical music for her dancing is provided by a "little xylophone of hollow

8. Leach, p. 223.

bones—the feet of a rhinoceros perhaps emptied by the ants" (97). With her "colossal thighs and hips" Mtalba makes a direct appeal to Henderson's flesh, and he acknowledges her power:

> Thus I realized as the night and the dancing wore on that this was enchantment. This was poetry, which I should allow to reach me, to penetrate the practical task of demolishing the frogs in the cistern. (98)

But Henderson turns single-mindedly back to the preparation of his bomb. As his porcine body reveals, he has already devoted too much of his life to the appetites. He is interested now in higher matters. He seeks, not gratification of the flesh, but gratification of the soul. He therefore turns away from the Siren's song.

The frogs Henderson intends to harrow are also music makers. When he first saw them in the cistern, "they crawled out and thrummed on the wet stone" (60). Henderson vowed then to be the agent of their destruction: "Just wait, you little sons of bitches, you'll croak in hell before I'm done" (60). Now, as he reconnoiters the cistern on the night before the bombing, he detects in their song a more appropriate note of doom:

> "These are really great singers. Back in Connecticut we have mostly cheepers, but these have bass voices. Listen," I said, "I can make out all kinds of things. Ta dam-dam-dum. Agnus Dei—Agnus Dei qui tollis peccata mundi, miserere no-ho-bis! It's Mozart. Mozart, I swear! They've got a right to sing miserere, poor little bastards, as the hinge of fate is about to swing back on them." (89)

Though Henderson is unaware of it, the doom in the voices of the frogs is for him as well as for themselves.

On the next morning the villagers gather expectantly but apprehensively for the fateful event, and at the appropriate moment Henderson tosses his bomb into the cistern: "The frogs fled from it and the surface closed again; the ripples traveled outward and that was all. But then a new motion began and I realized the thing was working" (108). It is a triumphant moment, and Henderson feels his soul "rise with the water." As the frog bodies shoot upward, Henderson exclaims, "Hallelujah! Henderson, you dumb brute, this time you've done it!" (108). With the strains of Handel's arias from the *Messiah* echoing recently through the narrative, Henderson's cry of joy suggests the "Hallelujah Chorus," the triumphant celebration of the coming of the savior. But Henderson's celebration is short-lived, his apotheosis premature. His "Hallelujah" dies in his throat as he realizes he has blown up the cistern as well as the frogs. As the last of the precious water trickles out of the crumbled stone walls, Henderson pulls his T-shirt over his face to hide his shame, his desire to serve and to save completely thwarted. Knowing more painfully now what it is to be "despised and rejected," he returns with Romilayu to the desert to seek deeper in the interior for an answer to his inner voice.

Leaving the meek, unlucky Arnewi, Romilayu takes the soul-sick Henderson on a ten-day journey to the land of the warlike, lucky Wariri, the "chillen darkness." Though lucky, they too live in a land cursed by drought, and their wasteland's Rain King is neither wounded nor impotent; he is dead. On Henderson is imposed the trying task of wrestling the large corpse into a ravine, though he is unaware of the identity of the dead man or the consequences of his act. He successfully meets the challenge, establishing his credentials as a strong man. This is his second wrestling match in Africa, the first being with Itelo, the very much alive Prince of the Arnewi. Henderson's physical struggles provide a parallel to his spiritual struggles, and both aspects of his striving are visible in his suffering face, "like an unfinished church," which is rendered even more craggy by his broken bridgework. Having successfully passed the Wariri's contrived trial by terror, Henderson is escorted into King Dahfu's courtyard. The procession into town is accompanied by a wild "fast march" played on "a rattle, a snare drum, a deeper drum, a horn blast, . . . a gunshot" (146). The tempo of this processional march sets the narrative pace for this section, for events begin to unfold rapidly, moving Henderson closer and closer to the transformation that will enable him to burst the spirit's sleep and satisfy the demands of his inner voice.

Henderson likes King Dahfu immediately. He sees him as "extended, floating," one of the "Being people," whereas Henderson sees himself as "contracted and cramped," one of the "Becoming people." "Enough! Enough!" Henderson exclaims, "Time to have Become. Time to Be!" (160). Henderson feels that Dahfu can help him to be, that they can "approach ultimates together" (156). He is convinced of the rightness of his feelings at the Rain King ceremony.

The momentum of events carrying Henderson along increases with the faster tempo of the background music. Amid frenzied sounds, Dahfu and Henderson are conveyed to the arena where the Rain King ceremony is to take place:

> The roars, the deep drum noises, as if the animals were speaking again by means of the skins that had once covered their bodies! It was a great release of sound, like Coney Island or Atlantic City or Times Square on New Year's Eve; at the king's exit from the gate the great cacophony left all the previous noises in my experience far behind. . . .
>
> The frenzy was so great it was metropolitan. There was such a whirl of men and women and fetishes, and snarls like dog-beating and whines like sickles sharpening, and horns blasting and blazing into the air, that the scale could not be recorded. The bonds of sound were about to be torn to pieces. (169)

During the ceremony, which is performed, as Dahfu says, to "prime the pumps of the firmament," Henderson is "pervaded by barbaric emotions" and in the spirit of the occasion he roars "like a great Assyrian bull" (171), pleasing the crowd. (He is later to roar in another form.) Then Henderson watches in awe as Dahfu performs an athletic dance with an Amazon priestess, using two human skulls in a skillful game of catch. The king is literally and symbolically defying his own death and thus testifying to his worthiness to live. Henderson's admiration is boundless, and in silently expressing the joy he feels, he alludes to art in general and music in particular. He thinks,

> "Oh, King, that was royally done. Like a true artist. Goddammit, an artist! King, I love nobility and beautiful behavior." . . .
> By mentioning the firmament, the king himself had shown me the way, and I might have told him a lot, right then and there.

What? Well, for instance, that chaos doesn't run the whole show. That this is not a sick and hasty ride, helpless, through a dream into oblivion. No sir! It can be arrested by a thing or two. By art, for instance. The speed is checked, the time is redivided. Measure! That great thought. Mystery! The voices of angels! Why the hell else did I play the fiddle? (175–76)

As exhibited in the dance, Dahfu's beauty and grace, his control and fullness of life, and his oneness with things as they are offer concrete, ordered evidence—the evidence of art—of the kind of existence which Henderson's inner voice has been demanding. His striving with the violin was his attempt to produce this form of existence for himself. Seeing it now in Dahfu, Henderson's spirits soar to the skies. He experienced a similar rise in spirits when Queen Willatale explained Grun-tu-molani to him and he shouted, "God does not shoot dice with our souls." His silent exclamation here, "that chaos doesn't run the whole show," parallels that earlier shout. In the earlier instance, however, Henderson's affirmation was undercut by his failure with the frogs. Here his affirmation is extended and enforced by his immediate success as the Rain King.

Inspired by Dahfu and caught up in the fervor of the ceremony, Henderson disregards all cautions and enters the contest to lift the largest goddess, Mummah, the goddess of the clouds. He acts in obedience to the dictates of his insistent inner voice:

Listen! Harken unto me, you schmohawk! You are blind. The footsteps were accidental and yet the destiny could be no other. So now do not soften, oh no, brother, intensify rather what you are. This is the one and only ticket—intensify. (187)

Amid the encouraging cries of the multitude, Henderson approaches the giant goddess, kneels (one knee), clasps her firmly, wrests her from the ground, and carries her the designated distance to the other gods. This is Henderson's third wrestling match, and this time he wrestles with a god—and wins! The crowd goes wild and Henderson becomes Sungo, the Rain King. "My spirit was awake and it welcomed life anew. Damn the whole thing! Life anew!" (193). The Wariri are "singing . . . and praising [him]"(192).

His duties begin at once. He is stripped and given a whip.

His nakedness is a symbol of his new birth, the beginning of the transformation he has been seeking. His birth, however, is a difficult one; at first he resists the running and the beating of others with the whip, but soon in his frenzy he too is flailing about and chanting "Ya-na-bu-ni-ho-no-mum-mah" to induce the heavens to pour forth rain. He had destroyed the pond of the Arnewi, he is now employed by the Wariri to cleanse ponds. He is thrown into muddy water and pulled out again, while he cries, "Mercy, have mercy!" In the background are "pounding drums" (199) mingling with the chanting, the mystical invocation to the sky. At last Henderson is forced to strike even the gods, and he capitulates completely: "Thy will be done!" Henderson cries, "Not my will, but thy will!" (199). Then the rains come. Dahfu assures Henderson that "the gods know us" [9] and that Henderson has "lost the wager" (202). Though he has lost the wager (that the ceremony would be unsuccessful), Henderson has reclaimed his soul. With the Arnewi Henderson had failed to lift the plague because he relied on an alien technology. Here he succeeds in overcoming the drought by acting in accordance with things as they are, by moving, as Dahfu says later of Atti, "completely within the given." What remains for Henderson is to refine his new spirit and give it direction under the guidance of King Dahfu.

To this point in the novel the narrative movement has been horizontal and its pace increasingly rapid. When the frenzied drums of the rain ceremony are no longer heard, however, the narrative strategy shifts. Now the movement is vertical, in accordance with Henderson's daily descent into Atti's den for his lion therapy, and the pace is much slower, in accordance with the philosophical nature of the discourse between Dahfu and Hunderson. The musical accompaniment changes accordingly.

As Henderson goes about his daily duties as Rain King, he is followed by a drummer: "The lone drum bumped after me; it seemed to warn people to stay away from this

9. At the conclusion of the wrestling match in which Henderson defeats Itelo, Itelo says to Henderson: "I know you now, sir. I do know you" (70).

Henderson, the lion-contaminated Sungo" (279). His duties also bring him into daily social intercourse with the Bunam, Horko, and their attendants. On these occasions mood music is provided in the background—African Muzak: "The old musician played his pendulum viol and others drummed and blew in the palace junkyard with its petrified brains of white stone and the red flowers growing in the humus" (279). The same musician—another fiddler—also provides music for the king:

> Beside one of the orange trees an old fellow was playing a stringed instrument. Very long, only a little shorter than a bass fiddle, rounded at the bottom, it stood on a thick peg and was played with a horse-hair bow. It gave thick rasping notes. . . . The instrument sobbed and groaned and croaked as the old fellow polished on it with his barbarous bow. Mupi, trying out the music, swayed two or three times, then raised her leg stiff-kneed, and when her foot returned slowly to the ground it seemed to be searching for something. (254–55)

But these occasions are merely light musical interludes which give Henderson some respite from his real business, the transformation of his body and attitude to conform with his newly acquired but imperfectly developed spiritual capacity. To this end, Henderson subjects himself to Dahfu's lion-therapy in accordance with his "core-rind" theory, that the flesh can be made to reflect the condition of the spirit, and vice versa.

To reform the piglike body which he has long abused, and to overcome the resistances built up over fifty-five years of maladjustment, Henderson must confront Atti in her den and imitate her fluid motions, her nobility of spirit, her "beingness." Under Dahfu's direction, he walks with her, runs with her, assumes her positions of rest, and, finally, roars like her:

> And so I was the beast. I gave myself to it, and all my sorrow came out in the roaring. My lungs supplied the air but the note came from my soul. The roaring scalded my throat and hurt the corners of my mouth and presently I filled the den like a bass organ pipe. (265)

A chief obstacle to Henderson's achievement of lion-ness is his monumental fear of Atti. During his sessions in the den he is a tangle of muscular, nervous, and respiratory spasms. His fear of the lion conflicts with his desire to burst the spirit's sleep and be worthy of Dahfu's confidence and friendship. The tension of these conflicting motives produces heaving Wagnerian strains of *Sturm und Drang* in the "bass organ pipe" of Henderson's voice, and in the music of his roaring he returns to familiar themes:

> Romilayu admitted he had hear me roar, and you couldn't blame the rest of the natives for thinking that I was Dahfu's understudy in the black arts, or whatever they accused him of practicing. But what the king called pathos was actually (I couldn't help myself) a cry which summarized my entire course on this earth, from birth to Africa; and certain words crept into my roars, like "God," "Help," "Lord have mercy," only they came out "Hooolp!" "Moooorcy!" It's funny what words spring forth. "Au secours," which was "Secooooooooor" and also "De profoooooondis," plus snatches from the "Messiah" (He was despised and rejected, a man of sorrows, etcetera). (274)

The anguish which attends the long process of Henderson's regeneration is great and is reflected in the music that slips into his roaring, the yearning for salvation. But he continues to strive because, as he explains to Romilayu, he will not "agree to the death of [his] soul" (277). Soon his progress becomes evident: He grows a mane—"black curls, thicker than usual, like a merino sheep, very black"—and his hands begin to look like paws—"very thick; each of my fingers felt like a yam" (273). In one of the final signs of his progress he writes to Lily, telling her that he is coming home and that she is to gain him admission into a medical school under the name, not of Eugene, but of Leo E. Henderson. His spirit greatly ennobled and his soul mostly restored, Henderson has found a direction for his service motive and the courage to implement his long-standing desire. As Elsie Leach observed, the "Rain King will become Medicine Man." [10]

"I am giving up the violin," he writes Lily. "I guess I will never reach my object through it. . . . I might as well do something in the interests of life, for a change" (284–85).

10. Leach, p. 223.

Then he thinks of his body metaphorically as an instrument in the orchestra of God: *"What is it, now, this great instrument? Played wrong, why does it suffer so? Right, how can it achieve so much, reaching even God?"* (285). But Henderson does not make any heavenly contacts, with his violin or his body and soul, until he receives unto himself the kingly spirit of Dahfu, who is killed by a lion while pursuing Gmilo, the lion in whom his father is supposedly reincarnated.

On the day of the hunt, the beaters gather for the procession into the bush. Henderson is at the side of Dahfu: "So with the bugles and drums and rattles and noisemakers of the beaters' party gathered around us, we were carried through the gates of the palace" (290). With this pulsating, raucous beginning, the pace of the novel picks up again, and the tension of the episode is represented by the musical sounds of insects: "I began to be aware of the tremble of insects as they played their instruments underneath the stems, down at the very base of the heat" (293). "The sounds of cicadas are going up in vertical spirals, like columns of thinnest wire" (304), and beneath this sustained sound is the "constant running of the drums" (302). As Henderson and Dahfu wait for the lion in the hopo, the bamboo blind, the sounds, like the situation, are full of suspense. When Dahfu falls and is killed by the lion— castrated, in appropriate wasteland tradition—Henderson is stained with his blood in a symbolic transmission of kinship and, to Henderson's astonishment, duty; for in the absence of a "child of age," the Sungo becomes king. The death of his friend and mentor and the fear of his new responsibilities cause a relapse in Henderson, a dark night of his soul, and this condition is compounded by the rigors of his escape journey with Romilayu from the burial hut of the king back to Baventai.

Taking with them the lion cub in whom the spirit of the deceased Dahfu is said to reside, Henderson and Romilayu flee the Wariri. "It's hard not to be king when It's in you and in the situation," Frost once said; but faced with the prospect of satisfying sixty-seven wives, Henderson is not sure it is in him, and besides he knows that Horko and his

henchmen will contrive his death just as they did Dahfu's.
He has had enough of death, and he has, moreover, another life to live. Henderson is still feverish, however, and
greatly distracted by his grief, and on the ten-day trek to
Baventai he becomes incoherent, reverting frequently to
his childhood and his childhood songs:

> As I ate the cocoons and the larvae and ants, crouching in the
> jockey shorts with the lion lying under me for shade, I spoke
> oracles and sang—yes, I remembered many songs from nursery
> and school, like "Fais do-do," "Pierrot," "Malbrouck s'en va-
> t'en querre," "Nut Brown Maiden," and "The Spanish Guitar,"
> while I fondled the animal, which had made a wonderful
> adjustment to me. (327)

In his madness here, Henderson approaches what Emily
Dickinson called "divinest sense," for, as every schoolboy
knows, "Except a man become again as a little child, he
cannot enter into the Kingdom of Heaven." Henderson
remembers Willatale telling him earlier that the world is
strange to a child but he is "not a child" (84); he understood
her implied distinction between the strangeness that the
child marvels at and the man dreads. Reporting this event
to Lily in his letter, Henderson thinks, *"The Kingdom of
Heaven is for children of the spirit. But who is this nosy,
gross phantom?"* (283). In this scene, with his lion cub and
his larvae pablum, Henderson returns through his songs to
the spirit of childhood, a state in which he can marvel at
the strangeness of the world. This reversion to childhood
leads him to a period of vivid lucidity and prepares the
way for his final triumphant scene of complete regeneration.

Coming into Baventai at last, Henderson exhorts the
standers-by: "Get the band. Get the music" (328). He tries
to assure Romilayu that he has returned to his senses. He
declares that "the sleep is burst" and he has come to himself, that he believes "there is justice, and that much is
promised," and that "you can't get away from rhythm"
(329), the rhythms of breathing, circulation, tides, sea-
sons—life. Dahfu had made a similar statement earlier to
Henderson, also using musical imagery, referring to "arrangement" where Henderson uses "rhythm":

"Even if, on supreme moments, there is no old and is no new, but only an essence which can smile at our arrangement—smile even at being human. That is so full of itself," he said. "Nevertheless a play of life has to be allowed. Arrangements must be made." (296)

A disciple now fully imbued with the spirit of his master and dwelling in clarity, Henderson is ready to journey back from the interior. He recovers his health, buys himself a dapper suit and hat, bids his faithful friend Romilayu a grateful goodbye, and boards a plane for home.

As he sits on the plane gazing out at the earth and sky, he contemplates the condition of his restored soul. He is at peace with the world, at one with the primal elements:

But I, Henderson, with my glowering face, with corduroy and Bersagliere feathers—the helmet was inside the wicker basket with the cub, as I figured he needed a familiar object to calm him on this novel, exciting trip—I couldn't get enough of the water, and of these upside-down sierras of the clouds. Like courts of heaven. (Only they aren't eternal, that's the whole thing; they are seen once and never seen again, being figures and not abiding realities; Dahfu will never be seen again, and presently I will never be seen again; but every one is given the components to see: the water, the sun, the air, the earth.) (333)

The world, of course, has not changed. It is still a place of "rhythms" where "arrangements" must be made, but Henderson's perception of it has changed. Now that he knows who he is and where he is going, now that he has achieved some degree of Being, the world no longer seems hostile to him; it is now a place of opportunity for service and a possible source of joy. His inner voice no longer cries "I want," for Henderson has silenced it by attuning himself—the instrument that is his life— to "the given."

He thinks of his terrifying roller-coaster rides as a boy with Smolak the bear—"Smolak was cast off and I [was] an Ishmael, too"—and how the bear comforted him because "somewhere in his huge head he had worked it out that for creatures there is nothing that ever runs unmingled" (339). As Smolak was then, so Henderson is now. The story of Smolak and his world-battered wisdom stands as an objective correlative for Henderson, who has achieved a similar wisdom and who now gives comfort in his turn to a Persian–American orphan aboard the plane—an act which compensates in part for the earlier rejection of Ricey's foundling. To the orphan, Henderson tries to convey a sense of the promise in the world, and to the stewardess he sings of the day of salvation:

> "Haven't you ever heard the song?" I said. "Listen, and I'll sing you a little of it." We were at the rear of the plane where I was feeding the animal Dahfu. I sang, "And who shall abide the day of his coming (the day of His coming)? And who shall stand when He appeareth (when He appeareth)?" (334)

The stewardess recognizes the music from the *Messiah*, and with this last sounding of the Messianic leitmotiv, the plane makes a refueling stop in a symbolic Newfoundland.

With the orphan in his protective arms, Henderson deplanes to run in the snow and to breathe the cold fresh air:

> I held him close to my chest. He didn't seem to be afraid that I would fall with him. While to me he was like medicine applied, and the air, too; it also was a remedy. Plus the happiness that I expected at Idlewild from meeting Lily. And the lion? He was in it, too. Laps and laps I galloped around the shining and riveted body of the plane, behind the fuel trucks. Dark faces were looking from within. The great, beautiful propellers were still, all four of them. I guess I felt it was my turn now to move, and we went running—leaping, pounding, and tingling over the pure white lining of the gray Arctic silence. (341)

This is the fully regenerate Henderson joyously celebrating the new life that he has discovered. His fluid, lionlike motion contrasts with the stillness of the landscape and the rigidity of the plane. It is a dance of life, his inner vision transforming the winter scene into the promise of spring. The scene is comically and happily pregnant with symbols of new life. The place is Newfoundland, covered with pure white snow; the time is morning, Sunday, the eve of Thanksgiving week. In Henderson's arms is a child whose eyes are "new to life altogether" (339), and on the plane is the lion cub, who represents the kingly spirit of Dahfu and the condition of pure Being. The scene is a riot of affirmation, a powerful celebration of all that is positive in life.

And the music? It can only be Handel's "Hallelujah Chorus" sung in this "arctic silence" by the "voice of angels" which Henderson had failed to produce through his groping efforts on his father's violin and which he had failed to earn at the Arnewi's cistern. Here he has earned the music in all its glory. Now that he has attuned himself to the universal rhythm of things, the music comes as a reward with his restored soul, his transformed vision. As Henderson cavorts around the plane, bearish but childlike, the air is filled with the heavenly sounds of a celestial choir celebrating the coming of the Messiah: "Hallelujah! Hallelujah! Hallelujah! Hallelujah!" it is a sweeping, majestic affirmation, and it is accomplished through a monumental piece of fictional inference, for every scene in the novel points to this resounding oratorical climax; yet not a sound is actually heard. The voices of angels thunder only in the soul, the soul of Henderson and that of the reader. Such music is not new, of course: "Heard melodies are sweet," Keats affirmed in his "Ode to a Grecian Urn," "but those unheard are sweeter."

The comic spirit is never absent in this majestic allusion, and it is especially evident in an implied pun. As the reborn Henderson, this Rain King, Medicine Man, and mock-Messiah, goes "leaping, pounding, and tingling over the pure white lining of Newfoundland," the refrain of Handel's most famous chorus keeps echoing in the mind's ear:

And He shall reign forever and ever.
And He shall reign . . .
And He shall reign . . .
And He shall reign . . .

6.

Herzog: Law of the Heart

"What this country needs," says Herzog, "is a good five-cent synthesis."[1] And Herzog's painful efforts to formulate such a synthesis to shore up his disintegrating life is the substance of Saul Bellow's sixth novel, a secular theodicy for our time. Unemployed, twice-divorced, out of touch with his children and his own wealthy siblings, unsure of his values and aspirations—in short, alienated—Herzog strives "to explain, to have it out, to justify, to put in perspective, to clarify, to make amends" (2). He seeks clarity and justice, and he appears to have the necessary credentials for the quest: a doctoral degree, professorial experience, and an impressive scholarly bibliography, including *Romanticism and Christianity,* an influential book dealing with the history of ideas. As a scholar-adventurer he has fared well in the mapping of intellectual horizons, but with the discovery that his wife and his best friend have made him a cuckold, Herzog finds himself lost in the wasteland of existential nothingness, "down in the mire of post-Renaissance, post-humanistic, post-Cartesian dissolution, next door to the Void" (93). This is alien country for a man of romantic temperament, and Herzog's journey back to familiar ground is a difficult one. His difficulties stem mainly from the dual nature of his character, from the conflict between his sensibilities and his intellect. His academic background compels him to acknowledge intellectually the conclusions required by evidence, and the chaotic evidence of his life shrieks support for the nay-sayers, the touters of the existential void. Yet as a man of feeling, Herzog clings desperately to the impulses of affirmation that come from his heart, the insistent voice of intuition.

1. Saul Bellow, *Herzog* (New York, 1964), p. 270. Subsequent page numbers, when necessary, will be supplied in parentheses.

The intellectual need to systematize and reconcile clashes with the emotional desire to believe on the basis of faith. Herzog is a romanticist in an existential world trying to relieve himself of a neoclassicist's burden, a task not easily done. He solves his problem, finally, by moving through existentialism to transcendentalism. Moreover, he earns his solution honestly, enduring the admonitions of a weird collection of "reality instructors," submitting manfully to the ministrations of a sexual priestess, confronting the void, and frantically writing letters to persons living and dead whose thoughts or actions have formed a part of the world in which he must reestablish his identity.

Between Herzog and his vision of a better life come the reality instructors, the real estate salesmen in the wasteland, the pragmatic everyday nay-sayers. To the "throb-hearted" Herzog they bring the assurance of iconoclasm, attempting to correct his vision and reduce his aspirations to the attainable level of negative possibility. They preach the gospel of nihilism, destruction for its own sake. Though Herzog is repelled by their doctrine, he is curiously drawn to them—as if he needs, in a Miltonic sense, to know evil in order to choose good. His bitterest lessons are learned from his second wife, Madeleine, who breaks his heart, yet bears him a daughter, June, "by a bungling father out of a plotting bitch, something genuine."

When his brother Will asks Herzog why he married Madeleine, he replies, "God ties all kinds of loose ends together. Who knows why! He couldn't care less about my welfare, or my ego, that thing of value" (305). At another time Herzog tries again to explain to Will his reason for marrying Madeleine:

> It's about time I stopped laboring with this curse—I think, I figure things out. I see exactly what I should avoid. Then all of a sudden, I'm in bed with that very thing, and making love to it. As with Madeleine. She seems to have filled a special need. . . . She brought ideology into my life. Something to do with catastrophe. (333–34)

But it is in a letter to Mermelstein that Herzog comes closest to articulating the subconscious motivation that has led him to many of his wrong choices, marriage included:

> People of powerful imagination, given to dreaming deeply and
> to raising up marvelous and self-sufficient fictions, turn to
> suffering sometimes to cut into their bliss, as people pinch
> themselves to feel awake. I know that my suffering . . . has
> often been like that, a more extended form of life, a striving for
> true wakefulness and an antidote to illusion. (317)

His goal (conscious or not) being wakefulness through suffering, Herzog becomes wide-eyed under the tutelage of
Madeleine.[2] Early in their marriage Herzog makes a sar-
castic suggestion to Madeleine: "Maybe I married you to
improve my mind!" " 'Well, I'll teach you, don't worry!'
said the beautiful, pregnant Madeleine between her teeth"
(125). Madeleine is intelligent but irresponsible, beautiful
but amoral, "proud but not well wiped." From her Herzog
learns something about envy, treachery, infidelity, lust,
and hate. "A bitch in time," Herzog notes after the divorce,
"breeds contempt" (21).

Along with Madeleine are the other reality instructors,
Gersbach, Simkin, and Himmelstein. Their personal relationships with Herzog are different, but their evaluations
of his character and their advice to him are essentially the
same. They see him as a "a real, genuine old Jewish type
that digs the emotions," whose "heart has been shat on,"
yet who feels that "everybody should love him. If not, he's
going to scream and holler." What he must do, they say, is
face facts, realize that the world is full of whores, that
there is no order in chaos, and that death negates all things.
Such is the message which Herzog, with fear and trembling, must consider: He questions,

> But what is the philosophy of this generation? Not God is dead,
> that point was passed long ago. Perhaps it should be stated

---

2. That Herzog is aware of his tendency to be drawn fatally toward the
wrong kind of person is clear from his response to a woman he sees on
the platform at Grand Central Station: "He saw . . . a woman in a shining
black straw hat which held her head in depth and eyes that . . . reached
him with a force she could never be aware of. . . . They were bitch eyes,
that was certain. They expressed a sort of female arrogance which had
an immediate sexual power over him; he experienced it again that very
moment—a round face, the clear gaze of bitch eyes, a pair of proud legs"
(34). Frequently, Herzog describes Madeleine in similar terms.

Death is God. This generation thinks—and this is its thought
of thoughts—that nothing faithful, vulnerable, fragile can be
durable or have any true power. Death waits for these things
as a cement floor waits for a dropping light bulb. The brittle
shell of glass loses its tiny vacuum with a burst, and that is that.
And this is how we teach metaphysics on each other. "You
think history is the history of loving hearts? You fool! Look at
these millions of dead. Can you pity them, feel for them? You
can nothing! There were too many. We burned them to ashes,
we buried them with bulldozers. History is the history of cruelty, not love, as soft men think. We have experimented with
every human capacity to see which is strong and admirable
and have shown that none is. There is only practicality. If the
old God exists he must be a murderer. But the one true god is
Death. This is how it is—without cowardly illusions." (290)

From "the unbearable intensity of these ideas," Herzog
experiences nausea, the condition Kierkegaard called the
"sickness unto death." The reality instructors are doing
their job; Herzog is being driven toward the abyss.

But Herzog has two defenses with which he resists, one
sexual, the other intellectual. His sexual defense is named
Ramona.

The function of Ramona in Herzog's life is distraction.
She provides the relief Herzog needs from the intensity of
his examination of the significance of his own life within
the general meaning of human existence.[3] With her "intox-
icating eyes and robust breasts, her short but gentle legs,
her Carmen airs," Ramona is ably equipped to divert him
in style. She transforms "his miseries into sexual excite-
ments" and turns "his grief in a useful direction" (157).

3. Several times in his musings Herzog refers to the following nursery
rhyme:

I love little pussy, her coat is so warm
And if I don't hurt her, she"ll do me no harm.
I'll sit by the fire and give her some food,
And pussy will love me because I am good. (118)

With the expectation of justice suggested by the poem and the sexual
meaning of *pussy* there is the merger here of the sex theme and the
quest-for-justice theme. It is worth remarking, also, that a similar merger
can be seen in the person of Valentine Gersbach, the unfaithful friend (a
symbol of injustice) who has a wooden leg (an obvious phallic symbol).
Suzanne Henning Uphaus, "From Innocence to Experience: A study of
Herzog," *Dalhousie Review,* 46 (Spring 1966), 71–72.

Though he can envision a possible permanence to their affair, Herzog has no illusions about the nature of their relationship nor about his need for sexual release:

> What I seem to do, thought Herzog, is to inflame myself with drama, with ridicule, failure, denunciation, distortion, to inflame myself voluptuously, esthetically, until I reach a sexual climax. And that climax looks like a resolution and an answer to many "higher problems." (208)

The hedonistic pleasure Herzog receives from Ramona is at variance with the compulsion to regain his identity which the ostensible collapse of old values has imposed on him, but of this too Herzog is aware:

> For when will we civilized beings become really serious? said Kierkegaard. Only when we have known hell through and through. Without this, hedonism and frivolity will diffuse hell through all our days. (151)

Herzog's second defense is his letters. It may be true, as Henry Adams asserted, that a teacher affects eternity; but such infinite evaluation is beyond the vision of an individual teacher, and even within the practical limits of his purview his contributions remain largely inestimable. He works with the hope that his efforts have some beneficially shaping influence, but he finds the extent of his influence—and therefore of his contribution—difficult to determine. If he cannot measure his influence, he cannot be certain of his control; and in an unsettled mind such a problem can assume epic proportions, calling into question his very reason for existence. Such is the case with Herzog. His letters are both an apology for his life and an attempt to regain his psychic balance through quixotic humor and a philosophic monologue.

Faced with the collapse of personal relationships, haunted by the snickering existential footmen urging him nearer to the void, and stripped of the insularity of the groves of academe, Herzog responds in the way most natural to a man of letters: He writes letters. Though never mailed, these letters are Herzog's desperate attempt to exert some control in a world that suddenly seems hostile and to counter an intellectual trend which, because of its persuasive claim to validity, threatens to undermine the system of values upon which he has built his life. Though products of his intellect, the letters are prompted by his heart; and they are produced in the anguish of a spirit which fears its efforts are futile.

Herzog's letters exhibit a wide-reaching social concern, ranging from common courtesy to natural resources, from racial strife to presidential elections. To an insolent clerk in a men's clothing store he writes,

> Dear Mack. Dealing with poor jerks every day. Male pride. Effrontery. Conceit. Yourself obliged to be agreeable and winsome. Hard job if you happen to be a grudging, angry fellow. . . . Must manage some civility. (20)

He checks out a rumor with the Secretary of the Interior:

> Dear Mr. Udall, A petroleum engineer I met recently in a Northwest jet told me our domestic oil reserves were almost used up and that plans had been completed for blasting the polar caps with hydrogen bombs to get at the oil underneath. What about that? (68)

He acknowledges the significance of the Negro's contribution to democracy:

> Dear Mr. King, The Negroes of Alabama filled me with admiration. White America is in danger of being depoliticalized. Let us hope this example by Negroes will penetrate the hypnotic trance of the majority. (67)

And to Adlai Stevenson he offers an evaluation:

> Dear Governor Stevenson, Just a word with you, friend. I supported you in 1952. Like many others I thought this country might be ready for its great age in the world and intelligence at last assert itself in public affairs—a little more of Emerson's "American Scholar," the intellectuals coming into their own. But the instinct of the people was to reject mentality and its images, ideas, perhaps mistrusting them as foreign. It preferred to put its trust in visible goods. (66)

Out of emotional necessity, Herzog's mind races, darts, probes, striving to restore order, to enforce propriety. "Things fall apart," as Yeats said; "the centre cannot hold."

But the comments which cost Herzog the most effort are

those in which he tries to shout down the prophets of dread, the preachers of alienation and anxiety. These letters, too, are prompted by emotional necessity, but they are demanded by intellectual duty, by the academic discipline which requires that truth be evaluated discursively. Although the dialogue between Herzog and his philosophic antagonists amounts at last to a monologue, it is carried out with the greatest seriousness, for Herzog's life is at stake. He takes Kierkegaard to task in a letter to Mermelstein:

> I venture to say Kierkegaard meant that truth has lost its force with us and horrible pain and evil must teach it to us again. . . . I do not see this. Let us set aside the fact that such convictions in the mouths of safe, comfortable people playing at crisis, alienation, apocalypse and desperation, make me sick. We must get it out of our heads that this is a doomed time, that we are waiting for the end, and the rest of it, mere junk from fashionable magazines. . . . But, to get to the main point, the advocacy and praise of suffering take us in the wrong direction and those of us who remain loyal to civilization must not go for it. (316–17

In the schemes of Gersbach, Herzog sees a travesty of the theistic existentialism of Martin Buber, and in the theories of Nietzsche he sees the destruction, not the survival, of the Dionysian spirit in its overexposure to "Decomposition, Hideousness, Evil." He finds himself "very tired of the modern form of historicism which sees in this civilization the defeat of the best hopes of Western religion and thought, what Heidegger calls the second Fall of Man into the quotidian or ordinary" (106), and in a comment on Spengler Herzog summarizes his opposition to the naysayers:

> The canned sauerkraut of Spengler's "prussian Socialism," the commonplaces of the Wasteland outlook, the cheap mental stimulants of Alienation, the cant and rant of pipsqueaks about Inauthenticity and Forlornness. I can't accept this foolish dreariness. We are talking about the whole life of mankind. (75)

Herzog does not earn the right to refute the wastelanders, however, until he has looked deep into their void, and he does that, significantly and ironically, in the citadel of justice, a courtroom.

As Herzog waits for his lawyer in a city courthouse, he witnesses several trials, and he learns firsthand what Nietzsche meant by "Hideousness, Evil." A Negro, a social derelict, is sentenced to jail for a petty crime; a young German intern finds his medical career jeopardized by an apparently impetuous act; a young male prostitute, without emotion, reveals the sordidness of his life and mindlessly submits to the ridicule and the sentence of the court. And finally Herzog audits a murder trial. A helpless child has been tortured and savagely slain by its demented, bestial mother and her subhuman Yahoo lover.

> The child screamed, clung, but with both arms the girl hurled it against the wall. On her legs was ruddy hair. And her lover, too, with long jaws and zooty sideburns, watching on the bed. Lying down to copulate, and standing up to kill. Some kill, then cry. Others, not even that. (240)

Stumbling from the courtroom, Herzog is overcome with a vague sickness; he has "an acrid fluid in his mouth [and a] repulsive headache, piercing and ugly." His malady is again existential nausea, Kierkegaard's sickness unto death. Whirled violently in the void at last, Herzog finds nothing, intellectual or emotional, to sustain him. In the reality of this negation, intellect, justice, and compassion are merely empty words. Herzog is "wrung, and wrung again, and wrung again, again." Herzog experiences here the dark night of his soul. The depth of his despair is a measure of his total exposure to the existential position. His plunge into the void convinces him that synthesis, justification, intellectual affirmation are impossible—but the realization that intellectual affirmation is unattainable enables Herzog to abandon his philosophic contention and paves the way for his move toward a transcendental affirmation of the heart.

Herzog's progress from the sickness unto death to the healthy condition of a man with all of his own faculties intact can be charted from the moment he decides not to shoot Gersbach, whom he finds bathing his little daughter, June. "As soon as Herzog saw the actual person giving an actual bath, the reality of it, the tenderness of such a buffoon to a little child, his intended violence turned into *theater,* into something ludicrous" (258). Despite the grotesqueness of Gersbach's character, his act is an act of love, which he performs on his knees, with the "faint wisps of powder" floating over his stooping head. It is a holy act, and Herzog, recognizing its holiness, steals quietly away.[4]

Satisfied for the moment that June is not being subjected to the abuse Herzog had imagined after his exposure to the wretchedness of the trial scene, Herzog leaves to visit Gersbach's wife, Phoebe. He offers to pay for a divorce suit against Gersbach if she will name Madeleine in her charge of adultery. She could thus get revenge for Gersbach's infidelity, Herzog argues, and he could perhaps get custody of June, since Madeleine would thus be proved an unfit mother. Phoebe rejects his offer, however. "You've been treated like dirt," she acknowledges. "That's true. But it's all over. You should get away. Just get away from this now" (264). She will not help him, but she offers him a semblance of pity. Herzog thinks, "Crumbs of decency—all that we paupers can spare one another." Phoebe's desire to keep up appearances and to avoid emotional turmoil strikes Herzog as a representative stance of modern man resulting from the highly mechanized age. Automatism has freed man from dependence on human feeling. Herzog does not feel himself really a part of this move toward what seems to him dehumanization: "My emotional type is archaic. Belongs to the agricultural or pastoral stages" (265). Suddenly Herzog experiences an epiphany that helps to relieve him of the now intolerable burden of systematic thought:

> He was only vastly excited—in a streaming state—and intended mostly to restore order by turning to his habit of thoughtfulness. Blood had burst into his psyche, and for the time being he was either free or crazy. *But then he realized that he did not need to perform elaborate abstract intellectual work*—work he

4. It is interesting to note that in both significance and dramatic structure, this scene is remarkably close to the scene in *Hamlet* in which Hamlet chooses not to kill Claudius while he is praying. The emphasis on *theater* in the quoted passage seems doubly to support such a parallel.

had always thrown himself into as if it were the struggle for survival. But not thinking is not necessarily fatal. Did I really believe that I would die when thinking stopped? Now to fear such a thing—that's really crazy. (265) [My italics.]

Like Henderson the Rain King, Herzog has burst the spirit's sleep. Having divested himself of the intellectual need to clarify and to justify, he is prepared to do a complete about-face. "Go through what is comprehensible," he asserts, "and you conclude that only the incomprehensible gives any light" (266).

The incomprehensible state accepted by Herzog's throbbing heart is not death, but life and love. At Lucas Asphalter's house, where he is staying so that he can visit June, he explains his position to Lucas, his oldest friend:

I really believe that brotherhood is what makes a man human. If I owe God a human life, this is where I fall down. Man liveth not by self alone but in his brother's face. . . . Each shall behold the Eternal Father and love and joy abound. When the preachers of dread tell you that others only distract you from metaphysical freedom then you must turn away from them. The real and essential question is one of our employment by other human beings and their employment by us. Without this true employment you never dread death, you cultivate it. And consciousness when it doesn't clearly understand what to live for, what to die for, can only abuse and ridicule itself. (272–73)

Having placed his feet once more on positive ground and finding himself in the company of one who shares his feelings and cares for his welfare, Herzog is able to sleep, a sign of his returning health.

The next day Herzog enjoys an afternoon idyll with June in Jefferson Park, but the day ends in near disaster when Herzog wrecks the rented teal-blue Falcon and is arrested on a charge of possessing firearms without a permit, the firearm being Father Herzog's old pistol with which Herzog, in a moment of madness, had intended to murder Gersbach and Madeleine. June is frightened but unhurt, but Herzog, bloody and in police custody, finds himself immersed in the whirlpool of quotidian chaos that he felt insulated from earlier as he sat, an auditor, in the courtroom scenes. He questions:

> Is this, by chance the reality you have been looking for, Herzog, in your earnest Herzog way? Down in the ranks with other people—ordinary life? By yourself you can't determine which reality is real? (287)

Later, reflecting in a jail cell as he waits for Will to come bail him out, Herzog realizes that this level of existence is a dimension of reality, certainly, but it is not the reality he desired nor what he is destined for: "This, Herzog realized, was not the sphere of *his* sins. He was merely passing through. Out in the streets, in American society, that was where he did his time" (303).

His experience in jail provides him not only with a glimpse into how far the law of the land may affect his fate but also with a striking insight into his true relationship to Madeleine. When she comes to pick up June in the police station, she tries to intensify Herzog's culpability in the eyes of the police, and she glares revealingly at Herzog:

> She seemed to realize that she must control her tic and the violence of her stare. But by noticeable degrees her face became very white, her eyes smaller, stony. He believed he could interpret them. They expressed a total wish that he should die. This was infinitely more than ordinary hatred. It was a vote for his nonexistence, he thought. (301)

The recognition that Madeleine truly hates him frees Herzog from her completely. Any residual love he has, any remaining commitment that he feels, is ended. In a note to Gersbach, one of his last, he makes explicit his escape from Madeleine: "*And you, Gersbach, you're welcome to Madeleine. Enjoy her—You will not reach me through her, however. I know you sought me in her flesh. But I am no longer there*" (318).

The broken rib that Herzog receives in the wreck, then, is a symbolic wound. Adam awoke with an ache in his side to find that Eve had been taken from his flesh, and this was the beginning. Herzog comes to an awareness that the marriage is finally and irrevocably ended, and this severance of flesh—one made into two—is accompanied by a broken rib; and this too is a beginning. The Adamic motif so introduced sets up the final section of the novel in which

Herzog, no longer in bondage to flesh or to intellectual compulsion, returns to the Ludeyville house in the Edenic Berkshires and to that "pastoral stage" which he has come to view as his appropriate state.

In control of himself now, though physically unsteady, Herzog returns to nature, basking in the sunshine, luxuriating among the trees and flowers, and lovingly sharing his old house, "Herzog's folly," with ants, spiders, owls, and mice. "He was surprised to feel such contentment . . . contentment? Whom was he kidding, this was joy! For perhaps the first time he felt what it was to be free from Madeleine" (313). For the first time also he is enjoying the exhilaration of being free from the intellectual compulsion to explain his life, to synthesize the complexities of experience with theoretical, systematic philosophies. He explores his new position and its attendant feeling in a letter to Rozanov:

> *A curious result of the increase of historical consciousness is that people think explanation is a necessity of survival. They have to explain their condition. And if the unexplained life is not worth living, the explained life is unbearable, too. "Synthesize or perish!" Is that the new law? But when you see what strange notions, hallucinations, projections, issue from the human mind you begin to believe in providence again. To survive these idiocies . . . Anyway the intellectual has been a Separatist. And what kind of synthesis is a Separatist likely to come up with?* Luckily for me, I didn't have the means to get too far away from our common life. I am glad of that. I mean to share with other human beings as far as possible and not destroy my remaining years in the same way. Herzog felt a deep, dizzy eagerness to *begin.* (322)

Herzog begins by making an attempt to clean up his place. This old house in its wild and decrepit state has come to stand as an objective correlative for the condition of Herzog's soul, and now, his soul restored, he appropriately begins to set his house in order. He begins in another way by discontinuing his letter-writing. He writes at last to God and to his dead mother, informing God that he has always tried to do His "unknowable will" and sending to his mother "out—out where it is incomprehensible" the "most loving wish" that he has in his heart (326). And then he has "no messages for anyone. Nothing. Not a single word" (341).

Herzog has returned to his house in Ludeyville to regroup his forces so that he can eventually sally forth again, a battered picaro, into the ambiguous world, at which time he will allow himself to be "deaf to the final multiplicity of facts." He has achieved the state Keats called (in a letter to George and Thomas Keats) "negative capability," the capability "of being in uncertainties, mysteries, doubts, without any irritable reaching after fact and reason." In a letter to Dr. Edvig, Herzog himself acknowledges the ability to accept ambiguity as a sign of health:

> Dear Edvig, he noted quickly. You gave me good value for my money when you explained that neuroses might be graded by the inability to tolerate ambiguous situations. . . . Allow me modestly to claim that I am much better now at ambiguities. I think I can say, however, that I have been spared the chief ambiguity that afflicts intellectuals, and this is that civilized individuals hate and resent the civilization that makes their lives possible. What they love is an imaginary human situation invented by their own genius and which they believe is the only true and the only human reality. How odd! But the best-treated, most favored and intelligent part of any society is often the most ungrateful. Ingratitude, however, is its social function. Now there's an ambiguity for you! . . . Dear Ramona, I owe you a lot. I am fully aware of it. Though I may not be coming back to New York right away. I intend to keep in touch. Dear God! Mercy! My God! Rachaim olenu . . . melekh maimis . . . Thou King of Death and Life! (304)

Herzog's progression here from mental analysis to emotional expression of gratitude is an indication of his awareness that he too has been an intellectual with his own somewhat narrow conception of human reality. But no more. To Ramona, he expresses thanks for the love she has given, and to his God, he acknowledges the gift of life, even with death, the most awesome ambiguity. Herzog cannot explain either life or death; he can only accept both, affirming despite overwhelming evidence to the contrary that life is still meaningful and that in the absence of an intellectual justification, he will accept an emotional one. Herzog's desire and capacity to affirm prevail over all resistances. His innocence is the "radical innocence" described by Ihab Hassan as the innocence that must constantly reassert itself against the evidence of negation. Such innocence affirms out of a need to affirm yet in full awareness that it can produce no all-encompassing rational justification for its stance.

Herzog moves, then, from existentialism to transcendentalism. He turns from what is negative in Spengler, Heidegger, Kierkegaard, and Nietzsche to what is positive in Emerson, Thoreau, Whitman, and Rousseau. His shift is neither an arbitrary nor a superficial one. It is proved on his pulses. Following Whitman, Herzog has "escaped from the life that exhibits itself" (324), and true to the Emersonian text of his high school address, he has finally allowed his life to "be open to ecstasy or a divine illumination" (160). Romantic, transcendental, humanistic, Herzog can finally affirm with Rousseau, "*Je sens mon coeur et je connais les hommes*" (340). Herzog celebrates finally the "law of the heart" which he had earlier planned to analyze in connection with *The Phenomenology of the Mind* (119). His affirmation is not fraudulent, and it is not cheap; it has been earned with all the turbulence of a human spirit in conflict with itself. He has endured alienation. He has suffered anguish and nausea. He has experienced the void in all its terror. And he has rejected the void—because it lacks a center, a heart, a positive force of which Moses Herzog can say (in the biblical language of a law-giver), "Thou movest me."[5]

5. Several reviewers have discussed the possible meanings of "Herzog" ("duke," "heart," "courage," etc.), but, as far as I know, only George Elliot has seen the significance of "Moses" as "law-giver." See "Hurtsog, Hairtsog, Heart's Hog?" *Nation,* 199 (October 19, 1964), 252. In the light of Herzog's final celebration of feeling and brotherhood, it seems that "law-giver of the heart" is one unavoidable interpretation of his name.

7.

Mr. Sammler's Planet:
Objectives Without Correlatives

I am Lazarus, come back from the dead,
Come back to tell you all, I shall tell you all.
　　　　"The Love Song of J. Alfred Prufrock"

. . . After the kingfisher's wing
Has answered light to light, and is silent, the light is still
at the still point of the turning world.

　　　　　　　　V

Words move, music moves
Only in time; but that which is only living
Can only die. Words, after speech, reach
Into the silence. Only by the form, the pattern,
Can words or music reach the stillness. . . .
　　　　　　"Burnt Norton"

Mr. Sammler's Planet is a disturbing book in many ways:
in its penetrating analysis of the malaise of our present age,
in its uneasiness about our future, in its stark confrontation
with final matters, and aesthetically, in its uneven relation
of theme to form. Irving Howe senses accurately that Bellow, like T. S. Eliot, fears "the derangements of the soul in
the clutter of our cities, the poverty of a life deprived of
order and measure."[1] Bellow makes no direct references to
Eliot, and the novel does not depend in any formal way on
parallels with Eliot's work, but it is illuminating, nevertheless, to feel the permeating spirit of Eliot in matters of
theme, tone, and point of view.

In its depiction of superficiality and moral decay, *Mr.
Sammler's Planet* shares the disturbing thematic vision of

1. Irving Howe, "Books: *Mr. Sammler's Planet*," *Harper's Magazine*,
240 (February 1970), 106.

The Waste Land. Yet the novel hints—however obliquely—at a transcendent order beyond the temporal one, an
inexplicable though knowable force at the center of things
corresponding to the thematic center of the *Four Quartets,*
built as they are around "the still point of the turning
world," the intersection of time with timelessness symbolized by the Incarnation. Like the Lazarus to whom Prufrock compares himself unfavorably, Mr. Sammler has
come back from the dead to "tell all"—an extraordinary
point of view—and like Prufrock himself, Sammler is detached and (at seventy-plus) "grows old": The heckler at
Columbia and later Angela Gruner tell Sammler that he
no longer has the physical credentials to make judgments
on the sexual ambience of the age, but Sammler comments
just the same. He has heard the "mermaids singing each to
each," though they no longer sing to him. Detached though
he is from many of his own circle, Sammler is not detached
from the reader, and thus he reveals a personal, meditative,
multifaceted voice comparable to the narrative persona of
the *Four Quartets.* The reader seems to be overhearing him
as much as to be hearing him and often has difficulty
distinguishing between Bellow and his protagonist. Where
Eliot was a royalist in politics, a classicist in literature, and
an Anglo–Catholic in religion, Sammler, a kind of Eliot
figure, is a Wellsian liberal in politics (a conservative position compared to the radicals and New Leftists Sammler
encounters), an arch-classicist in literature (he reads mainly the Bible and Meister Eckhardt, cites Shakespeare, Dostoevski, and Proust often and finds Marcuse and Norman
O. Brown "worthless fellows"), and a nondoctrinaire qua-
si-orthodox Jew in religion. The overtones of Eliot lend a
literary richness and a kind of cultural authenticity to
Sammler's narrative.

Such is the nature of the central intelligence through
whom Bellow chooses to present a view of the world. That
Sammler sees the world through a single eye does not
signify a narrowness of vision but both a form of scrutiny
and a duality of perspective—and, at the aesthetic level, a
narrative strategy. Sammler sees outward and inward. His
good right eye records characters, actions, and events in

the world around him. His blind left eye symbolically subjects current events to introspective analysis, to historical and philosophical perspective. "The damaged left eye seemed to turn in another direction, to be preoccupied separately with different matters."[2] Thus the novel moves cyclically from action to reflection, and within that general strategy there are complementary movements from past to present, from private to public, from life to death. Sammler's predecessor in Bellow's canon is Queen Willatale of *Henderson the Rain King,* also a one-eyed character of great though primitive wisdom from whom Henderson learns the secret of grun-tu-molani, man want to live. As a "woman of Bittahness," Queen Willatale was able to achieve a kind of secular transcendence over the plague of frogs and the drought in the Arnewi wasteland, but of course Willatale was only a supporting character, not a central intelligence. Sammler's mental detachment gives him some distance from the chaos around him, but the distance is never transformed into transcendence. Sammler remains painfully involved in his world, partially through his actions in it, but mainly through his thoughts about it.

Sammler's thoughts—and thus the themes of the novel—are as varied as the subject matter of Herzog's letters,[3] but the main issues are these: sexual madness, crime, distortions of the self, advanced technology in a void, and death. The events and characters designed to embody these themes are brought to and often imposed upon Sammler in accordance with his role as recording observer; he does not seek them out, and thus Sammler is the still point of the turning action:

> Things met with in this world are tied to the forms of our perception in space and time and to the forms of our thinking.

2. Saul Bellow, *Mr. Sammler's Planet* (New York, 1970), p. 31. Page numbers hereafter refer to the Viking hardcover edition and will appear in parentheses in the text.
3. In fact, D. P. M. Salter has discussed Sammler as the logical continuation of Herzog's development. He sees Herzog's last letter to God, for example, as comparable in theme and strategy to Sammler's prayer over Elya's body: "Optimism and Reaction in Saul Bellow's Recent Work," *Critical Quarterly,* 14, 1 (Spring 1972), 57–66.

We see what is before us, the present, the objective. Eternal being makes its temporal appearance in this way. The only way out of the captivity in the forms, out of confinement in the prison of projections, is through freedom. Sammler thought he was Kantian enough to go along with this. (57)

Kantian-fashion, then, Sammler constantly relates the phenomenal world to the noumenal one. He both participates in and stands back from the events that revolve around him, sorting them out, classifying them, comparing them, judging them, and then questioning his judgments.[4] Like *Seize the Day, Mr. Sammler's Planet* can be divided into scenes, specifically twenty-two scenes in six chapters, each scene built around Sammler's perceptions in "space and time" and involving a movement between action and reflection, and each scene focusing on some facet of a world going mad under the moon, a lunatic planet. Doubting the ability of his perceptive powers to keep pace with his allotted space and time, Mr. Sammler summarizes the accelerating frenzy of his age:

Because of the high rate of speed, decades, centuries, epochs condensing into months, weeks, days, even sentences. So that to keep up you had to run, sprint, waft, fly over shimmering waters, you had to be able to see what was dropping out of human life and what was staying in. You could not be an old-fashioned sitting sage. You must train yourself. You had to be strong enough not to be terrified by local effects of metamorphosis, to live with disintegration, with crazy streets, filthy nightmares, monstrosities come to life, addicts, drunkards, and perverts celebrating their despair openly in midtown. You had to be able to bear the tangles of the soul, the sight of cruel dissolution. You had to be patient with the stupidities of power, with the fraudulence of business. Daily at five or six a.m. Mr. Sammler woke up in Manhattan and tried to get a handle on the situation. He didn't think he could. Nor, if he could,

---

4. In an excellent review that justifiably got a good deal of exposure, Benjamin DeMott argued that Sammler's objectivity is seriously flawed and "that the root of the book's trouble, both as argument and as art, is a defect of sympathy." Sammler's detachment, he declares, "attains insufficient substance for the reader, seemingly belonging only to the surface structure of his hesitations, sounds faint, as from the wings, whereas his scorn and vituperation come forth strongly as from the center." "Saul Bellow and the Dogmas of Possibility," *Saturday Review*, 53 (February 7, 1970), 27.

would he be able to convince or convert anyone. (74)

Despite his professed lack of confidence, Mr. Sammler expends substantial energy in his attempts to "get a handle on the situation." In fact, getting a handle on the situation seems to be what the novel is finally all about.

One of Sammler's earliest reflections concerns the sexual excesses of the age. Waking up in his room in the first scene, which fills the first thirty-nine pages of the novel, Sammler allows his thoughts to range over most of the book's major themes, but the emphasis is on sexuality run amuck:

> The labor of Puritanism now was ending. The dark satanic mills changing into light satanic mills. The reprobates converted into children of joy, the sexual ways of the seraglio and of the Congo bush adopted by the emancipated masses of New York, Amsterdam, London . . . the privileges of aristocracy (without any duties) spread wide, democratized, especially the libidinous privileges, the right to be uninhibited, spontaneous, urinating, defecating, belching, coupling in all positions, tripling, quadrupling, polymorphous, noble in being natural, primitive, combining the leisure and luxurious inventiveness of Versailles with the hibiscus-covered erotic ease of Samoa. (32–33)

In a later scene (180–92) with Wallace Gruner, Sammler acquiesces to Wallace's claim that women are animals. "Temporarily," Sammler says, "there is an animal emphasis" (185). And to Angela Gruner in the next-to-last scene (294–307) Sammler admits, "New York makes one think about the collapse of civilization, about Sodom and Gomorrah, the end of the world" (304). As in most of his reflections, Sammler makes historical, philosophical, and cultural comparisons, seeking clarity like Herzog, exercising both his outward and his inward vision. In a short view, one of those condensed statements envied by Govinda Lal, Sammler capsules his judgment on the sexual ambience of the age he has lived so improbably into: "A sexual madness was overwhelming the Western World" (66).

At the level of dramatic action, Sammler's observation is supplied with ample supportive detail. H. G. Wells, Sammler remembers, carried his sexual passion for young girls well into his seventies (71), and attending Picasso's last exhibit at the Museum of Modern Art, accompanied by Angela, Sammler discovers,

> Old Picasso was wildly obsessed by sexual fissures, by phalluses. In the frantic and funny pain of his farewell, creating organs by the thousands, perhaps tens of thousands. Lingam and Yoni. Sammler thought it might be enlightening to recall the Sanscrit words. Bring in a little perspective. But it didn't really do much for such a troubled theme. (66)

The "troubled theme" is disturbing enough to Sammler in the lives of public men like Wells and Picasso or in the various forms of perversity he sees all around him in the human wreckage of New York; it is most disturbing, however, as it touches him privately, in the confessions of Walter Bruch and Angela Gruner and in his own confrontation with the black pickpocket.

Walter Bruch comes to Sammler to confess his surreptitious sexual activity, his fetish for women's arms, especially arms that are "dark, heavy" (like the penis of the pickpocket). In the subway or drugstore in the Puerto Rican section he places himself close to a woman with such arms and masturbates against his attaché case. Tearfully, he confesses his shame to Sammler. "Uncle Sammler, what shall I do? I am over sixty years old" (60). Bruch is a boyman, seeking punishment from an authority figure but enjoying forbidden fruit, "Walter Bruch, with his old urchin knuckles in his eyes sat in his room and sobbed, having told on himself" (61). Yet, as Sammler knows, Bruch is at the same time carrying on a proper relationship with a refined lady, having his forbidden fruit and eating it, too, both a victim and an exploiter of the double standard. Sammler tells him, mock-seriously, that he has "an old nineteenth-century Krafft-Ebing trouble" (60).

If Bruch, of an older generation, moves within a double standard, Angela, of the younger generation, has abolished standards altogether. Like Bruch, Angela comes to Sammler to confess her sexual exploits, after visits to her analyst. "Putting together the ideal man" for Sammler on one such visit, she claims, "A Jew brain, a black cock, a nordic beauty . . . is what a woman wants" (66–67). She "swings" freely and often. With her current lover, Wharton Horricker, she swaps partners in Mexico with a couple they meet on the beach. According to her brother, Wallace, Angela "let that twerp in Mexico ball her fore and aft in front of Wharton, with who-knows-what-else thrown in free by her. In a spirit of participation" (187). Her confessions to Sammler appear to be as compulsive as Bruch's, but they are not remorseful. She flaunts her freedom. Her dying father quips to Sammler that she can be found in the hospital "frenching an orderly, or in a daisy chain" and then describes her with deadly seriousness as having "fucked-out eyes" (178). Sammler is finally dismayed that Angela can be "gay, amorous, intimate with holiday acquaintances," can practice "diversions, group intercourse, fellatio with strangers" but that she can "not come to terms with[her]father at the last opportunity" (306). She shows, as Sammler observed earlier, all the libidinous privileges of aristocracy without any of the duties. The situation is even worse. In Angela—and, it is implied, those like her of her generation—there is no longer any sense of duty. Hedonism is all, Dionysiac frenzy.

Dionysianism—especially phallic worship—culminates in the ostensibly incongruous act of the pickpocket. Forcing Sammler to look at his exposed penis as a warning, the pickpocket provides focus for the random sexual energy Sammler feels all around him. No Freudian virility surrogates like a knife or a gun here: The pickpocket reveals the thing-in-itself. He does so in a "princely" fashion, with "lordliness," a certain "majesty is assumed." Sammler is not in the land of the blind, where a one-eyed man can be king; he is in the land of the sexually mad, where the plenipotent is king:

> At any rate, there was the man's organ, a huge piece of sex flesh, half-tumescent in its pride and shown in its own right, a prominent and separate object intended to communicate authority. As, within the sex ideology of these days, it well might. It was a symbol of superlegitimacy or sovereignty. It was a mystery. It was unanswerable. The whole explanation. . . . And yet, such sensitive elongations the anteater had, too, un-

complicated by assertions of power, even over ants. But make Nature your God, elevate creatureliness, and you can count on gross results. (55)

It is as though the pickpocket has assumed the throne created by the racial myths that the black male is super virile, that black is necessarily beautiful. He arrogates all the myths to himself, believes in them, and forces Sammler to bear witness to his apotheosis. He becomes Sexual Force. (We are reminded here, by his attitudes, his situation, and his dress, of Rinehart in Ralph Ellison's *Invisible Man*, who learned, cynically, to turn chaos and racial myths into a source of personal power.) The event generates much interest. Margotte speculates about the Black's background and psychological make-up, Wallace in intrigued, Eisen is amused, and Feffer is delighted and wants pictures: "New York is really a gas city" (122). In reflection, Sammler returns often to this event.

In addition to the role he plays in the development of the sexual theme, the pickpocket is equally involved in the development of the criminal theme, an issue which Sammler confronts both dramatically and reflectively. He is appalled by the rampancy of criminal behavior as one more manifestation of a general decline in moral standards. It is most vivid in the pickpocket's activities on the uptown bus, but it is also evident in widespread vandalism and the indifference of both the police and the general public.

The pickpocket, a kind of criminal Nietzschean *Ubermensch*, has set himself above the common law, like Raskolnikov, whom Sammler thinks of often in this context. Yet the pickpocket himself acts from instinct, not philosophy. The animal imagery which Sammler uses to describe the pickpocket reveals the primitive nature of his predatory activities, the counterpart to his primitive sexual force. He preys on the unwitting or terrified bus passengers like a "great black beast" (14), with "the effrontery of a big animal" (5), as quiet as "a puma" (49) on a bus that takes curves "with a growl of flabby power" (6), working streets that look as though they have turned up an "asphalt belly" (9, 134). It is, of course, a jungle, and the animal imagery becomes an almost constant motif in Sammler's observations of life in New York (presented as a representative city in the United States and thus the glittering facade of "Uncle Sam's Planet"). The first time Sammler sees the pickpocket at work, he is unable in three blocks to find an operable pay phone so that he can report the crime. Vandals have robbed the boxes, smashed the instruments, used the booths for urinals. Calling in the crime finally from his home phone, Sammler encounters only jaded indifference from the police. The implication is that nothing will be done—perhaps that nothing can be done.

It is the sense of powerlessness that dominates Sammler's reflections on crime. He is mentally indignant that the pickpocket's victims do nothing in their defense, for the Black can take "the slackness, the cowardice of the world for granted" (47). Sammler does not "give a damn for the glamour, the style, the art of criminals"; they are not "social heroes to him" (10); yet when the pickpocket confronts him in the lobby, Sammler is equally powerless to resist, as he is powerless to act in the fight between Feffer, Eisen, and the Black:

> Sammler was powerless. To be so powerless was death. And suddenly he saw himself not so much standing as strangely leaning, as reclining, and peculiarly in profile, and as a *past* person. . . . Someone between the human and the not-human states, between content and emptiness, between full and void, meaning and not-meaning, between this world and no world. (289–90)

Sammler's paralysis is intensified by the curious passiveness of the crowd, their calm unwillingness to help avert violence, their "beatitude of presence" at a scene where someone was "going to get it" (289). The pressures of the city, the dehumanization, the anonymity—all create frustrations that demand an outlet, a ritual sacrifice, and *any* sacrifice will do. Here each participates in the sacrifice vicariously, imposing his own meaning on it, without bearing any responsibility for it. A voice in the crowd—perhaps The Voice of the Crowd—cries, "He'll kill that cocksucker!" (291) and the crowd, like gallows watchers, looks on, forming the moral void whose center is agonizingly occupied by Mr. Sammler. In an earlier reflection Sammler had accounted for the desire for violence he encounters here:

> One thing, though, the disciplined hate the undisciplined to the point of murder. Thus the working class, disciplined, is a great reservoir of hatred. Thus the clerk behind the wicket finds it hard to forgive those who come and go their apparent freedom. And the bureaucrat, glad when disorderly men are killed. All of them, killed.[5] (147)

Though Sammler is no newcomer to violence, killing, or crime, he is horrified to confront such things in bright daylight on the streets of one of the New World's largest cities and be helpless to influence the turn of events for the better. Like Joseph of *Dangling Man*, Sammler becomes lost in a crater of the spirit.

In addition to sexual madness and crime, Mr. Sammler must try to come to terms with the various distortions of the self created by a complex and pressure-filled world, and the distortions are legion. In the people Sammler sees or interacts with daily, Bellow provides textbook cases of the kinds of distortion of the self that David Riesman described in *The Lonely Crowd* or, more recently, Wylie Sypher in *The Loss of the Self*. Sammler judges the cause of the trouble to be the high premium presently placed on unlimited freedom and personal individuality or originality:

> What one sees on Broadway while bound for the bus. All human types reproduced, the barbarian, redskin, or Fiji, the dandy, the buffalo hunter, the desperado, the queer, the sexual fantasist, the squaw; bluestocking, princess, poet, painter, prospector, troubadour, guerrilla, Che Guevara, the new Thomas à Becket. Not imitated are the businessman, the soldier, the priest, and the square. The standard is aesthetic. As Mr. Sammler saw the thing, human beings, when they have room, when they have liberty and are supplied also with ideas, mythologize themselves. They legendize. They expand by imagination and try to rise above the limitations of the ordinary forms of common life. (147)

Mr. Sammler's point is that the cruel myths of unlimited

---

5. Mark Harris's latest novel, *Killing Everybody*, follows a similar track.

personal freedom and opportunity for development of the self have led individuals to try—often desperately—to avoid imitation and to gratify every whim and desire. Since an imperfect world does not grant such gratification—Madison Avenue pitchmen, notwithstanding—people are driven despite their desire to debased forms of imitation and originality, debasing both themselves and the forms they employ:

> More possibility, more actors, apes, copycats, more invention, more fiction, illusion, more fantasy, more despair. Life looting Art of its wealth, destroying Art as well by its desire to become the thing itself. Pressing itself into pictures. Reality forcing itself into all these shapes. Just look (Sammler looked) at this imitative anarchy of the streets—these Chinese revolutionary tunics, these babes in unisex toyland, these surrealist warchiefs, Western stagecoach drivers—Ph.D.s in philosophy, some of them. . . . They sought originality. They were obviously derivative. And of what—of Paiutes, of Fidel Castro? No, of Hollywood extras. Acting mythic. Casting themselves into chaos, hoping to adhere to higher consciousness, to be washed up on the shores of truth. Better, thought Sammler, to accept the inevitability of imitation and then to imitate good things. (148–49)

What Sammler laments here is the absence of what is close to an Aristotelian concept of mimesis in art and life, and he terms this madness "the attempted liberty of people who feel themselves overwhelmed by giant forces of organized control" (146). "Sore at heart" for the failure of individuality he witnesses, Sammler describes the irrationality of this miserable contemporary creature, characteristically, in animal imagery: "a volatile and restless animal, such a high-strung curious animal, an ape subject to so many diseases" (146). In the same vein he notes "a female bum drunkenly sleeping like a dugong, a sea cow's belly rising, legs swollen purple; a short dress, a mini-rag" (106).

In his observations on the values and life-styles of contemporary young people Sammler sees further distortions of the self, and he continues his animal imagery. The dirty, indolent, badly educated collegiate readers whom Sammler no longer employs he describes as having "the helpless vital pathos of young dogs with their first red erections" (37). The radically active youth, confronting technology he cannot understand, is, like an "uncomprehending Congo savage," "setting fires to libraries" in the name of irrationality and "wholeness" (182). Others, not activists, are simply practicing a kind of mindless escapism, also in the name of irrationality: "Innocent, devoid of aggression, opting out much like Ferdinand the Bull. No *corrida* for them; only smelling flowers under the lovely cork tree" or, as Wells saw them, "lovely young human cattle hearded by the cannibalistic Morlocks" (106). The words, attitudes, gestures, and values of the young heckler at Columbia suggest to Sammler "Barbary ape howling.[6] Or like the spider monkeys in the trees . . . defecating into their hands, and shrieking, pelting the explorers below" (43). Sammler feels he is in a Yahoo world where there is a good deal of "doggish hind-sniffing" (117) going on.[7]

Moving from public to private observations, Sammler finds the same kinds of distortion of the self in the lives of those closest to his own, and again the irrationality, the compensations, the instinctual excesses are rendered in animal imagery. Angela has sacrificed all other standards for sexual freedom and instinctual gratification. Despite her name, her father calls her "a cow" (78); to her brother she is "a pig . . . a swine" (186); she calls herself "a skunk. So many odors, Uncle" (71). In her turn, Angela calls Wallace, with all his crazy rebellion-against-the-father

6. One critic views the scene with the heckler as symptomatic of a fundamental flaw in the novel: "This outburst, meant to characterize the student movement and the consciousness of the New Left, characterizes more than anything else what has gone wrong with this novel. When an artist who is no blunderer—and Bellow is a supreme artist—furnishes so false a moment, it is something of a revelation. Bellow has failed to give credibility to the opposition.

"The point of course is that opposition is just what it is: The student is recognizable only as a nasty caricature. He is part of a whole corpus of signs and tendencies that this novel is proclaiming against. He is being used." Beverly Gross, "Dark Side of the Moon," *The Nation*, 210 (February 9, 1970), 153–55.

7. Bellow, of course, does not free Sammler himself from the animal metaphors. Sammler's eyebrows overhang like "some breeds of dog" (4) and, dog-fashion, Sammler does some hind-sniffing of his own: "[Wallace] often transmitted to Sammler in warm weather (perhaps Sammler's nose was hypersensitive) a slightly unclean odor from the rear. The merest hint of fecal carelessness" (87).

schemes, a "kinky cat" (88). Jewish-Catholic Shula hides her loneliness and nonfulfillment in eccentricity. Married to "poor dog-laughing Eisen," she and her husband appear to Sammler as "two cuckoos in their whitewashed Mediterranean cage" (294). Divorced, she intensifies her eccentricity and feeds her illusions about Sammler's work on H. G. Wells, haunting old bookstores in a wig made of "yak and baboon hair" (34), collecting junk in a shopping bag like "a scavenger or magpie" (162), an "ingenuous animal" with "ears like a fox" (201). And Walter Bruch, a successful musicologist with a refined lady friend, also nourishes his arm fetish, masturbates compulsively, enjoys playing dead, buys children's toys for himself and plays with them secretly in his room, writes contentious and vindictive letters to music reviewers, and confesses tearfully to Sammler his remorse over his lost life. Sammler recalls that Bruch twisted his trunk "apelike" (60, 284), that in his confessions "he gobbled, he quacked, grunted, swallowed syllables" (57). In a statement that could serve as a summary of the distortions of the self as they assume animal form, Sammler recalls Cleopatra's words to the dying Antony that this world "in thy absence is no better than a sty" and "There is nothing left remarkable/Beneath the visiting moon" (197).

The moon serves in the novel as the central symbol for both the goal of advanced technology and the future of Man. But, in Sammler's view, the technological advances appear to be occurring in a moral void, and thus the future of Man is uncertain, another major theme. The frequent references in the novel to the Apollo moon shot provide the surface dramatic action which serves as the ground for discussion of technology, but mainly the theme is treated in the complementary reflections of Dr. Govinda Lal and Mr. Sammler.

To Sammler's growing suspicions of the apparent impossibility of ethical order, Lal, a scientist, poses the certainty of biological order:

> Biological science is in an extraordinary state of progress. . . .
> To participate is a privilege. This chemical order, which is a

fundamental of life, is of great beauty. (216)

Lal favors inhabitation of the moon as a manifestation of scientific progress, the earth being simply a stage in a vast evolutionary spiral, though he acknowledges other considerations as well. He knows, for example, that the United States' leadership in the space race is good public relations and that some financial wastefulness is unavoidable, but he thinks there will be spillover research value for related sciences, "fruitful gaspillage," and he speculates that the adventures of opening a new frontier will relieve overcrowded conditions on earth and perhaps even "introduce new sobriety" (217). Sammler, less sure, acquiesces to Lal's judgments with much uncertainty.

Sammler's reflections on the future of man vis-à-vis the moon and advancing technology are troubled. He reiterates the failures of individuality and originality and the dreadful distortions of the Self:

> The idea of the uniqueness of the soul. An excellent idea. A true idea. But in these forms? Dear God! With hair, with clothes, with drugs and cosmetics, with genitalia, with round trips through evil, monstrosity, and orgy, with even God approched through obscenities? How terrified the soul must be in this vehemence, how little that is really dear to it it can see in these Sadic exercises. (229)

In Sammler's saddened view, Western civilization has failed to realize its dream. It has created a nightmare. Space, then, offers an uncertain possibility for another chance; that is, if there is uncertainty, there may be hope. Though Sammler, as a philosopher, has little interest in the engineering aspects of the expedition, he ventures to hope that man can make of technological advance a new Manifest Destiny:

> So I suppose we must jump off, because it is our human fate to do so. If it were a rational matter, then it would be rational to have justice on this planet first. (237)

Sammler's experiences in Poland, in Israel, and on the streets of New York have shown him the remoteness of "justice first"; consequently, he joins Lal in hoping for a better day tomorrow, another time, another space.

Water imagery is a major unifying device in this long philosophical scene (201–37), and both Sammler and Lal use it. Lal suggests that crowded conditions create the desire to be a Baudelairean "drunken boat," and he thinks of the move into space as a "voyage" that "does not necessarily have to be a death-voyage," that we need to know in our beleaguered state that "there is a universe into which we can overflow" (219). "To plunge" into the immensity of space, Lal continues, makes "sea-depth petty, the leviathan no more than a polliwog" (222). And Sammler describes inundation by teeming numbers and ideas:

> They say our protoplasm is like sea water. Our blood has a Mediterranean base. But now we live in a social and human sea. Inventions and ideas bathe our brains, which sometimes, like sponges, must receive whatever the currents bring and digest the mental protozoa. (227)

Consequently we "lie under and feel the . . . weight of the world" (227). It is oppressive, suffocating. Trying to act human in such circumstances, people go "swimming and boating in that cloudy, contaminated, confusing, surging medium of human feelings, taking the passion waters, exclaiming over their fate" (234). In another passage, Sammler describes death as going under the surface never to reappear:

> We watch these living speed like birds over the surface of a water, and one will dive or plunge but not come up again and never be seen any more. And in our turn we will never be seen again, once gone through that surface. But then we have no proof that there is no depth under the surface. (236)

Water imagery is appropriate to this section for several reasons. First, because water occupies two-thirds of the earth's surface, it is a suitable metaphor for the overcrowded conditions which both Sammler and Lal describe. The turbulence of the water matches the turbulence of the teeming multitudes, frantically seeking gratification or release, even in the form of escape to another planet; and the mystery of the sea is equivalent to the mystery of human death, which Sammler ponders. The moon exerts influence on the tides just as human behavior and direction are affected by the prospects of advanced technology leading to inhabitation of the moon, the subject matter of this section. The scene ends appropriately with Wallace flooding the house, a microcosmic counterpart, however comical, to The Flood, which according to biblical account God sent to destroy sinful man. Sammler fears, of course, that we are nearing that point again. Blundering despite his "blueprints" of the plumbing, Wallace furthermore enacts a technological disaster; Sammler can imagine the same effect from the space race. Modern man may not be ready to go or, getting there, he may find the moon as vacuous as earth seems depleted.

Against the theme of myriad human life zanily seeking direction or escape, Bellow sets the theme of death. Like Prufrock, Sammler has "heard the Eternal Footman hold his coat and snicker," and he has been afraid. He describes himself as preoccupied with "dying, the mystery of dying, the state of death" (273), and his preoccupation takes many forms. In the plot of the novel it is Sammler's painful awareness, in the background of every other event, that Dr. Gruner, his distant relative but close friend and benefactor, is dying. And in his memories and reflections death is the counterpoint to almost every other thought. He turns frequently to his memories of Poland. Leaving the body of his dead wife behind, Sammler crawled out of a mass grave and escaped, blinded in one eye, to a cemetery, where, paradoxically, he returned to life in a tomb cared for, paradoxically again, by an anti-Semitic Pole. In Zamosht forest, starving and persecuted, he took the life of a Russian soldier. Because of the personal provocation he felt, he did so without remorse and, because remorselessly, with even a kind of ecstacy. The experience taught him something about the relation of political power to killing (144). He relives his war experiences when he covers the Israeli Six-Day War as a kind of ad-hoc correspondent. The images of death he retains are, as they must be, grim, grotesque. He remembers a "sound of shovel-metal, gritting" (273) in his mass grave, the kind of grave that made Eichmann sick from "the fresh blood welling up at his shoes" (137). On the Russian soldier he killed Sammler "saw the soil already sprinkled on his face. He saw the grave on his skin" (139).

In Gaza, death was deterioration:

> In the sun the faces softened, blackened, melted, and flowed away. The flesh sank to the skull, the cartilage of the nose warping, the lips shrinking, eyes dissolving, fluids filling the hollows and shining on the skin. A strange flavor of human grease. Of wet paper pulp. Mr. Sammler fought his nausea. (251)

Such memories prompt Sammler now to think of "Ussher underground, in this or that posture, of this or that color or physical condition. As he thought of Antonina, his wife" (206) or to say of Eisen's portraits that "everybody looked like a corpse, with black lips and red eyes, with faces a kind of leftover cooked-liver green" (65).

"Humankind marks certain people for death," Sammler believes, and he feels "deformed" (230) that he was so marked and escaped. He believes Elya Gruner to be similarly marked now by the symbolic *X* Sammler sees on a condemned tailor shop (89). Like the Russian soldier, Gruner also shows "soil on his face" (141). Sammler's preoccupation with death, then, results from his experiences, past and present, his "deformity," his age, and, of course, his humanity. The theme of death is concluded with the death of Elya Gruner.

While Sammler is trying to persuade Angela to decency and Shula to honesty, Elya dies. Sammler feels that "this famous truth for which he was so keen, he had it now, or it had him" (312). The detachment Sammler has tried to maintain gives way. Weeping, he sees himself as a great iceberg dissolving in a vast sea (the sea of humanity, apparently, that he and Lal had discussed): "He felt that he was breaking up, that irregular big fragments inside were melting, sparkling with pain, floating off. . . . One more reason to live trickled out" (312). Standing over the still body of Elya in the post-mortem room, Sammler prays:

> Remember, God, the soul of Elya Gruner. . . . He was aware that he must meet, and he did meet—through all the confusion and degraded clowning of this life through which we are

speeding—he did meet the terms of his contract. The terms which, in his inmost heart, each man knows. As I know mine. As all know. For that is the truth of it—that we all know, God, that we know, that we know, we know, we know, we know. (313)

Sammler makes two points here that seem to summarize the substance of the novel. One is that life is dominated by "confusion and degraded clowning"; the bulk of the novel has been devoted to documenting this point. The other point is that there is something positive beyond the chaos of the finite that every man yearns toward, a still point of a turning world, and Elya, despite his vanity and underworld connections (which Shula's call has just verified), achieves a kind of essential virtue in accordance with this transcendent order.

In Sammler's view, Elya has become fully human through his love of family, decency, sense of duty and tradition, protective benevolence, and calm in the face of death. Such achievement, Sammler tells Angela, requires great effort because "only the capacity is natural" (30). But Sammler has insisted throughout the novel that each man knows in his heart of hearts the conditions he must satisfy to become fully human, to achieve virtue, or, in other words, to make peace with his God. "A few may comprehend," Sammler thinks, "that it is the strength to do one's duty daily and promptly that makes saints and heroes" (93). Despite the absurdity of human existence, Sammler admits that "almost daily" he has "strong impressions of eternity" and if there were nothing after death he would mainly miss his "God adumbrations in the many daily forms" (237). Each spirit, Sammler believes feels similarly in the midst of chaos:

> The spirit feels cheated, outraged, defiled, corrupted, fragmented, injured. Still it knows what it knows, and the knowledge cannot be gotten rid of. The spirit knows that its growth is the real aim of existence. (236)

Sammler declares further, "About essentials almost nothing could be said. . . . And, anyway, we know *what is what*" (261). In defense of his plea for decency, he affirms to Angela, "I only believe that there are things everyone knows, and must know" (307). This knowledge, of final and essential matters, forms the basis of Sammler's prayer over Gruner and is set against the overpowering negative aspects of the novel. Gruner may not seem to the reader the pillar of virtue that Sammler paints him, but it is Sammler's evaluation the novel offers, and that is the one we must take or leave. Sammler's prayer may suggest Herzog's last letter to God as D. P. M. Salter suggests (footnote 2), but the scene seems to me closer to the final scene of *Seize the Day*, in which Tommy Wilhelm weeps over the body of a stranger, symbolically drowning himself but expressing a desire to escape the madness of a pretender soul, to become better than he is. Water imagery is used in similar ways in both scenes.

With Sammler's prayer the novel ends, thus bringing to a conclusion the movement from actions to reflections—involving sexual madness, crime, distortions of the self, technology in a void, and death—that has constituted the basic narrative strategy. Sammler agrees to refer to his discourse in the long philosophical scene (201–37) as a recital, and the novel itself, at least formally, has something of that quality, a staged performance.[8] Animal imagery is employed appropriately, though perhaps heavy-handedly, to depict human bestiality, savagery, and grotesqueness. Water imagery is used skillfully to suggest overpopulation, immensity, turbulence, mystery, death, and the influence of the moon on the earth. There is an imbalance, however, between reflections and actions: The novel is heavy on ideas, light on fictional concretions, thematic embodiments.[9] Characterization, for example, is weak.

8. There is, in fact, extensive use made of imagery involving actors, acting, the stage, the theater, the arts, but this image-motif seemed too obvious to require examination in detail. Sammler does make several noteworthy observations in this context. He calls Wagner's music, for example, "background music for a pogrom" (136) and describes computer-generated music as "Art groveling before Science" (137).

9. In this regard, David Galloway charges Bellow with a lack of innovation, a failure of imagination, a falling back on stock situations and character-pairings: "*Mr. Sammler's Planet:* Bellow's Failure of Nerve," *Modern Fiction Studies*, 19, 1 (Spring 1973), 17–28.

With the exception of Mr. Sammler, the characters seem merely walk-on functionaries, as though they are bearing signs declaring their thematic significance: Angela as "Sad but Determined Sexual Liberation," Shula as "Quirky and Unfulfilled Modern Woman," the heckler as "Radical Campus Activist," Wallace as "Defiant Prodigal Son," Gruner as "Forgivably Flawed Human Virtue," and so on. The novel lacks the vital characterization and the density of texture that enriches, say, *The Adventures of Augie March.* The plot, too, is very loose. Despite occasional strategic juxtapositioning of parallel scenes,[10] there is no clearly established organic relationship between the pickpocket plot, the stolen-manuscript plot, and the death-of-Gruner plot. And the book reveals a paucity of the usual Bellow wit, perhaps because wit and indignation mix well only in satire.[11]

Since this chapter began by calling attention to the pervasive spirit of T. S. Eliot's poetry in the theme, tone, and point of view of Bellow's novel, it seems appropriate to conclude by applying one of Eliot's critical principles to an evaluation of Bellow's book. Here the unsatisfactory relationship between theme and form in the novel results from Bellow's failure to find adequate "objective correlatives," a set of concretions which embody his ideas and emotions

10. A few representative examples: Sammler's war experiences in Poland are compared with those of the Israeli Six-Day War; after passing through the wholesale butcher section of New York, Sammler witnesses Eisen's butchery of the pickpocket; Angela's sexy outfit at the death scene of her father reminds Sammler of the sexy English girls, with Italian photographers, cowering in bomb craters—absurd eroticism in the face of death in both cases.

11. In the review cited above, DeMott takes Bellow to task for not truly employing satire: "As a 'pure' gallery of fools, an enclosed world with a little of the flavor of a seventeenth-century 'humours' comedy or Enlightenment dunciad, an instructive catalogue of the puerilities of 'cultural revolution,' *Mr. Sammler's Planet* would have edge and point. . . .Instead of accepting itself as satire, a distorting mirror, it undertakes to pass itself off as a genuine imaginative encounter with, and penetration of, forces and beings it despises" (28). On the other hand, in a misreading of Bellow's tone that is either blatantly wrongheaded or tongue-in-cheek, another critic sees the success of the novel resting on Bellow's employment of sardonic humor and ironic modes: James Neil Harris, "One Critical Approach to *Mr. Sammler's Planet,*" *Twentieth-Century Literature,* 18 (October 1972), 235–50.

in coherent and organic fashion. Eliot brought a similar charge against Shakespeare's *Hamlet.* Finally, Gruner as a realized character is inadequately developed to carry the thematic weight of essential virtue that Sammler imposes upon him, as the peripheral characters are too clearly functionaries for various kinds of pronouncements. Thus contraries, the weight of opposition, are not given fair play and therefore the final vision is not earned. Mr. Sammler's detachment acts mainly to camouflage his indignation— Bellow's main point—and is consequently adventitious, and the use of animal and water imagery seems ultimately too pat in the movements between reflection and action. The ideas are important, frequently expressed with eloquence, and often intensely felt, but the form is thin. Consequently, one's intellectual faculties and critical sensibilities find themselves responding more to an essay than to a novel, more to actual objectives than to virtual objects. That it is a novel by Saul Bellow that occasions such responses is a matter of not a little disappointment.[12]

12. R. R. Dutton disagrees. In an adumbrated reading of the novel according to the cyclical theories of history of Spengler and Toynbee, Dutton sees the novel as built around four time spans from the Middle Ages to the present, and he judges the book to be "Saul Bellow's highest technical achievement." *Saul Bellow* (New York, 1971), p. 164. I genuinely wish I could agree with Professor Dutton. Brigitte Scheer-Schazler sees the form of the novel as "indicative of Bellow's present inclination for the 'nonfiction philosophical novel' as well as his modification of a literature courting silence." *Saul Bellow* (New York, 1972), p. 128. For a similar evaluation, see Peter Buitenhuis, "A Corresponding Fabric: The Urban World of Saul Bellow," *Costerus,* 8 (1973), 13–35.

8.

Bellow's Vision:
To Live and Not Die

> I went to the woods because I wished to live deliberate-
> ly, to front only the essential facts of life, and see if I
> could not learn what it had to teach, and not, when I
> came to die, discover that I had not lived.
> —Henry David Thoreau

In these concluding remarks I should like to move from
the critical description that has characterized the preced-
ing chapters to more evaluative observations in a comparative review of Bellow's heroes, who provide, collectively,
an insight into Bellow's vision of man. I shall thus establish
a standard according to which Bellow's human contribution as an artist can be assessed. Then I should like briefly
to place Bellow's creative vision in a literary tradition that
I am calling *neo-transcendentalism*. First, though, I feel I
must anticipate an objection that might be raised against
my procedure and respond to that objection—but without
bogging the reader down in critical polemics.

*   *   *   *   *

It is not unusual for the detractors of formalist criticism
to define formalism as narrowly as possible and then damn
it for its narrowness, especially for its alleged separation
of aesthetic qualities from human content.[1] The practice

1. F. W. Bateson is representative: "The New Critics have tended to
approach poetry, not as the embodiment of human values, but as a museum of emphasis and memorability devices, a kind of syntax." *Essays in
Critical Dissent* (Totowa, N. J., 1971), p. 12. See also Ihab Hassan, "Beyond a Theory of Literature: Intimations of Apocalypse?" *Comparative
Literature Studies*, 1 (1964), 261–71; and Joseph N. Riddle, "Against Formalism," *Genre*, 3 (1970), 156–72.

is unfair, and the charge is invalid. No major formalist is guilty of such aesthetic insularity either in intent or methodology. In fact, the "human" element is perhaps best approached through the aesthetic, as Robert Frost's poem "Stopping by Woods on a Snowy Evening" demonstrates:

> Whose woods these are I think I know.
> His house is in the village, though;
> He will not see me stopping here
> To watch his woods fill up with snow.
>
> My little horse must think it queer
> To stop without a farmhouse near
> Between the woods and frozen lake
> The darkest evening of the year.
>
> He gives his harness bells a shake
> To ask if there is some mistake.
> The only other sound's the sweep
> Of easy wind and downy flake.
>
> The woods are lovely, dark, and deep,
> But I have promises to keep,
> And miles to go before I sleep,
> And miles to go before I sleep.

One major distinction between the man and the horse in the poem is that the man has the capacity for an aesthetic experience, a feeling response to beauty. (The capacity for such response may never be highly developed, as the poem suggests in its contrast between the man enjoying the woods and the man who owns the woods but lives in the village.) Despite the cold and the pressure of his practical responsibilities ("promises to keep"), the man is transfixed by the beauty of the scene before him. The reflective tone of the last line intimates, too, that the man is attracted, at least subconsciously, to the eternal rest of death. The horse wants his oats, some rest, and the warmth of the barn; the man wants only, and temporarily, to contemplate the beauty and mystery of the snow and the woods and the falling of night. Engaged by patterns, textures, and quietude, the man is led to ponder meanings that remain, in the poem, concretely presentational: Nature, Beauty, Mortality, Responsibility, Eternality. Not only can the man be intellectually and emotionally engaged by beauty, as the horse cannot, the man can also foresee his own death, as the horse cannot. The man's contemplation defines his humanity.[2]

Contemplating the poem, the reader defines his humanity and enlarges its possibilities. The confrontation of the man with the snowy evening has its analogue in the reader's confrontation with the poem. The aesthetic experience of the poet's persona *in* the poem leads the reader to an equivalent aesthetic experience *of* the poem. What remains presentational in the contemplation of the man in the imagined woods becomes philosophically discursive in the contemplation and response of the reader of the poem. Universal human meanings about Nature, Beauty, Mortality, Responsibility, and Eternality emerge more explicitly in criticism, but they emerge only through the formal strategies of the poem: the contrasts between man and horse, man and man, man and nature, the linking rhyme scheme, the images of "easy wind" and "downy flake," and the woods as quiet, lovely, dark, deep, and cold (an image pattern that suggests, to the critic, a grave, a metonymy for the death which the man in the poem subconsciously yearns toward momentarily). The formalist critic certainly deals with such human content, but he gets at it through form. As Brooks said in the fifth "article of faith": "Form is meaning."

Geoffrey H. Hartman has carefully enunciated the notion that form and meaning are inseparable and that, therefore, statements about human values are ultimately made by formalist criticism. Though Hartman has some reservations about the scope of formalist criticism, he defines it fairly as

a method . . . of revealing the human content of art by a study of its formal properties. This definition does not say that form and content are separable, nor does it infer that the human and

2. The substance of this discussion grew out of a conversation with Cleanth Brooks on the afternoon of April 26, 1968, on the road to Corvallis, Oregon, where he was to lecture in the evening on Faulkner. The humanity of Professor Brooks on that evening (in his lecture and afterward) was gratifying evidence that formalist criticism is not at variance with humane values.

the formal could not be caught and exposited by a great inter-
preter. It does suggest that the literary scholar establishes a
priority which has procedural significance, and which engages
him mediately and dialectically with the formal properties of
the work of art.[3]

The point is worth repeating: The critic studies the formal
properties of art and thus discovers its human content. The
emphasis in this study has been on the formal properties
of Bellow's art, and each novel has been treated for the
most part as a discrete work. It seems appropriate to turn
now to a comparative look at Bellow's heroes in the interest of evaluation and a more explicit statement of human
content.

*   *   *   *   *

Joseph is the least appealing of all Bellow's heroes, I
think, and *Dangling Man* is the least satisfying novel. The
first judgment accounts for the second in part, but the
flaws go well beyond characterization. The reason Joseph
fails to move us as, say, Tommy Wilhelm does, is that his
suffering is too blatantly cerebral and self-centered. The
journal form in which the novel is written is appropriate
to the intellectual nature of the protagonist, certainly, but
it is in effect too personal, and the device of the "Spirit of
Alternatives" emerges as somewhat contrived. The dialogue with *Tu As Raison Aussi* and some of the entries in
the journal move very close to pure essay and thus threaten
the integrity of the novel. The structure of the book too
often escapes the shaping power of its texture.

Joseph's stance at the end of the novel, too, is problemat-
ical. Like Melville's Ahab and Bartleby, Joseph is surrounded by metaphorical walls, barriers to understanding
the principles according to which the world at large operates in relation to the individual. Failing to square actuality
with his "ideal construction," Joseph is first prompted, like
Ahab, to defiance, and then, like Bartleby, to withdrawal.
When his alienation becomes unendurable, he turns toward accommodation through service to the national

3. "Beyond Formalism," *Modern Language Notes*, 81, 5 (1966), 542.

cause, showing himself at the end to be a mellowed Ahab, a more courageous Bartleby. This is movement in the right direction, certainly, but it is very abrupt and somehow not in keeping with Joseph's character. That a man of Joseph's intellectual abilities could truly hope to answer the question, "How should a good man live?" and to reach others through "violence" and the "regimentation" of military service seems an excessive irony that cannot be attributed either to his youth or to his previous insularity.

Asa Leventhal, by contrast, is a fully realized artistic creation, and *The Victim* is second only to *Seize the Day* in unity and powerful totality of effect. *The Victim*, as its title suggests, is also the most naturalistic of Bellow's novels, and Leventhal the most realistic protagonist. He is not a hyperintellectual like Joseph or Herzog, nor is he a larky, optimistic free spirit like Augie March. He is too impassive, too earthbound and gloomy, to fit into either of these categories. He most closely resembles Henderson in his size and his earnest desire to live meaningfully and to do what is right, but he has none of Henderson's riotous comic spirit or powerful drive. There is no element of caricature in his characterization. Leventhal exhibits average middle-class ambitions for success and reveals, accordingly, an appropriate fear of failure through his own acts, through acts of others that reflect on him, or through the capriciousness of the system under which he lives. Because he is not a systematic conceptual thinker, he does not attempt to understand the world in terms of abstract theories; he tries only to discover a practical stance that will enable him to live in the world with some degree of peace. After much genuine anguish, Leventhal comes to terms with Mickey's death, with his own fear of failure from the caprice of fate or from an anti-Semitic world, and with the problem presented by Allbee. He comes to a more accurate conception of who he is, and he strikes an existential balance between what he owes to himself and what he owes to others. It is, however, a psychological adjustment mainly, not a philosophical justification; but it is all Leventhal needs and all, really, the reader expects of him. At the realistic level of the novel, this development is handled very skillfully through revealing situations, unifying metaphors, and convincing depth of psychological motivation.

Leventhal's success in striking a psychological balance in his own life does not, however, affect the imbalances in the larger world in which he lives. Implicit in Leventhal's personal problems are the ultimate metaphysical problems of Death, Evil, and Injustice. These concerns are handled unobtrusively at the symbolic level of the novel through literary and mythical allusion, but never at the expense of the realistic vehicle or its protagonist. Some persons escape the inequities of the system, the book acknowledges, but millions do not, and their victimization is often arbitrary and ineluctable. Leventhal's affirmation at the end is severely qualified, and his awareness of its limitations lends further weight to the book's larger vision and to the interaction of the realistic and symbolic levels. Bellow's achievement here is a "concrete universal" of the first order.

In Augie March, Bellow has created one of the most engaging and charming figures in American literature. Augie is the smiling, adoptable, easygoing perpetual adolescent. His quest for a worthwhile fate is the journey of every man toward a satisfying life. That he does not find the fate he seeks—the fulfillment of his vision of life lived according to the "axial lines"—within the course of the novel does not deter him from continuing to search, though he continues with less fervor and a more realistic sense of the world's imperfections and his own limitations. Instead of a worthwhile fate, what Augie discovers is a worthwhile attitude with which to deal with fate: a persistent optimism strengthened by laughter, the *animal ridens* in him. Despite the substantial evidence of disappointment with life in those all around him, Augie refuses to lead a disappointed life. He is not blind or indifferent to misfortune; he just will not allow his life to be built on it or his attitudes shaped by it.

Because it is a picaresque novel, *The Adventures of Augie March* does not even approach the unity of *The Victim* or *Seize the Day*, yet it does have a unity of its own. The strategy of opposites the novel employs gives to Augie's development both direction and coherence. His optimism and desire for freedom are exposed to many characters and situations that are inimical to his temperament, his aspirations, and his philosophical stance; but he emerges from the exposure largely unaffected. The extent of the exposure, though, serves finally to validate the quality of his continued optimism. His positive vision at the end is an aware—and thus an earned—vision. Not every episode or character in the novel contributes directly to this strategy, and consequently there appears to be a good deal of extraneous material, but even this usually adds to the book's charm. Whatever unity is lost through expansiveness is recovered through the compensating scope of human wisdom thus revealed. A more serious flaw is perhaps the uneasy line the novel walks between realism and romance, the Chicago scenes involving Augie at home being starkly different in kind from the exotic scenes in Mexico in which the bewildered Augie helps Thea in her attempts to catch iguanas with eagles. Nevertheless, it is a first-rate novel, and it clearly contains the seeds that later blossomed into *Henderson the Rain King* and *Herzog.*

In terms of structure and organic unity *Seize the Day* is without doubt Bellow's most successful work. The themes of failure, suffering, and painful rebirth are skillfully rendered in the texture of each scene and unified around the central image of drowning, which stands clearly as the termination of one kind of life, the beginning of another. The embodiment of structure in texture through the intrareferential elements within scene is enhanced even further by the cross references between scenes. A sustained tone of profound human emergency, moreover, imbues the total narrative with a moving poetic intensity.

Seize the Day is significant, of course, beyond the limits of its unity. The depiction of Tommy Wilhelm with all his flaws, his unsatisfied hungers, and his suffering is painfully vivid, and the people who reject or exploit him—Adler, Tamkin, Margaret—are frighteningly representative of the ambience of our age.[4] That Bellow can find in Wilhelm

4. "The ultimate consideration of the novel is a moral one. It concerns the human condition, the problem of the meaning of man's humanity in the world of the mid-twentieth century.

and in his plight a definition of the human and a basis for
hope, despite the surrounding forces of negation, is a measure of both Bellow's own humanity and his philosophical
wisdom. The vision is dark here, certainly, and there is no
celebration; but there is a hopeful awareness that darkness
does not cover the earth—at least not all day nor everywhere at once.

The celebration comes in *Henderson the Rain King*, the
exuberance of which may have resulted in part from a
reaction against the sustained depression that suffuses its
predecessor, for Bellow must contain like Augie March, a
large measure of the *animal ridens*, the laughing creature.
Henderson is the life-driven quester after profound experience and meaningful values, the spirit of us all seeking to
carry our lives to a certain height. He is both mock Messiah
and *Mensch*, at once a *shlemiel*, a *shlimazl*, and a savior.
The celebration of Henderson's achievement, his transformed vision and triumphant affirmation, is attended by
all the literary pomp and ceremony that Bellow can mus-
ter, and he musters a phenomenal amount. The many levels of parody that run through the novel merely add to the
playfulness appropriate to the childlike quality of Henderson's eagerness and his ultimate new vision.
Henderson's final qualified apotheosis is properly accentuated by the silently thundering sounds of an implied
celestial choir that is no less joyous for being also comic.
Henderson is a rugged 230-pound testament to the possibility for joy in an imperfect world. The force of Henderson's
affirmative stance and the intense reality of his character
testify to the validity of the positive vision he represents.

Some critics, among them Norman Mailer, have com-

"To understand Dr. Adler's cold detachment from his son's misery, one
must understand the essential nature of Dr. Tamkin, who stands as a
symbol for the new man of a new age of opportunism. Here is Bellow's
presentation of what man has become in a world which gives its most real
admiration to the image of success. . . . He[Tamkin] is a man who has
learned the weaknesses of the human condition and who puts his knowledge to practical use. He is presented as not only devoid of sympathetic
understanding but as one for whom the possibility of it has ceased to
exist." William J. Handy, "Saul Bellow and the Naturalistic Hero," *Texas
Studies in Literature and Language*, 5 (Winter 1964), 541.

plained that the book generates expectations it never sat-
isfies, that Henderson's affirmative last scene based on his
new vision of community and his commitment to human
service is too trite and superficial to satisfy the demands
growing out of his exposure to the profundity of Willatale
(Grun-tu-molani), Dahfu and Atti (pure Being), and the
ageless, exotic African interior. Such criticism, I think, is
invalid. That such an expectation has been created and
that these readers have felt Bellow capable of satisfying the
expectation, even though they think he fails, can surely be
taken, on the one hand, as a measure of Bellow's power
and, on the other, as an indication of his recognition of the
limitations of his subject matter and his art. Evidence for
affirmation in an imperfect world is peculiar to each man's
experience in the world; it does not lend itself to universal
revelations or programmatic formulas, however desirable
such programs might be. Furthermore, to take Henderson
from his celebratory last scene on to medical school and
further testing of his mettle would be, obviously, to involve
him in further struggles and perhaps other affirmations.
But that would be another novel. In this novel, Bellow
earns Henderson's affirmation, not so much by an accumulation of specific evidence for a positive universal vision, but by the superbly imaginative creation of a single
spectacular affirmer. In the awe-inspiring presence of
"Leo" Henderson, Rain King and Medicine Man, dancing
triumphantly around a plane in snowy Newfoundland to
the strains of the "Hallelujah Chorus," affirmation is a
demonstrated fact—the evidence on which it rests is relatively insignificant. Henderson is a monumental fictional
creation, worthy to take his place alongside Hester, Huck,
and Holden in the American literary canon.

Perhaps even Herzog is eligible to joint this list, for the
Joseph of *Dangling Man* comes to full maturity in the novel
that showcases the character of Moses E. Herzog. Here,
too, is the happy blending of the probing, introspective,
well-made novel of ideas with the fast and loose, free-
swinging picaresque quest novel. The journey, though, is
a journey of the mind, and the pace is set by the anxious
intellect groping for a reconciliation of theoretical wisdom

with actual pain. The transcendental solution of the heart that Herzog achieves is not a negation of the intellect, but an elevation of feeling to a status equal to that of ideas, a shift in values which the academically oriented Herzog had been reluctant to accept out of a sense of intellectual obligation. What makes Herzog a more appealing character than Joseph is the greater depth of his intelligence and his ability to distance himself from his emotional pain through humor, the psychic defense of a comic stance. Herzog is also more capable than Joseph of experiencing genuine deep feeling for other human beings and is more tolerant of their shortcomings. His humanity, in short, bears a more convincing stamp of authenticity.

Like Tommy Wilhelm, Herzog suffers greatly; but unlike Wilhelm, Herzog can detach himself from his suffering and attempt to put it in some kind of philosophical perspective. Like Augie March, Herzog is both in flight and on a quest, but his path is neither as broad nor as exotic as Augie's. Like Leventhal and Henderson, Herzog reaches an affirmation, but his affirmation is not as severely qualified as Leventhal's and not as spectacular as Henderson's. In a quiet way, Herzog represents the culmination of most of the Bellovian heroes who have preceded him, and he exhibits in modern qualified-heroic measure that passion for life which is at the very center of Bellow's vision of man, what Ihab Hassan called, in speaking of the new hero in contemporary fiction, "man's quenchless desire to affirm, despite the voids and vicissitudes of our age, the human sense of *life*." [5] Bellow's novels speak of many things, of course, but the dominant impression left by the experience of each of his heroes is of the vibrant "unabstracted bodiness" of the "human sense of *life*!"

Even *Mr. Sammler's Planet*, death-ridden and chaos-riddled as it is, speaks through its outrage for a return to the human possibilities for a sane and satisfying life. Mr. Sammler is Bellow's reflective hero. He is too old, too experienced, and too wise to be subject to new revelations or dramatic transformation of character, but he is not so

5. Ihab Hassan, *Radical Innocence* (Princeton, 1961), p. 6.

old that he no longer cares about himself and others and the quality of their lives. His ostensible detachment is constantly vitiated by the gravitational pull of the human beings around him—however grotesque most of them are. Like Herzog, Sammler desires that each life be completed in some meaningful way before death (though his detachment may vitiate his sympathy), and from this desire comes his love for Gruner, his anxiety over Shula, his advice to Wallace, his admonitions to Angela, his compassion for the pickpocket, and his anger over the mindlessness of mass society. So pathetically short of realizing their potential for a meaningful life are most of the people in Sammler's world that they are not even aware that such potential exists. Thus the bleakness of the book and thus, formally, the disparity between theme and form, the spilling-over of outrage into didacticism.

Mr. Sammler describes his stance as a "vivid shuffle with its pangs of higher intuition from the one side and the continual muddy suck of the grave underfoot" (261). In the name of the "higher intuition," the transcendent order beyond what Augie learned to call *moha* (the Bronx cheer of the conditioning forces), Sammler has offered resistance to chaos and to the intimidation of inescapable death, but the resistance grows harder as he grows older and the forces of chaos hurl him with terrifying centrifugal force away from the still center. There is no *animal ridens* to generate saving laughter here, nor a newfound land to occasion a celebrative dance, nor even the momentary repose of a Thoreauvian Ludeyville. All Sammler can do is assert through his prayer that the human heart can still find its way to transcendent order and a meaningful life, and there rests his commitment, and Mr. Sammler's prayer serves as the temporary benediction to Bellow's novelistic canon. Huck Finn said it, and Bellow's fiction reaffirms the truth: "You can't pray a lie." In the thick of the fray, a prayer may be thin stuff, but it is on the side of Right, it is genuine, and it is far better than maniacal laughter, silent despair, or screaming death. Finally, Bellow's novelistic stance suggests a firm alignment with the nineteenth-century American transcendentalists.

*　　*　　*　　*　　*

In a recent book on contemporary American fiction, Tony Tanner perceptively identifies two opposing impulses in American writers:

> I shall try to show that there is an abiding dream in American literature that an unpatterned, unconditioned life is possible, in which your movements and stillnesses, choices and repudiations are all your own; and that there is also an abiding dread that someone else is patterning your life, that there are all sorts of invisible plots afoot to rob you of your autonomy of thought and action, that conditioning is ubiquitous. The problematical and ambiguous relationship of the self to patterns of all kinds—social, psychological, linguistic—is an obsession among recent American writers.[6]

The notions of a "dread" and a "dream" echo, it seems to me, a long-standing polarity in American literature. In the broadest terms, the polarity is the pessimistic versus the optimistic traditions.

The pessimistic tradition can be traced back to Puritanism and then through Naturalism to current Black Humor fiction. The Puritan God, if we can believe Jonathan Edwards, was wrathful and arbitrary, and His Grace was, at best, enigmatic. No matter how the Puritan rationalized the justice of his fate, he must have felt himself the victim of a theological determinism. The course of his life had been determined for him by nebulous, albeit divine, forces without regard for his individual merit or aspirations. In the literature of the American naturalists—Crane, Dreiser, Norris, London, and others—theological determinism was augmented by scientific determinism. Heredity and environment became the determinants. Predestination, original sin, and eternal damnation took the forms of sociological and biochemical determinism, human weakness, and inescapable—and final—death. Man was a victim of forces that he could neither understand nor control. In the metaphors of the time he was "a ship without a rudder," "a wisp in the wind," "a flower in a mud puddle," "a pawn

6. Tony Tanner, *City of Words* (New York, 1971), p. 15.

on the chessboard of fate." From Darwinian theories of evolution grew the naturalistic dread that man was being manipulated like any other creature by an indifferent cosmic process. The most recent popular spokesmen in the pessimistic tradition are the Black Humorists: John Barth, Kurt Vonnegut, J P. Donleavy, Joseph Heller, Bruce Jay Friedman, John Hawkes, and others. Instead of total depravity, wrathful divinity, and various forms of deterministic damnation, they chant the doctrines of Absurdity, Alienation, Dehumanization, Despair, and Entropy. In fact, Black Humor might well be called Neo-Puritanism.[7] The Puritan's arbitrary God in all His wrath has been replaced by modern technocracy in all its mindlessness, but man is still a victim. The Puritan expressed his despair in meek submission; The Black Humorist expresses his in mocking laughter, yet they are brothers under the skin. In the pessimistic tradition, then, man has been viewed as a victim of several kinds of deterministic forces: theological, sociological and biological, and technological.

The pessimistic vision, though, has coexisted with an optimistic counterpart that views man as a resistant hero, or at least as a possessor of free will with the capacity for heroism. In the beginning of our literary tradition, Puritanism enjoyed the status of orthodoxy, but it had to exist in the face of several resistant heterodoxies: Arminianism, Quakerism, Deism, Unitarianism, and Universalism. These positive visions rejected predestination, inherited guilt, the loss of free will, everlasting punishment, vicarious atonement, and the notion of mortal separation from an arbitrary and wrathful God. In short, they restored human possibilities. Their faith in the Divine included faith in the

7. Following Leslie Fiedler, one might also make a case for calling it "Neo-Gothicism," since it mocks middle-class ideals and shifts the focus from the triumph of virtue ("the persecuted principle of salvation") to the power of darkness ("the persecuting principle of damnation"); *Love and Death in the American Novel* (New York, 1960), pp. 106–48. Whatever one calls Black Humor, it is only fair to say that it has received more positive treatment that I have given it here. See, for example, Robert Scholes, *The Fabulators* (New York, 1967); Charles B. Harris, *Contemporary American Novelists of the Absurd* (New Haven, 1971); and Raymond M. Olderman, *Beyond the Waste Land* (New Haven, 1972).

human. The creeds of these groups were never as rigidly
codified as the Puritan creed, and codification became
even harder to approach in their successors, the New England transcendentalists. Seeing the visible world as symbolic of a higher spiritual reality, the transcendentalists
affirmed a belief in the strength, imagination, dignity, and
moral perfectibility of man, a teleologically inspired cor-
respondence between man and nature, a faith in democratic ideals (if man would rise to them), and thus a fervent
hope for human growth and progress.[8] Emerson urged
self-reliance, Thoreau applauded individual dignity and
heroism and, with Emerson, celebrated nature; and Whitman saw the nation—and the world—spiralling ever upward toward an eventual union with the Divine. The "Divine" was a universal, creative, permeating force or spirit,
not an anthropomorphic deity susceptible to petitions or
propitiations. Attuning himself to such a spirit, man could
become capable of unlimited moral growth. The writers of
recent fiction who are continuing in the spirit of Emerson,
Thoreau, and Whitman are Ralph Ellison, Bernard Mala-
mud, Ken Kesey,[9] and Saul Bellow—the neo-transcenden-
talists. Discussion of the first three writers is appropriate
subject matter for another effort elsewhere. I mention
them here only to indicate that Bellow does not work alone
in the optimistic tradition.

To work in the spirit of the transcendentalists is as much

8. Even within the ranks of the transcendentalists there was polarity.
Hawthorne and Melville believed that the visible world was symbolic of
an invisible world all right, but they had serious reservations about the
nature of that other realm. Hawthorne did not want to commit himself
about it, though he did speculate gloomily about all the possibilities, but
Melville was issuing "no's" in various degrees of thunder from Bartleby's
"I would prefer not to" to Ahab's barbed defiance of the white whale
whether he were agent or principal. The active defiance typified by Ahab
gave way toward the end of the nineteenth century to a largely passive
despair in the form of literary naturalism. The bifurcation of transcendentalism into positive and negative traditions is treated by C. C. Walcutt
in *American Literary Naturalism: A Divided Stream* (Minneapolis, 1956).

9. Kesey is frequently—but erroneously—classified as a Black Humorist. Such classification rests on his use of surrealistic techniques and
occasional *caricatura* but ignores his themes of self-reliance, individual
heroism, brotherhood, and the renewal of universal contacts (through
rivers, geese, trees, the moon, etc.).

as a writer can do, since transcendentalism was more an attitude than an explicit systematic philosophy. It was certainly not a program, and the critic who attempted to formulate one for it would be guilty of monumental temerity. What one can do is point to the themes and attitudes that Bellow has in common with the transcendentalists as a way of fitting him into a central literary tradition, although it is clear that Bellow's work can be related to several traditions (Russian realism, for example, or Yiddish humor). The justification for drawing a parallel between Bellow's novels and transcendentalism must come from Bellow's work, and there, as we have seen, transcendentalist quotations and allusions abound. Leventhal's situation in *The Victim* parallels Dimmesdale's in Hawthorne's *The Scarlet Letter* ; Augie's optimism restates that of Emerson and Whitman; Wilhelm affirms an oversoul when he declares, "There is a larger body, and from this you cannot be separated" (84); Henderson's opposition to hunting and materialism comes from Thoreau, and his trip to Africa is, in a sense, glossed by *Walden* ; Herzog is led through the philosophical tangle of Reality Instructors by the wisdom of Emerson, Thoreau, and Whitman, whom he quotes throughout the novel; and Mr. Sammler can reach his "still center" only by an act of transcendence, a rising above the mass of men leading lives of "quiet desperation" all around him.

Like his predecessors, Bellow as neo-transcendentalist sounds again and again the themes of nature, self-reliance, freedom, individual heroism, and renewal of universal contacts, yet he affirms the possibilities of democracy and civilization while lamenting the failure of Americans to realize all of their possibilities. He knows well the problems of the individual versus society. The paradox of the one in counterpoise with the many is at the center of Emerson's "Self-Reliance," Thoreau's "Civil Disobedience," and Whitman's *Leaves of Grass*, in which he both sang the "simple separate person" and emphasized the words "en masse" and "democratic." Whitman's metaphor "the float forever held in solution" expressed at once the relation between the individual and the mass, the temporal and the eternal, the soul and the oversoul. Similar tensions between individual needs and social and metaphysical exigencies complicate the lives of Joseph, Leventhal, Wilhelm, Herzog, and Mr. Sammler. The delicate balance between what a person owes himself and what he owes to others, Bellow shows, is never easily reached, and it must constantly be reconfirmed in the light of the Other, what Herzog calls the "incomprehensible" that makes life more than "a cloud of particles, more facticity" (266).

It is in the affirmative tone of celebration, however, that Bellow most resembles the transcendentalists. Augie learns to overcome the conditioning forces of the finite *(moha)* through love, and he transforms the final winter scene into happiness through laughter. Henderson's turbulent spirit finds peace in its newly discovered service motive. His resolution leads him singing through the African wilds and sets him dancing in honor of his new life on the frozen ground of Newfoundland. Herzog moves through existential terror to transcendental peace and discovers joy in the restoration of his pastoral soul in accordance with the law of the heart. Commenting on this hopeful strain in recent fiction, Richard Rupp "takes an Emersonian view: 'We ought to celebrate this hour by expressions of manly joy. . . . When all is said and done, the rapt saint is found the only logician. Not exhortation, not argument becomes our lips, but paeans of joy and praise.' " Following Emerson, Rupp concludes that "the best of our novelists seem to move *toward* celebration, although that move is tentative, groping, and fleeting. Our most responsible fiction manifests an assent to reality, a willingness to live."[10] Unquestionably one of our best novelists, Bellow has clearly committed himself in his fiction to the cause of

10. *Celebration in Postwar American Fiction* (Coral Gables, Fla., 1970), p. 9. Though they do not use the term *neo-transcendentalism*, a number of critics have written on the optimistic strain in contemporary fiction and have mentioned frequently, but not systematically, the names, the concepts, and the terminology of the nineteenth-century transcendentalists. Each critic has a different name for the positive impulse, but each one is focusing on a resistant, creative, affirmative, celebrative spirit in contemporary American fiction. In addition to Rupp, see Marcus Klein, *After Alienation* (Cleveland, 1962); Ihab Hassan, *Radical Innocence* (New York, 1961); Howard Harper, *Desperate Faith* (Chapel Hill, N.C., 1967);

celebration, reaffirming like the transcendentalists before him the human possibilities of the dream despite the power of the dread.

*   *   *   *   *

Bellow's vision of the dream would be meaningless, of course, unless he also acknowledged the reality of the dread. Every wish, Augie learned, lives in the face of its opposite, and a writer, as Robert Penn Warren demonstrated, must "make his peace with Mercutio," must earn his vision. Bellow earns his vision with every novel. He gives more than fair play to the forces of dread in the derelicts that haunt Leventhal, in the mess of Wilhelm's life, in the anguish of Herzog, in the sordid madness of the city in which Mr. Sammler must seek balance, but Bellow puts his money on the dream. His fiction testifies to the resiliency and the aspiration of the human spirit and, in a nondoctrinaire way, to a force larger than the individual somewhere "out where it is incomprehensible." Herzog "can only pray toward it" (326) as does Mr. Sammler in the midst of his pain. God, Love, Prime Mover, Life Force, *Élan Vital*, or simply Creative Spirit, it is a Universal that has the power, properly intuited, to give meaning to human existence, to inspire brotherhood, to sustain the dream.

A reader does not need to believe in an orthodox divinity in order to understand and appreciate Bellow's fiction, but he will find it helpful, I think, to know something about the Yellow Brick Road and the Second Star to the Right. He will also need to be attentive to venerable flesh overlapping elbows as a sign of character, and he should be capable of gratitude that all children have cheeks and all mothers have handkerchiefs and spittle to keep them clean. Bellow's "message" is clear. Through Herzog, he asks, "Let life continue—we may not deserve it, but let it continue" (51); and with Auden, he urges that we love our crooked neighbors with our crooked hearts, that in the midst of eros and dust, negation and despair, we show an affirming flame.

Max T. Schulz, *Radical Sophistication* (Athens, Ohio, 1969); Helen Weinberg, *The New Novel in America* (Ithaca, N. Y., 1970).

Bibliography

Reviews of *Dangling Man*

Chamberlain, John, *New York Times*, March 25, 1944, p. 13.
De Vries, Peter, *Chicago Sun Bookweek*, April 9, 1944, p. 3.
Fearing, Kenneth, *NYTBR*, 49 (March 26, 1944), 5, 15.
Hale, Lionel, *Observer*, January 12, 1947, p. 3.
Heppenstall, Rayner, *New Statesman and Nation*, n.s. 32 (December 28, 1946), 488–89.
Kristol, Irving, *Politics*, 1 (June 1944), 156.
Kupferberg, Herbert, *NYHTBR*, 20 (April 9, 1944), 11.
Mayberry, George, *New Republic*, 110 (April 3, 1944), 473–74.
O'Brien, Kate, *Spectator*, 178 (January 3, 1947), 27.
Rothman, N. L. *SRL*, 27 (April 15, 1944), 27.
Schorer, Mark, *Kenyon Review*, 6 (Summer 1944), 459–61.
Schwartz, Delmore, *Partisan Review*, 11 (Summer 1944), 348–50.
Time, 43 (May 8, 1944), 104.
TLS, January 11, 1947, p. 21.
Trilling, Diana, *Nation*, 158 (April 15, 1944), 455.
Wilson, Edmund, *The New Yorker*, 20 (April 1, 1944), 78, 81.

Reviews of *The Victim*

Downer, Alan S., *NYTBR*, 52 (November 30, 1947), 29.
Farrelly, John, *New Republic*, 117 (December 8, 1947), 27–28.
Fiedler, Leslie, *Kenyon Review*, 10 (Summer 1948), 519–27.
Gibbs, Wolcott, *The New Yorker*, 28 (May 10, 1952), 58 (drama).
Greenberg, Martin, *Commentary*, 5 (January 1948), 86–87.
Hale, Lionel, *Observer*, June 13, 1948, p. 3.
Hardwick, Elizabeth, *Partisan Review*, 15 (January 1948), 108–17.
Match, Richard, *NYHTBR*, 24 (November 23, 1947), 10.
Poore, Charles, *New York Times*, November 22, 1947, p. 13.
Smith, R. D., *Spectator*, 180 (June 4, 1948), 686, 688.
Straus, Ralph, *Sunday Times* (London), June 6, 1948, p. 3.
Time, 50 (December 1, 1947), 111–12.
Trilling, Diana, *Nation*, 166 (January 3, 1948), 24–25.
Wilson, Edmund, *The New Yorker*, 23 (December 13, 1947), 139 –40.

Reviews of *The Adventures of Augie March*

American Scholar, 23 (Winter 1953–1954), 126.

Amis, Kingsley, *Spectator*, 192 (May 21, 1954), 626.

Cassidy, T. E., *Commonweal*, 58 (October 2, 1953), 636.

Connole, John, *America*, 90 (October 31, 1953), 133.

Crane, Milton, Chicago *Sunday Tribune Magazine of Books*, September 20, 1953, p. 4.

Davis, Robert Gorham, *NYTBR*, 58 (September 20, 1953), 1, 36.

Finn, James, *Chicago Review*, 8 (Spring–Summer 1954), 104–11.

Geismar, Maxwell, *Nation*, 177 (November 14, 1953), 404.

Harwell, Meade, *Southwest Review*, 39 (Summer 1954), 273–76.

Hicks, Granville, *New Leader*, 36 (September 21, 1953), 23–24.

Hopkinson, Tom, *London Magazine*, 1 (August 1954), 82, 84, 86.

Hughes, Riley, *Catholic World*, 178 (December 1953), 233–34.

Kristol, Irving, *Encounter*, 3 (July 1954), 74–75.

Mizener, Arthur, *NYHTBR*, 30 (September 20, 1953), 2.

Newsweek, 42 (September 21, 1953), 102, 104.

Pickrel, Paul, *Yale Review*, n.s. 43 (Autumn 1953), x.

Podhoretz, Norman, *Commentary*, 16 (October 1953), 378–80.

Popkin, Henry, *Kenyon Review*, 16 (Spring 1954), 329–34.

Prescott, Orville, *New York Times*, September 18, 1953, p. 21.

Priestley, J. B., *Sunday Times* (London), May 9, 1954, p. 5.

Pritchett, V. S., *New Statesman and Nation*, n.s. 47 (June 19, 1954), 803.

Rolo, Charles J., *Atlantic*, 192 (October 1953), 86–87.

Rosenberg, Dorothy, San Francisco *Sunday Chronicle*, October 25, 1953, p. 18.

Schorer, Mark, *Hudson Review*, 7 (Spring 1954), 136–41.

Schwartz, Delmore, *Partisan Review*, 21 (January-February 1954), 112–15.

Time, 62 (September 21, 1953), 114, 117.

TLS, June 4, 1954, p. 357.

Walbridge, Earle F., *Library Journal*, 78 (September 15, 1953), 1529–30.

Warren, Robert Penn, *New Republic*, 129 (November 2, 1953), 22–23.

Webster, Harvey Curtis, *SRL*, 36 (September 19, 1953), 13–14.

West, Anthony, *The New Yorker*, 29 (September 26, 1953), 140, 142, 145.

West, Ray B., Jr., *Shenandoah*, 5 (Winter 1953), 85–90.

Wilson, Angus, *Observer*, May 9, 1954, p. 9.

Reviews of *Seize the Day*

Allen, Walter, *New Statesman and Nation*, n.s. 53 (April 27, 1957), 547–48.

Alpert, Hollis, *SRL*, 39 (November 24, 1956), 18, 34.
Baker, Robert, *Chicago Review*, 11 (Spring 1957), 107–10.
Bayley, John, *Spectator*, 198 (June 7, 1957), 758.
Bowen, Robert, *Northwest Review*, 1 (Spring 1957), 52–56.
Crane, Milton, Chicago *Sunday Tribune Magazine of Books*, December 30, 1956, p. 7.
Fenton, Charles A., *Yale Review*, 46 (Spring 1957), 452.
Fiedler, Leslie, *The Reporter*, 15 (December 13, 1956), 45–46.
Flint, R. W., *Partisan Review*, 24 (Winter 1957), 139–45.
Gill, Brendan, *The New Yorker*, 32 (January 5, 1957), 69–70.
Gilman, Richard, *Commonweal*, 78 (March 29, 1963), 21 (drama).
Gold, Herbert, *Nation*, 183 (November 17, 1956), 435–36.
Hicks, Granville, *New Leader*, 39 (November 26, 1956), 24–25.
Hogan, William, San Francisco *Chronicle*, November 15, 1956, p. 27.
Hopkinson, Tom, *Observer*, April 21, 1957, p. 11.
Kazin, Alfred, *NYTBR*, 61 (November 18, 1956), 5, 36.
Lynch, John, *Commonweal,* 65 (November 30, 1956), 238–39.
Newsweek, 48 (November 19, 1956), 142–43.
Pickrel, Paul, *Harper's*, 213 (December 1956), 100.
Rolo, Charles J., *Atlantic*, 199 (January 1957), 86–87.
Rugoff, Milton, *NYHTBR*, 33 (November 18, 1956), 3.
Schwartz, Edward, *New Republic*, 135 (December 3, 1956), 20–21.
Swados, Harvey, *New York Post Weekend Magazine*, November 18, 1956, p. 11.
Swan, Michael, *Sunday Times* (London), April 21, 1957, p. 7.
Time, 68 (November 19, 1956), 122.
TLS, May 10, 1957, p. 285.
West, Ray B., Jr., *Sewanee Review*, 65 (Summer 1957, 498–508.
Wyndham, Francis, *London Magazine*, 4 (August 1957), 66.

Reviews of *Henderson the Rain King*

Baker, Carlos, *NYTBR*, 64 (February 22, 1959), 4–5.
Cruttwell, Patrick, *Hudson Review*, 12 (Summer 1959), 286–95.
Curley, T. F., *Commonweal*, 70 (April 17, 1959), 84.
Gold, Herbert, *Nation*, 188 (February 21, 1959), 169–72.
Hardwick, Elizabeth, *Partisan Review*, 26 (Spring 1959), 299–303.
Hicks, Granville, *SRL*, 42 (February 21, 1959), 20.
Hogan, William, San Francisco *Chronicle*, February 23, 1959, p. 25.
Jacobson, Dan, *Spectator*, 202 (May 22, 1959), 735.
Kogan, Herman, Chicago *Sunday Tribune Magazine of Books*, February 22, 1959, p. 3.
Leach, Elsie, *Western Humanities Review*, 14 (Spring 1960), 223–34.
Maddocks, Melvin, *Christian Science Monitor*, February 26, 1959, p. 11.

Malcolm, Donald, *The New Yorker*, 35 (March 14, 1959), 171–73.
Newsweek, 53 (February 23, 1959), 106.
Pickrel, Paul, *Harper's*, 218 (March 1959), 104.
Podhoretz, Norman, *NYHTBR*, 35 (February 22, 1959), 3.
Prescott, Orville, *New York Times*, February 23, 1959, p. 21.
Price, Martin, *Yale Review*, n.s. 48 (Spring 1959), 453–56.
Rolo, Charles J., *Atlantic*, 203 (March 1959), 88.
Scott, J. D., *Sunday Times* (London), May 24, 1959, p. 15.
Stern, Richard G., *Kenyon Review*, 21 (Autumn 1959), 655–56.
Swados, Harvey, *New Leader*, 42 (March 23, 1959), 23–24.
Time, 73 (February 23, 1959), 102.
TLS, June 12, 1959, p. 352.
Wain, John, *Observer*, May 24, 1959, p. 21.
Waterhouse, Keith, *New Statesman*, n.s. 57 (June 6, 1959), 805–6.
Weales, Gerald, *The Reporter*, 20 (March 19, 1959), 46–47.
Whittemore, Reed, *New Republic*, 140 (March 16, 1959), 17–18.
Wilson, Angus, *Observer*, "Books of the Year," December 27, 1959, p. 8.

Reviews of *Herzog*

Barrett, William, *Atlantic*, 214 (November, 1964), 192, 196.
Battaglia, Frank, San Francisco *Chronicle*, March 7, 1965, p. 43.
Capon, Robert F., *America*, 112 (March 27, 1964), 425–27.
Chevigny, Bell Gale, *Village Voice*, October 8, 1964, pp. 6, 17.
Curley, Thomas, *Commonweal*, 81 (October 23, 1964), 137–38.
Davenport, Guy, *National Review*, 16 (November 3, 1964), 978–79.
Elliot, George P., *Nation*, 199 (October 19, 1964), 252–54.
Ellmann, Richard, *Chicago Sun-Times Bookweek*, September 27, 1964, p. 1.
Gill, Brendan, *The New Yorker*, 40 (October 3, 1964), 218–22.
Gross, J., *Encounter*, 25 (July 1965), 64–65.
Hicks, Granville, *SRL*, 47 (September 19, 1964), 37–38.
Howe, Irving, *New Republic*, 151 (September 19, 1964), 21–26.
Kermode, F., *New Statesman*, 69 (February 5, 1965), 200–201.
Klein, Marcus, *The Reporter*, 31 (October 22, 1964), 53–54.
Maddocks, Melvin, *Christian Science Monitor*, September 24, 1964, p. 7.
Moynahan, Julian, *NYTBR*, 69 (September 20, 1964), 1, 41.
Newsweek, 64 (September 21, 1964), 114.
Pickrel, Paul, *Harper's*, 229 (October 1964), 128.
Poirier, R., *Partisan Review*, 32 (Spring 1965), 264–71.
Pritchett, V. S., *New York Review of Books*, 3 (October 22, 1964), 4–5.
Rahv, Philip, *New York Herald Tribune Book Week*, September 20, 1964, pp. 1, 14, 16.
Rovit, Earl, *American Scholar*, 34 (Spring 1965), 292, 294 ff.

Scott, N. A., *Christian Century*, 81 (December 16, 1964), 1562–63.
Solotaroff, Theodore, *Commentary*, 38 (December 1964), 63–66.
Time, 84 (September 25, 1964), 105.
TLS, February 4, 1965, p. 81.

Reviews of *Mr. Sammler's Planet*

Bayley, John, *The Listener*, 84 (July 9, 1970), 51–52.
Braine, John, *National Review*, 22 (March 10, 1970), 264–66.
Broyard, Anatole, *NYTBR*, February 1, 1970, pp. 1, 40.
DeMott, Benjamin, *Saturday Review*, 53 (February 7, 1970), 25–28, 37.
Epstein, Joseph, *Book World*, February 1, 1970, p. 1.
Fletcher, Janet, *Library Journal*, 95 (February 1, 1970), 511.
Gray, P. E., *Yale Review*, 69 (March 1970), 432–33.
Gross, Beverly, *Nation*, 210 (February 9, 1970), 153–55.
Howe, Irving, *Harper's*, 240 (February 1970), 106, 108, 110, 114.
Katz, Phyllis R., *Best Seller*, 29 (February 1, 1970), 409–10.
Kazin, Alfred, *New York Review of Books*, 15 (December 3, 1970), 3–4.
Kiely, Robert, *Christian Science Monitor*, February 5, 1970, p. B–11.
Lindroth, James R., *America*, 122 (February 21, 1970), 190.
Lurie, Alison, *New Statesman*, 80 (July 10, 1970), 19.
Newsweek, 75 (February 2, 1970), 77.
Oates, Joyce C., *Critic*, 28 (May 1970), 68–69.
Opdahl, Keith, *Commonweal*, 91 (February 13, 1970), 535–36.
Samuels, C. T., *New Republic*, 162 (February 7, 1970), 27–30.
Sissman, L. E., *New Yorker*, 45 (January 31, 1970), 82, 85–87.
Stock, Irwin, *Commentary*, 49 (May 1970), 89–90, 92–94.
Time, 95 (February 9, 1970), 81–84.
TLS, July 9, 1970, p. 749.
VaQR, 46 (Spring 1970), xl–xli.

Articles

Allen, Michael. "Idiomatic Language in Two Novels by Saul Bellow," *Journal of American Studies*, 1 (October 1967), 275–80.
Alter, Robert. "The Stature of Saul Bellow," *Midstream*, 10 (December 1964), 3–15.
Baim, Joseph, "Escape from Intellection: Saul Bellow's *Dangling Man*," *University Review*, 37 (1969), 28–34.
Baker, Sheridan. "Saul Bellow's Bout with Chivalry," *Criticism*, 9 (Spring 1967), 109–22.

Bellow, Saul. An interview with Jay Nash and Ron Offen. *Chicago Literary Times* (December 1964), p. 10.

———. "Laughter in the Ghetto," *Saturday Review,* 36 (May 30, 1953), 15.

———. "How I Wrote Augie March's Story," *NYTBR* (January 31, 1954), pp. 3, 17.

Bergler, Edmund. "Writers of Half-Talent," *American Imago,* 14 (Summer 1957), 155–64.

Bezanker, Abraham. "The Odyssey of Saul Bellow," *Yale Review,* 58 (Spring 1969), 359–71.

Bradbury, Malcolm. "Saul Bellow's *The Victim,*" *The Critical Quarterly,* 5 (Summer 1957), 155–64.

———. "Saul Bellow and the Naturalist Tradition," *Review of English Literature,* 4 (October 1963), 80–92.

Buitenhuis, Peter. "A Corresponding Fabric: The Urban World of Saul Bellow," *Costerus,* 8 (1973), 13–35.

Chapman, Abraham. "The Image of Man as Portrayed by Saul Bellow," *College Language Association Journal,* 19 (1967), 285–98.

Chase, Richard. "The Adventures of Saul Bellow," *Commentary,* 27 (April 1959), 323–30.

Clay, George R. "Jewish Hero in American Fiction," *The Reporter,* 17 (September 19, 1956), 43–46.

Cook, Bruce. "Saul Bellow: A Mood of Protest," *Perspective,* 12 (February 1963), 47–50.

Crozier, Robert D. "Theme in *Augie March,*" *Critique,* 7 (Spring 1965), 18–32.

Detweiler, Robert. "Patterns of Rebirth in *Henderson the Rain King,*" *Modern Fiction Studies,* 12 (Winter 1966–67), 405–14.

Deuesberg, Jacques C. "Un jeune romancier Amercain: Saul Bellow," *Synthesis,* 10 (May–June, 1955), 149–50.

Donoghue, Denis, "Commitment and the *Dangling Man,*" *Studies: An Irish Quarterly Review,* 53 (Summer 1964), 174–87.

Downer, Alan S. "Skulduggery in Chungking and Manhattan," *NYTBR,* 52 (November 30, 1947), 29.

Eisinger, Chester E. "Saul Bellow: Love and Identity," *Accent,* 18 (Summer 1958), 179–203.

Elliot, George. "Hurtsog, Hairtsog, Heart's Hog?" *Nation,* 199 (October 19, 1964), 252–54.

Fiedler, Leslie A. "The Breakthrough: The American Jewish Novelist and the Fictional Image of the Jew," *Midstream,* 4 (Winter 1968), 15–35.

Fossum, Robert. "The Devil and Saul Bellow," *Comparative Literature Studies,* 3, 2 (1966), 197–206.

Frank, Joseph. "Spatial Form in Modern Literature," *Sewanee Review,* 53 (1945), 221–40, 433–56, 643–53.

Frank, Reuben. "Saul Bellow: The Evolution of a Contemporary Novelist," *Western Review* (Winter 1954), 101–12.

Freedman, Ralph. "Saul Bellow: The Illusion of Environment," *Wisconsin Studies in Contemporary Literature*, 1 (Winter 1960), 50–65.

Frohock, W. M. "Saul Bellow and his Penitent Picaro," *Southwest Review*, 53 (Winter 1968), 36–44.

Galloway, David G. "*Mr. Sammler's Planet:* Bellow's Failure of Nerve," *Modern Fiction Studies*, 19 (Spring 1973), 17–28.

———. "The Absurd Man as Picaro: The Novels of Saul Bellow," *Texas Studies in Language and Literature*, 6 (Summer 1964), 226–54.

Glicksberg, Charles I. "The Theme of Alienation in the American Jewish Novel," *Reconstructionist*, 23 (November 29, 1957), 10.

Goldberg, Gerald J. "Life's Customer, Augie March," *Critique*, 3 (Summer 1960), 15–27.

Goldfinch, Michael A. "Journey to the Interior," *English Studies*, 43 (October, 1962), 439–43.

Guttman, Allen. "Bellow's Henderson," *Critique*, 7 (Spring 1965), 33–42.

Handy, W. J. "Criticism of Joyce's Works: A Formalist Approach," in *James Joyce: His Place in World Literature.* Proceedings of the Comparative Literature Symposium, 11 (Lubbock, Texas, 1969), 53–90.

———. "Saul Bellow and the Naturalistic Hero," *Texas Studies in Literature and Language*, 5 (Winter 1964), 538–45.

Harris, James Neil. "One Critical Approach to *Mr. Sammler's Planet*," *Twentieth-Century Literature*, 18 (October 1972), 235–50.

Hassan, Ihab. "Saul Bellow: Five Faces of a Hero," *Critique*, 3 (1960), 28–36.

Howe, Irving. "Mass Society and Post-Modern Fiction," *Partisan Review*, 26 (Summer 1959), 420–36.

Hughes, Daniel. "Reality and the Hero: *Lolita* and *Henderson the Rain King*," *Modern Fiction Studies*, 6 (Winter 1960–1961), 345–64.

Klein, Marcus. "A Discipline of Nobility: Saul Bellow's Fiction," *Kenyon Review*, 24 (Spring 1962), 203–26.

Leach, Elsie. "From Ritual to Romance Again: *Henderson the Rain King*," *Western Humanities Review*, 14 (Spring 1960), 223–24.

Lehan, Richard. "Existentialism in Recent American Fiction: The Demonic Quest," *Texas Studies in Literature and Language*, 1 (Spring 1959), 181–202.

LePellec, Yves. "New York in Summer: Its Symbolical Function in *The Victim*," *Caliban*, 8 (1969), 101–10.

Levenson, J. C. "Bellow's *Dangling Man*," *Critique*, 3 (Summer 1960), 3–14.

Levine, Paul. "Saul Bellow: The Affirmation of the Philosophical Fool," *Perspective*, 10 (Winter 1959), 163–76.

Mailer, Norman, "Modes and Mutations: Quick Comments on the

Modern American Novel," *Commentary*, 41 (March 1966), 37–44.

Mathis, J. C. "Theme of 'Seize the Day,' " *Critique*, 7 (Spring 1965), 43–45.

Miller, Karl. "Leventhal," *New Statesman*, 70 (September 10, 1965), 360–61.

Morrow, Patrick. "Threat and Accomodation: The Novels of Saul Bellow," *Midwest Quarterly*, 8 (1967), 389–411.

Pierce, Richard. "The Walker: Modern American Hero," *Massachusetts Review*, 5 (Summer 1964), 761–64.

Porter, M. Gilbert. "*Henderson the Rain King:* An Orchestration of Soul Music," *New England Review*, 1, 6 (Spring 1972), 24–33.

———. "*Herzog:* A Transcendental Solution to an Existential Problem," *Forum*, 7 (Spring 1969), 32–36.

Quinton, Anthony. "The Adventures of Saul Bellow," *The London Magazine*, 6 (December 1959), 55–59.

Rans, Geoffrey. "The Novels of Saul Bellow," *Review of English Literature*, 4 (October 1963), 18–30.

Ransom, John Crowe. "The Concrete Universal: Observations on the Understanding of Poetry," in *Poems and Essays*. New York, 1955.

———. "The Content of the Novel: Notes Toward a Critique of Fiction," *The American Review*, 7 (April 1936), 301–18.

———. "Criticism as Pure Speculation," in *Literary Opinion in America*, Rev.ed. Morton D. Zabel, ed. New York, 1951.

———. "The Understanding of Fiction," *Kenyon Review*, 12 (Spring 1950), 189–218.

Ross, Theodore J. "Notes on Saul Bellow," *Chicago Jewish Forum*, 18 (Winter 1959), 21–27.

Salter, D. P. M. "Optimism and Reaction in Saul Bellow's Recent Work," *Critical Quarterly*, 14, 1 (Spring 1972), 57–66.

Samuel, Maurice. "My Friend, the Late Moses Herzog," *Midstream*, 12 (April 1966), 3–25.

Schorer, Mark. "Fiction and the 'Matrix of Analogy,' " *Kenyon Review*, 11 (Autumn 1949), 539–60.

Schulman, Robert. "The Style of Bellow's Comedy," *PMLA*, 83 (March 1968), 109–17.

Stevenson, David L. "Fiction's Unfamiliar Face," *Nation*, 187 (November 1, 1958), 307–9.

———. "The Activists," *Daedulus*, 92 (Spring 1963), 238–49.

Stock, Irvin. "The Novels of Saul Bellow," *Southern Review*, 3 (January 1967), 395–403.

Tanner, Tony. "Saul Bellow: The Flight From Monologue," *Encounter*, 24 (February 1965), 58–70.

Tate, Allen, "Techniques of Fiction," *Sewanee Review*, 41 (Winter 1944), 210–25.

"A Place in the Sun," *TLS* (June 12, 1959), 352.

"A Vocal Group: The Jewish Part in American Letters," *TLS*, November 6, 1959, p. xxxv.

Trachtenberg, Stanley. "Saul Bellow's *Luftmenschen:* The Compromise with Reality," *Critique*, 9 (Summer 1967), 37–73.

Trowbridge, Clinton W. "Water Imagery in *Seize the Day*," *Critique*, 9 (Spring 1968), 62–73.

Uphouse, Suzanne Henning, "From Innocence to Experience: A Study of *Herzog*," *Dalhousie Review*, 46 (Spring 1966), 67–78.

Way, Brian. "Characters and Society in *The Adventures of Augie March*," *British Association for American Studies Bulletin*, No. 8 (1964), 36–44.

Weatherhead, A. Kingsley. "Structure and Texture in Henry Green's Latest Novels," *Accent*, 24 (Spring 1959), 111–12.

Weber, Ronald. "Bellow's Thinkers," *Western Humanities Review*, 22 (Autumn 1968), 305–13.

Weiss, Daniel. "Caliban on Prospero: A Psychoanalytic Study on the Novel *Seize the Day*," *American Imago*, 19 (Fall 1962), 277–306.

Widmer, Kingsley. "Poetic Naturalism in the Contemporary Novel," *Partisan Review*, 26 (Summer 1959), 467–72.

Young, James Dean. "Bellow's View of the Heart," *Critique*, 7 (Spring 1965), 5–17.

Books

Aldridge, John W. *In Search of Heresy*. New York, 1956.

Alter, Robert. *Rogues' Progress: Studies in the Picaresque Novel*. Cambridge, Mass., 1964.

Balakian, N., and C. Simmons, ed. *The Creative Present*. Garden City, N. Y., 1963.

Baumbach, Jonathan. *The Landscape of Nightmare*. New York, 1965.

Bellow, Saul. *The Adventures of Augie March*. New York, 1953.

———. *Dangling Man*. New York, 1944.

———. *Henderson the Rain King*. New York, 1965.

———. *Herzog*. New York, 1964.

———. *Mosby's Memoirs and Other Stories*. New York, 1968.

———. *Mr. Sammler's Planet*. New York, 1970.

———. *Seize the Day*. New York, 1956.

———. "Some Notes on Recent American Fiction," in *The American Novel Since World War II*, Marcus Klein, ed. Greenwich, Conn., 1969.

———. *The Victim*. New York, 1965.

Blackmur, R. P. *Eleven Essays in the European Novel*. New York, 1943.

Booth, Wayne C. *The Rhetoric of Fiction.* Chicago, 1961.

Brooks, Cleanth, and Robert Penn Warren. *Understanding Fiction.* New York, 1943.

Cohen, Sarah Blacher. *Saul Bellow's Enigmatic Laughter.* Illinois, 1974.

Clayton, John J. *Saul Bellow: In Defense of Man.* Indiana, 1968.

Cowley, Malcolm. *The Literary Situation.* New York, 1954.

Detweiler, Robert. *Saul Bellow.* Grand Rapids, Mich., 1967.

Dutton, Robert R. *Saul Bellow.* New York, 1971.

Eisinger, Chester E. *Fiction of the Forties.* Chicago, 1963.

Eliot, T. S. *Collected Poems and Plays.* New York, 1962.

Fiedler, Leslie. *Love and Death in the American Novel.* New York, 1960.

Frye, Northrop. *The Anatomy of Criticism.* Princeton, N. J., 1957.

Galloway, David G. *The Absurd Hero in American Fiction.* Austin, Tex., 1966.

Geismar, Maxwell. *American Moderns: From Conformity to Rebellion.* New York, 1958.

Gold, Herbert, ed. *Fiction of the Fifties.* New York, 1959.

Goldberg, Gerald J., and Nancy M. Goldberg, ed. *The Modern Critical Spectrum.* Englewood Cliffs, N. J., 1962.

Gordon, Caroline, and Allen Tate. *The House of Fiction.* New York, 1950.

Hall, James. *The Lunatic Giant in the Drawing Room.* Indiana, 1968.

Handy, W. J. *Kant and the Southern New Critics.* Austin, Tex., 1963.

Harper, Howard M., Jr. *Desperate Faith.* North Carolina, 1967.

Hassan, Ihab. *Radical Innocence.* Princeton, N. J., 1961.

Hemingway, Ernest. *The Sun Also Rises.* New York, 1926.

Hicks, Granville, ed. *The Living Novel.* New York, 1957.

Hoffman, Frederick J. *The Modern Novel in America.* Chicago, 1951.

Hutchens, Robert M., and Mortimer J. Adler, ed. *The Great Ideas of Today.* Chicago, 1965.

Kazin, Alfred. *Contemporaries.* Boston and Toronto, 1962.

Klein, Marcus. *After Alienation.* Cleveland, Ohio, 1965.

Langer, Susanne K. *Feeling and Form.* New York, 1953.

Lemon, Lee T., and Marion J. Reis, eds. *Russian Formalist Criticism.* Lincoln, Nebr., 1965.

Lewis, R. W. B. *The American Adam.* Chicago, 1955.

Ludwig, Jack. *Recent American Novelists.* Minneapolis, 1962.

Mailer, Norman. *Advertisements for Myself.* New York, 1966.

———. *Cannibals and Christians.* New York, 1966.

Malin, Irving, ed. *Saul Bellow and the Critics.* New York, 1967.

———. *Saul Bellow's Fiction.* Carbondale, Ill., 1969.

Moore, Harry T., ed.*Contemporary American Novelits.* Carbondale, Ill., 1964.

Morgan, Bayard Q., trans. Johann von Goethe's *Faust.* New York, 1954.

Muir, Edwin. *The Structure of the Novel.* London, 1928.

Opdahl, Keith. *The Novels of Saul Bellow: An Introduction.* University Park, Pa., 1968.

Ortega y Gasset, José. *The Dehumanization of Art.* New York, 1956.

Podhoretz, Norman. *Doings and Undoings.* New York, 1964.

Ransom, John Crowe. *The World's Body.* New York, 1938.

Rovit, Earl. *Saul Bellow.* Minnesota, 1967.

―――. *Saul Bellow: A Collection of Critical Essays.* New Jersey, 1974.

Rupp, Richard H. *Celebration in Postwar Fiction.* Coral Gables, Fla., 1970.

Salinger, J. D. *The Catcher in the Rye.* New York, 1951.

Scheer–Schäzler, Brigitte. *Saul Bellow.* New York, 1972.

Scholes, Robert. *Approaches to the Novel.* San Francisco, 1961.

Schulz, Max F. *Radical Sophistication.* Athens, Ohio, 1969.

Scott, Nathan A., Jr. *Three American Moralists: Mailer, Bellow, Trilling.* Notre Dame, 1973

Stallman, Robert N., ed. *Critiques and Essays in Criticism.* New York, 1949.

Tanner, Tony. *City of Words.* New York, 1971.

―――. *Saul Bellow.* Edinburgh, 1965.

Walcutt, C. C. *Man's Changing Mask: Modes and Methods of Characterization in Fiction.* Minnesota, 1966.

Waldmeir, Joseph J., ed. *Recent American Fiction.* Boston, 1963.

Warfel, Harry R., ed. *American Novelists of Today.* New York, 1951.

Wasserstrom, William. *Heiress of All the Ages.* Minneapolis, 1959.

Weinberg, Helen. *The New Novel in America.* Ithaca, N. Y., 1970.

Wellek, René, and Austin Warren. *Theory of Literature.* New York, 1956.

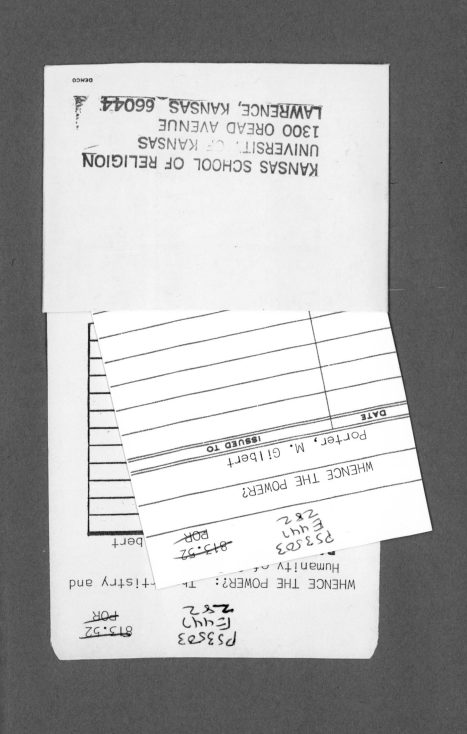